THE
YOUNG LEADER'S GUIDE

To Internships, Scholarships, and Fellowships in
Washington, D.C., and Beyond

THE
YOUNG LEADER'S GUIDE

To Internships, Scholarships, and Fellowships in
Washington, D.C., and Beyond

BY STEEVE SIMBERT

www.steevesimbert.com

THE YOUNG LEADER'S GUIDE TO INTERNSHIPS, SCHOLARSHIPS, AND FELLOWSHIPS IN WASHINGTON, D.C. AND BEYOND

Copyright © 2018 Steeve Simbert

Published: August 5, 2018

ISBN: 9781731002884

Editorial Team

Laura Pruett, Sheeva Azma, and Deborah Ling

Steeve Simbert

This guide may be purchased in quantity and/or special sales by contacting the publisher, Steeve Simbert:

www.steevesimbert.com/contact

Find out more about the author:

Website: http://steevesimbert.com/contact/

Table of Contents

Acknowledgments...1
How to Use This Guide...3

SECTION 1: Preparing for Success..7
    Chapter 1: A Positive Mindset 8
    Chapter 2: Ten Golden Rules..17

SECTION 2: Mastering the Application Process 21
    Chapter 3: A Winning Cover Letter..23
    Chapter 4: An Amazing Résumé 25
    Chapter 5: Your Network...27
    Chapter 6: The Art of the Interview 31

SECTION 3: Interning in the Nation's Capital and Beyond...........33
    Part I: U.S. Government Internships and Fellowships................37
    Chapter 7: Executive Branch — White House..............................41
    Chapter 8: Executive Branch — Departments and Agencies....43
    Chapter 9: Legislative Branch..53
    Chapter 10: Judicial Branch...59

    Part II: Nonprofit-Sector Internships 61
    Chapter 11: Advocacy Organizations and Foundations...........63
    Chapter 12: Public Policy Research Organizations 71
    Chapter 13: International Organizations.....................................83

    Part III: Private-Sector Internships...93
    Chapter 14: Media Outlets for Politicos.....................................95
    Chapter 15: Leading Companies..101
    Chapter 16: Political and Business Consulting Firms.............113
    Chapter 17: Top Law Firms...119

SECTION 4: Financing Your College and Graduate Education ...125
    Chapter 18: U.S. Scholarships and Fellowships.......................131
    Chapter 19: Women's Scholarships and Fellowships...............145
    Chapter 20: Diversity Scholarships and Fellowships...............153
    Chapter 21: Scholarships and Fellowships for Study
            Abroad 159

Chapter 22: Pre-Law Programs and Law School
       Scholarships..179
Chapter 23: STEM Scholarships and Fellowships 187
Chapter 24: Women's and Diversity STEM Scholarships
       and Fellowships...199

SECTION 5: Living in the Nation's Capital.................................207
Chapter 25: University Summer Housing.................................209
Chapter 26: District of Columbia, Maryland, and
       Virginia Neighborhoods...210
Chapter 27: Other Housing Resources....................................215

SECTION 6: Thriving in the Nation's Capital (and Beyond)........219
Chapter 28: Developing a Sustainable Lifestyle 221
Chapter 29: Insider's Delights in Washington, D.C.................225
Chapter 30: Coping with Rejection 229
Chapter 31: A Parting Thought...231
Epilogue: Call to Action 233

SECTION 7: Appendices..235
Appendix A: Sources and Resources.......................................237
Appendix B: Cover Letter Examples 243
Appendix C: Résumé Examples...249
Appendix D: Miscellaneous Email and Letter Samples..........261

About the Author 263

"There's no such thing as a self-made man."

— George Matthew Adams, American newspaper
columnist

Acknowledgments

This quotation has always spoken to me, as I truly believe that I am a product of those who have mentored and supported me. From the womb of my mother to attending the University of Oxford, as well as working on Capitol Hill and at the State Department, I have been blessed by the goodwill and kindness of friends, philanthropists, and even strangers.

I want to thank all of the administrators from all of the schools I have attended — St. Thomas University, Georgetown University, and the University of Oxford — for awarding me full scholarships. I also want to thank my former internship supervisors, teachers, mentors, and friends, who have had a tremendous positive impact on my life.

Additionally, I would like to thank a few people individually:

- Juan Casimiro, my first mentor when I moved to the United States after the earthquake in Haiti, who taught me to challenge myself and aim for greatness;
- Dr. Joe Holland, my teacher at St. Thomas University, who has been my steadfast supporter and taught me the true meaning of the pursuit of knowledge;
- Alice W. Muehlhof, my statistics professor from Princeton University's Woodrow Wilson School of Public and International Affairs, who is the kindest and sweetest person ever to believe in me;
- and Paul O'Neill, my mentor from the Georgetown Scholarship Program, who taught me the value of hard work and who became a father figure to me.
- Last, but not least, I would like to thank my incredible editorial team, especially Laura Pruett, Sheeva Azma, and Deborah Ling, who gave me valuable feedback and made countless contributions to this guide. In addition, there were dozens of students and friends who have remained incredibly patient with me and generous with their time in the face of my endless questions.

I dedicate this book to all of the people who have invested their time and energy in me. From the rubble of Haiti's earthquake, to attending Oxford, to working on Capitol Hill and within the State Department, I truly could not have done it on my own. The time has come for me to use my education to help others and make the world a better place than I found it. I will remain eternally grateful to every person and institution that has invested in and supported me.

"When I was in college, I wanted to be involved in things that would change the world."

— Elon Musk, American business magnate, investor, and founder of SpaceX

How to Use This Guide

For an ambitious young leader, arriving in a bustling city like Washington, D.C., can be a daunting experience. While it is critical to meet face-to-face with people who can share their professional experiences, when I found myself at this stage in my career a few years ago, I often wished there was a comprehensive resource to help me find my way.

This book is exactly that: a guide to help you, the young leader, navigate the maze of Washington, D.C., and find the perfect place for your talents.

But what makes you a young leader?

With your spark and passion, you shine like a star. You do not simply major in a field such as political science or public policy. Instead, you understand that gaining a wide range of experience in other fields, from consulting and law, to science and technology, will enhance your ability to produce effective change.

America needs young leaders with well-rounded skill sets like yours, in order to produce effective public policy that improves people's lives by balancing competing interests and finding common ground. In the United States, unlike in many other countries, public policy professionals often move from the government to the private sector to the academic community, and back again.

Successful Mindset

A young leader must stand guard at the door of his or her mind. Your ultimate success relies on your perception of yourself. You must doggedly work to improve yourself, while also conditioning your mind and learning from the giants who have come before you. We have dedicated the first section of this guide to sharing with you the mindsets of ultra-successful people, which will guide you toward your educational and career success.

Application Process

For the application process, you will need a résumé, a cover letter, letters of recommendation, your exam scores, etc. In this section, we share with you unique strategies to simplify the application process and make your application shine.

Internships

In this guide, we provide you with all the resources you need to acquire skills and experience through internships — not only within the government and the nonprofit community, but also in the private sector, including consulting firms, law firms, technology industries, and a wide array of companies, from Adobe to YouTube. We present these listings in a way that is easy to navigate and fun to read.

To the best of our research team's abilities, each listing includes the following information:

- What the organization or company does
- What interns do there
- What types of students can apply — e.g., juniors and above, master's students only, certain majors only
- What benefits the internships include (financial or otherwise)
- What time of year internships are available (summer only, or year-round)

We have marked a couple of types of internships with symbols to make them easy to find. These symbols appear to the left of the listing title:

^^ An opportunity that emphasizes grassroots activism, working with the disadvantaged, and/or social entrepreneurship

¶ An opportunity that requires an essay, personal statement, writing sample, and/or letter(s) of recommendation

Unless otherwise indicated, all internships listed are full time or at least 30 hours a week.

Scholarships and Fellowships

As a bonus, we have included a substantial section on financing your college and graduate education. It lists hundreds of scholarships and fellowships, from the highly prestigious to the lesser-known, that are available to you as an undergraduate, graduate student, or recent graduate. (See the introduction to each section for important information on how you can use the listings most effectively given your individual situation.)

- To the best of our research team's abilities, each listing includes the following information:
- A brief introduction to the company or organization
- Whether the internship or fellowship is paid or unpaid
- The amount of the award
- The types of students who can apply — e.g., juniors and above, master's students only, certain majors only

We have marked several awards with symbols to make them easy for you to find. These symbols appear to the left of the listing title:

** An especially prestigious award (in Section 3 only; all awards in Section 2 are highly prestigious)

\$\$ An award of \$25,000 or more and/or one that waives tuition for two years or more

Clickable Links

To save you time, the links in the Table of Contents are clickable, allowing you to navigate easily to the most relevant chapters for your circumstances. Similarly, each of the over 800 internship, scholarship, and fellowship listings in the guide includes a clickable link to a specific webpage with more information, so you won't need to start from the homepage of the website and search for the applicable page. Our team has conducted extensive research to ensure that all information and links are up to date and actionable. For the sake of brevity, the website links appear in a shortened form.

Insider's Tips

Throughout this book, we share key resources and tips with you that only Washingtonians know about. For example:

Insider's Tip: These two online resources, popular with Washington, D.C., job seekers, hint at the dizzying array of employers in our nation's capital, not only within the federal government but also within the local government, advocacy organizations, trade associations, political action committees, universities, embassies, law firms, consulting firms, and more:

- TheHill.com's online job board (http://thehill.com/resources/classifieds/ employer)
- Public affairs jobs blog (https://publicaffairsjobs.blogspot.com/)

Additional Resources

The closing section of this book provides information to assist you with the challenging task of finding housing in the Washington, D.C., area, along with a guide to lesser-known sights and events in Washington, D.C., to enjoy in your leisure time and tips on healthy practices for developing a sustainable lifestyle.

The appendices include full citations and links to the sources we utilized while compiling this guide, as well as additional resources we recommend for your exploration. In addition, this section provides examples of résumés, cover letters, useful email, and letter samples.

~ ~ ~

Many people have helped me on my journey thus far, and I feel I have a duty to pay it forward by mentoring others along the way. Having availed myself of the numerous opportunities available to me, I want to help you gain a competitive edge as well.

If you are a young leader who wants to excel in your career, achieve your dreams, and change the world — this is the guide for you!

"Every struggle in your life has shaped you into the person you are today. Be thankful for the hard times; they can only make you stronger."

— Keanu Reeves, actor, director, and philanthropist

SECTION 1:
Preparing for Success

At the pinnacle of your educational career, you might think you are on top of the world. You may have developed a preconceived notion that all doors will be opened for you. After all, school administrators have constantly reminded you that you are among the best and brightest minds of the world. Relatives and friends have told you how special you are. Strangers have randomly contacted you to tell you how much they look up to you. On the other hand, you may face your own internal battle, questioning whether your skills and abilities are adequate for attaining your goals.

Unfortunately, most people simply see the finish line. They have no idea of the journey you took to get there or of the challenges you have faced. In fact, most people don't care. Had you failed to attain your goal, most people would not take the time to learn from your mistakes. On the other hand, many people will be excited to learn about your failures if you become a successful person who overcame your struggles.

What all successful people have in common is their attitude when they face adversity. Life is not just about the crises that you face. All of us have faced similar crises to yours. The big question is, *"What will you do about yours?"* In other words, your attitude is what will differentiate you from most people.

I have probably received only 1 percent of the opportunities I have applied for, which means that 99 percent of the time, I have been rejected. When I am rejected, I tell myself that God has something better in store for me. As a result of this outlook, I become eager to apply for even more opportunities. The first step in becoming successful as an intern is learning how to apply for one.

Many internships require only a cover letter, a résumé, and sometimes a list of references to apply. Others, especially the more competitive and prestigious ones, may require additional materials, such as transcripts, letters of recommendation, and/or a personal essay or statement. Media internships may require a writing or video sample. Some may also require a journal article or, in the case of STEM opportunities, a copy of a research proposal that you have written.

Applying for an internship is similar to applying for a part-time job, and you should treat it as such. Create weekly goals and commit to accomplishing them. Make time to reach out and connect with the right people. Meet with prospective employers for coffee, and remember always to follow up with a genuine thank-you note. Talk to your extended contacts and ask them to reach out to your potential employer as well. You will be amazed at how creative you can be. Take risks and try different strategies that your peers are not doing. Also, always be yourself. I would much rather be happy and get a job where I can be myself than pretend to be someone I am not. Stay true to yourself, take risks, and have fun in the process.

You may need to apply anywhere from three months to a year prior to when your internship actually begins. On the other hand, some internships may accept you within as little as a week or two of submitting your application. Check each internship organization's webpage to learn more about its unique requirements and procedures.

While some internships select interns based on applications alone, most internships also involve some form of interview. Interviews may be conducted by phone, via a video chat service such as Skype, or in person. They may be one-on-one interviews or panel interviews, in which many different people will ask you about your life and credentials.

The interview process allows the internship organization to get to know you and connect a personality (and, if the interview is conducted by video chat or in person, a face) with your application. You should familiarize yourself with some common interview questions and prepare your answers in advance. It may be helpful to practice your interview with a trusted friend or family member who can provide you with feedback so that you do not feel as nervous on interview day. If you can't find anyone else to help you, practice with your pet or in front of the mirror. Record yourself (e.g., on your smartphone) answering questions, and then listen to your answers so you can critique your own interview skills.

You should hear from the internship organization within days or weeks of your application submission and/or interview. For a better idea of when you will hear back, ask about the approximate timeline when you submit your application. If you don't hear back in a reasonable amount of time, you may wish to follow up with them.

"Success is walking from failure to failure
with no loss of enthusiasm."

— Winston Churchill, British prime minister

Chapter 1:
A Positive Mindset

Necessity is the mother of invention. As an immigrant to the United States, following the massive Haitian earthquake of 2010, I had to be innovative and sell anything (legal) I could to acquire additional money and cover my living expenses. At one point, I almost got into trouble with the law when I was trying to sell my friend's Miami Marlins baseball tickets.

To find a buyer, I visited a range of businesses, block by block. I ended up at a huge supermarket, where I started pitching the baseball tickets to customers. As I was selling them and taking the cash, an employee asked me to leave. The next thing I knew, they had called the police, who told me I was not allowed to do that. I freaked out to the point that the police officer began reassuring me that it was not a serious situation and that I was not in trouble with the law.

My greatest fear as an immigrant has always been being arrested. I have always thought that if I were arrested, my life would be over. Therefore, I have always been determined to obey the law and to treat our police officers with the utmost respect. In addition, I try my best to wear suits almost every day. I always keep a smile on my face, and I try to treat everyone I meet with respect.

Although some people may disagree with the extreme measures I take, I don't ever want to be shot by the police or be arrested. At the same time, it is important to hustle legally to make ends meet. To gain an edge in life, you will never be able to create true wealth from just your daily 9 a.m. to 5 p.m. routine. If you simply rely on living paycheck to paycheck, you will die broke. Therefore, it is crucial to innovate; use your brain to develop creative ideas to generate extra income.

Prior to graduating high school, I purchased various accessories from Haiti to sell in Miami. As I was selling them at the Little Haiti Cultural Complex, I met a motivated young woman who thought I would be a perfect candidate for the Ultimate Life Entrepreneurship Camp that she had registered to attend the following week. Given that I didn't have the financial means to cover the cost of the camp, after I pleaded my case to the founder, he allowed me to attend. The winner of the business camp's plan competition would receive seed capital toward their venture.

Prior to attending the camp, I was just a typical teenager. I had never won anything and had certainly never been recognized for winning something. However, I knew from the start that this camp would be special and would have a long-lasting impact on my life. I told myself that if I won first place at this camp, it would be the beginning of a long winning career.

In short, I partnered with the girl who had invited me, and we launched an accessories business called "Les Merveilles" — The Marvelous. We won first place by presenting our business plan to a panel of judges that consisted of prominent leaders from Doral in Miami-Dade County, Florida.

We then had the opportunity to attend the Ultimate Life Summit at Walt Disney World. This camp changed my entire life perspective. It was during this enlightenment period that I was exposed to the "Seven Mindsets for Living an Ultra-Successful Life," which has played an integral role in my personal life and professional success.

Since then, I have tried every day to apply these seven mindsets, as well as the invaluable lessons that I learned from my mentors and the founders of the Magic Wand Foundation – Juan P. Casimiro, Mitchell Schlimer, Scott Shickler, and Jeff Waller:

1. Everything Is Possible

Believing that Everything Is Possible means that you understand that everyone can live an extraordinary life. After all, everything that humans have ever made was only an idea until someone supported that idea enough to turn it into a reality. Accepting this basic tenet of the Seven Mindsets will allow you to believe in the possibility that you can live a wonderful life, help raise your overall expectations, and empower you to take charge of your life.

2. Passion First

The idea behind Passion First is that we, as humans, are unique individuals who should share that uniqueness with the world. To that end, you must pursue your most genuine goals with passion and zest, overcoming any obstacles in your path.

3. We Are Connected

When you understand that We Are Connected, you will also realize that everyone you meet can help you achieve your dreams. As such, you will discover how to explore your relationship with others, look beyond physical and material differences, and enjoy competing with friends and acquaintances with the understanding that a healthy competition offers a learning opportunity for everyone involved.

4. 100 Percent Accountable

Being 100 Percent Accountable means that you are responsible for your past, present, and future life. No one else is to blame for your mistakes, but no one else can take credit for your successes either. You are what you choose to be, and no one can take that away from you. Adopting this mindset will allow you to move beyond your preconceived notions, as well as any imaginary boxes you have drawn yourself into. You will be a free agent who can achieve anything that anyone else can achieve.

5. Attitude of Gratitude

With an Attitude of Gratitude, you will learn to look at the bright side of life and find something positive in even the most negative circumstances. Although every situation includes bad and good aspects, continually searching for the bad parts will set you on a self-destructive path. On the other hand, looking for the silver lining will always bring you joy and success.

6. Live to Give

When you begin to Live to Give, you will realize that everything in life operates in a continual cycle. As they say, "What goes around comes around." When you show kindness and generosity toward those around you, they will often return that kindness in whatever way they can. In other words, using your talents to help others will inspire them to return the favor. Expand that idea to a worldwide perspective, and you will see that making a positive impact in the world will reward you in return.

7. The Time Is Now

When you realize that The Time Is Now, you will learn to embrace the present. Since the future is uncertain and the past is unchangeable, the only time that you can produce any effect on your world is right now. If you want to improve your future, you must begin today, at this moment, and without delay.

These seven mindsets have been my foundation. I truly believe in these seven mindsets. In fact, the moment I started at St. Thomas University, I created the first chapter of the Ultimate Life Club. I wanted to share with other students about the mindsets, to help other people achieve their own goals. I take great pride and joy in helping others achieve their dreams. No matter what else I do in life, helping empower other and motivating them to believe in their own potential is something that I will always pursue. It is my passion and my calling, and I love it!

Role vs. Tasks

To understand your internship role, as opposed to your tasks, you must first develop the proper mindsets. Think about Capitol Hill. The chief of staff, the most senior manager, manages a team of people toward achieving a common cause or a shared vision. An intern, on the other hand, is a trainee or student who is striving to acquire work experience in their field of choice. The two will often perform completely different tasks and responsibilities.

However, take a step back, and observe the commonalities between a successful intern and a chief of staff. At their core, they both need to ensure the effective and efficient management of their role. Both must meet the needs of their coworkers and colleagues. In other words, even when you are only a simple intern, YOU matter, YOU are worthy, YOU are valuable, YOU can make an impact, and YOU can make a difference.

Adopting this attitude will enable you to take your role seriously, even though your tasks might be mundane at times. Whether you are an intern or a chief of staff, your ultimate role is to add value to your team so that you can advance the goal of the organization as a whole. Every decision you make in your position should reflect that goal. When you are striving to improve the organization you are interning at, your coworkers, other interns, and your superiors will notice your efforts. Ultimately, if you are truly valuable, you will be rewarded for your value, worth, and contribution.

Character vs. Qualifications

Now that you know you matter and that you can be valuable, what else do you need that will set you apart from other interns? You will want to show your employer that you are not only qualified for the position, but also that you possess the right character to be a part of the team. Whether during an interview or while writing your cover letter or personal statements, always highlight your unique qualities in an innovative fashion.

Character

Your character sets the tone by defining your behaviors and the nature of your interactions with people. These character-defining elements will help you stand out from your peers. To demonstrate to your employer that you possess the ideal character, highlight the following six qualities whenever you have the opportunity to express yourself. To establish an ideal character, be passionate, remain honest at all times, use common sense, be a team player, display a humble attitude, and demonstrate loyalty.

Passion

Passion is a strong feeling of enthusiasm or excitement for something or about doing something. In the workplace, you demonstrate your passion by how you handle everyday situations and the stress that may accompany them. When you feel passionate, instead of feeling bored by the mundane tasks and everyday assignments required by your position, you will feel excited by them. When a stressful situation comes along, instead of panicking, you will attack the issue head-on, knowing you have the skills to manage the situation.

Honesty

As an intern, be someone who colleagues can trust, not only with work-related tasks, but with other information as well. Preserving the trust of those around you will show that you are dependable, which will enable others to listen to you and solicit your opinion whenever necessary. This quality also reflects well on your capacity to complete any tasks assigned.

Displaying any degree of dishonesty, whether to a client, a fellow peer, or to your superior, may lead people to question your moral integrity. To your superiors, this may warrant micromanaging you, at which point you may feel your freedom and personal space infringed upon. These types of awkward situations can be easily avoided by maintaining an honest moral character. Honesty and trustworthiness go hand-in-hand.

Trustworthiness

Being trustworthy reflects upon your abilities, reiterates your personal benevolence, and is the hallmark of integrity. This quality will help you establish the positive legacy you need to leave behind as an intern, while also shaping your future career path in ways that transcend the internship. You need to be the embodiment of honesty and trustworthiness in order to navigate the dynamics of a given setting without encountering conflicts and with exceptionally high output.

Common Sense

You may wonder if you should use your common sense to complete certain tasks within your internship, as opposed to waiting for your supervisor's directions. However, an intern typically fulfills specific roles, which are clearly allocated. Often, your supervisor will be keen on understanding your approach to achieving the goals you have been assigned. As such, exploit your common sense in certain situations. Waiting for your supervisor's directions, even on simple decision-making tasks, will make you dispensable. However, consult with your superiors when you are uncertain.

Additionally, practice what you know, but also show your creativity and innovativeness. Do not feel limited by the scope of your responsibilities. Creativity is like a muscle; if you do not use it, you will lose it. Showing your innovativeness and creativity will help you win the hearts and minds of the people within the organization, provided you work toward the benefit of the organization.

However, how can you assess your acumen? It boils down to checking the results of your past choices. Have they made you a better person within your society, or have they caused harm to you or your society? Pay attention to the manner in which you make decisions. You do not want those within your internship organization to see you as someone who is always indecisive or who is slow at making choices.

On the other hand, you don't want to be seen as someone who makes poor choices, either, so consider your choices well, but quickly reach a conclusion. Developing your compassion and critical thinking will go a long way toward ensuring you make the best decisions whenever presented with a situation that calls for good acumen.

Team Player Attitude

Teams are the hallmark of the contemporary workplace. As such, surviving will require you to adapt to team roles. Identify the type of teamwork required by any task, whether it's a collaboration or mutual reinforcement, and align its topmost goals and missions with the activities it entails. Effective team players are flexible, show genuine commitment, possess the ability to take on responsibility, are reliable, and are upfront problem-solvers.

However, as an intern, being a team player does not mean giving people the latitude to take advantage of you. Do not be the go-to person for all menial jobs, such as washing dishes. While it is okay to help with such tasks occasionally, in fulfillment of team spirit, watch out for any tendency by others to push you toward those types of duties on a regular basis. If you find yourself being taken advantage of, stand up for yourself. Learn to say "no" at times so that people don't abuse your goodwill.

Humility

Humility is a word that almost everyone understands, yet rarely demonstrates in its most basic form. If you are distracted by your phone, enamored with your own self-importance, and hardly paying attention to a conversation someone is trying to have with you, you are not behaving in a humble manner. The subtle aspects of any interaction define humility.

There are three pertinent areas where you need to show humility. The first is planning, during which you seek out existing information; the second is disseminating information, during which you seek to ensure everyone understands the message you are trying to deliver; and the third is continual learning, during which you seek to learn skills (especially from others and the environment around you) that enable you to develop your technical attributes and your emotional intelligence.

Simply put, while confidence gives you the ability to stand out within a crowd, humility gives you the ability to stand back and make room for other people's ideas and thoughts. Overconfidence, on the other hand, is what many describe using the Lake Wobegon effect, often termed illusory superiority. This simply refers to an individual's tendency to overestimate their positive qualities and capabilities, while underestimating, or completely ignoring, their negative traits in relation to those of others. Drawing the line between the two is not easy, in part because the average person believes themselves to be better than average. Discerning whether this is a confidence problem or a humility one is, therefore, not a simple task.

The secret lies in how you convey these two traits. Overconfidence will manifest itself in the manner in which you treat servers, drivers, and other service personnel; your focus on your personal interests when engaging in any conversation; your curiosity when interacting with others; and your tendency to elevate your accomplishments in any conversation. Humility, on the other hand, displays opposite symptoms of overconfidence, and therein lies the balance.

Qualifications

Once your employer knows that you possess the right character, demonstrate the following five critical qualities to show that you retain the qualifications and expertise necessary to succeed and thrive in your internship. As an intern, demonstrate that you are a learner, you perform quality work, you are innovative, you take the lead, and you take the time to learn about the organization with which you are interning.

Be a Learner

To be a learner, you must possess a specific mindset. Someone who is a learner is, as the name implies, willing to learn from others. As a learner in the workplace, you will want to learn all you can from your coworkers, your supervisor, and your boss. No one can take away your knowledge. The more you learn in the position you are at now, the more you will be able to take to your next project, internship, or job. Nothing can replace on-the-job training (OJT).

Perform Quality Work

Pertaining to quality work, internship organizations seek complexity, authenticity, and craftsmanship. Complex work tends to be rigorous, aligns with the objectives of the organization, and often exceeds the expected bare minimum. It shows an astute understanding of new concepts and contexts, and leverages multiple perspectives. Authentic work, on the other hand, concerns creativity; namely, your ability to find simple solutions to complex problems.

You can demonstrate your craftsmanship through your attention to detail and accuracy, as well as the resulting sophistication of the product. Always strive to go beyond what is required of you. Any projects you handle must leave your station when they are almost complete, requiring minimal touches before they are sent out to the client.

Be Innovative

The value you add to your internship organization will demonstrate your resourcefulness. The organization at which you are interning is already operational, and has been producing the goods or delivering the services without your input. Therefore, to convince the organization's management to include you on the team, show them that what you have to offer is of great value, and might be revolutionary in the long term. Do not simply go through the motions of your position for the sake of the internship. Rather, show off your unique skills as you embark upon your career journey.

To be resourceful, remain rational when handling your tasks. A case in point is an intern who was asked to run an errand that was basically a physical delivery of a package. With all the details provided except the location, the intern chose to ask the supervisor the location of the building, something they could have easily researched on Google. Principally, you should strive to make the job easier for your superior by rationally filling in certain gaps, but not necessarily thinking on behalf of them. Being resourceful demands that you be both rational and astute.

Take Initiative

While taking initiative will set you apart as enthusiastic and passionate, be careful not to overstep your boundaries by infringing on someone else's job. Be creative and innovative with your initiatives so that no one sees your actions as an attempt to sabotage them. At the same time, don't make yourself the workhorse of the organization by taking on each and every task that comes your way, as this might work against you. You don't want to be the poster child of a know-it-all at this stage in your career.

Learn About the Organization

Knowing as much about the organization as you can should be your first goal as a new intern. Learn and understand the diction that defines the business setting. Your knowledge of the different stakeholders, the politics at play within the organization's setting, and any other self-seeking or universal initiatives will enable you to navigate your internship environment with ease. Given how dynamic business environments are, always demonstrate a willingness to learn more about the organization as you seek to grow your knowledge base daily.

"Success is no accident. It is hard work, perseverance, learning, studying, sacrifice, and most of all, love of what you are doing or learning to do."

— Pelé, Brazilian soccer player elected Athlete of the 20th Century by the International Olympic Committee

Chapter 2:
Ten Golden Rules

A recent study by Georgetown University's Center on Education and the Workforce reported that more than 70 percent of college students have worked or interned while attending school. In addition to providing an excellent opportunity for beginning your professional career, interning will provide you an opportunity to gain valuable skills and expand your expertise in a specific field.

To maximize your internship experience, follow these 10 golden rules.

1. Build Relationships

Most internships will last only a few months. Make the most of your time by nurturing relationships with colleagues and superiors, who may prove tremendously helpful to you in the future when you apply for jobs or graduate school. After meeting someone for the first time, follow up with a thank-you note or an email to express your gratitude. This simple act will help differentiate you from other interns.

While you should be genuine when connecting with people, take care not to become too easy-going or personal. Exhibit respect, use professional language, and acknowledge your superiors. The best way to build relationships with others is by offering your services to them. You can get anything you want in life by first helping others get what they want; in return, they will often be willing to help you.

2. Be Professional

Professionalism can be defined as the collective set of skills and behaviors you need to adopt in order to act like a career employee in the workplace. This includes dressing suitably, performing tasks exceptionally well, and maintaining a businesslike tone with colleagues. It is crucial for success as an intern.

Demonstrating professionalism will improve both your personal reputation and the reputation of your organization. It will also solidify your colleagues' view of you as a reliable individual. Be professional not only with your boss and colleagues but also with clients and with anyone else you encounter in the workplace.

Be professional in the quality of your work — even with something as simple as checking your spelling and grammar when submitting a report. Being a professional is about demonstrating high standards and producing projects that you take pride in.

Do not become too informal in the workplace. Be mindful that others are observing you. This extends to dressing for success. Typically, you will be informed of the office dress code before your internship begins. Offices that are more formal will require you to wear a suit each day, whereas more relaxed ones may prefer business casual. If you are not sure about your office's dress code, ask your colleagues.

3. Be Punctual

To excel in your career, you must arrive on time and meet deadlines. Being punctual shows others that you value their time, you are a reliable person who keeps your word, and you can be trusted. People will appreciate your punctuality and regard you as organized and disciplined.

4. Be Resourceful

As a high-performing intern, show your resourcefulness by finding creative ways to execute your ideas successfully. Before asking for help, try to find the answers or solutions on your own, since your colleagues are busy people. Then present a few alternatives to your boss and ask which solution they prefer.

Do not be a nagging intern who asks incessantly for additional projects. Instead, if you have spare time, try to create innovative projects on your own. You can start by asking your colleagues if they need any help with their tasks. Be mindful that you must prove yourself in order to earn the trust of your colleagues and superiors.

When you begin your internship, develop a plan detailing what you want to obtain from the opportunity. Early on, try to think concretely about how you want your experience to look on your résumé and what kinds of skills you want to acquire from it. Develop a plan of action!

5. Listen More and Keep Your Opinions to Yourself

People often spend too much time talking and too little time listening, which can lead to miscommunication. When you speak, try to speak with substance instead of sharing every thought that comes to mind. Silence, at times, is golden. Refrain from trying to impress people by asking a lot of irrelevant questions, as it may damage your reputation in the workplace.

Do not discuss highly controversial or personal topics in the workplace. This is an important aspect of professionalism. Especially in a political setting such as a Capitol Hill internship, discussing your personal opinions might alienate your colleagues and affect your standing in the workplace. Leave your opinions in your personal life and, instead, discuss them with your friends.

When disagreeing with a colleague or superior, carefully listen to their argument to find some common ground that you agree on, and build the dialogue from there. Be careful not to publicly shame anyone.

6. Observe, Learn, and Adapt

Think of every organization or office as having its own specific culture. You must be adaptable and versatile to survive and thrive. You also must take time to learn how your colleagues and superiors operate in order to successfully navigate the workplace and advance your career.

During this process, maintain a positive attitude. Do not be the type of person who darkens the room when they walk in. Be a breath of fresh air and give people reasons to want you as their colleague. Focus on sharing this positivity, and use your strengths to increase your performance. Establish a monthly, weekly, and daily plan to give yourself deadlines and remind yourself of the skills you want to acquire.

7. Ask Great Questions

The best way to showcase your intellectual curiosity and willingness to work is by asking great questions. When asking a question, make certain that the answer could help clarify a specific subject that you do not understand. Be mindful not to speak just for the sake of speaking or showing off. Keep your questions thoughtful and genuine.

8. Maintain Realistic Expectations

The best way to maximize your internship experience is to maintain realistic, attainable expectations. To imagine that you will be performing high-level tasks like those of full-time staffers from the outset is to set yourself up for grave disappointment.

Be ready to handle whatever tasks you are assigned. People will assign you greater responsibilities as time goes on.

9. Be Humble and Work Hard

While displaying confidence in the workplace is important, take care not to appear arrogant. No one likes a know-it-all who treats colleagues as inferiors.

If you make a mistake, acknowledge it and focus on fixing the issue. Reach out to others for help if necessary. No one was born knowing everything. Everyone has a learning curve; embrace yours, while trying your best to improve every day. Invite constructive criticism, and do not take it personally. Listen to it attentively, learn from it quickly, and continue moving forward.

At the same time, be aware of your value and potential, and do not let anyone abuse you by being disrespectful or inconsiderate to you. If you are unhappy at an internship, leave it and do something else. Life is short, so live it to the fullest.

Work hard, try your best to help people along the way, and serve your colleagues. People notice those who get things done and give their best. Ask questions so you do not make easily avoidable mistakes; this will convey your dedication to performing high-quality work. Try to have your colleagues' backs when they need you, and maintain good working relationships with them. Do your best to stay calm, focused, respectful, and positive.

Finally, show respect to everyone in the office, regardless of his or her status. The way you treat others says much about you and your character.

10. Control Your Social Media Usage

Research indicates that 70 percent of employers use social media to screen candidates before hiring. Capitalize on social media to stand out from your peers and showcase your personality and professionalism.

That said, always think before you post something on social media, because you never know if your current or future employer is watching. Your reputation is your greatest asset, especially if you hope to be hired on completion of your internship. Do not post inappropriate pictures, be too negative, or criticize others on social media; instead, be true to yourself and post content consistent with your values and personality.

You may also wish to change your privacy settings so that casual visitors to your social media see a limited public profile.

"Don't be afraid to fail. Don't waste energy trying to cover up failure. Learn from your failures and go on to the next challenge. It's OK to fail. If you're not failing, you're not growing."

— H. Stanley Judd, author

SECTION 2:
Mastering the Application Process

The application process is like an art. Think of it as a meal you are cooking in the comfort of your beautiful kitchen. For the meal to taste truly excellent, you need to put a variety of ingredients in it. You might need pepper, salt, spices, oil, water, and so forth. Moreover, you need to combine the ingredients in the perfect ratio to produce a truly excellent meal.

To achieve the perfect blend of ingredients during your application process, you will need a résumé, a cover letter, letters of recommendation, exam scores, etc. The perfect amalgamation of these different parts will determine your success and ability to thrive during the application process. Therefore, in this section, we share with you unique strategies to make your application shine, including how to write a winning cover letter and an amazing résumé, how to utilize your network to your greatest advantage, and how to showcase your best self in your internship interviews.

"Adversity has a way of introducing a man to himself."

— Shia LeBeouf, American actor and filmmaker

Chapter 3:
A Winning Cover Letter

Imagine a chief of staff in Congress who is reviewing hundreds of applications for a position in the office. Most of the applicants have a background in political science. Most have interned on the Hill. Most have been to top schools. Some have campaign experience. Most have made top grades. How do you persuade that chief of staff that you should be called in for an interview? Let's begin with your cover letter.

Writing a standout cover letter is an important way to differentiate yourself from your competitors. While you may not have extensive professional work experience, you can use other strategies to highlight your passion, character, and qualifications in ways that connect with your prospective employer. One way to connect is to do your due diligence in finding out about the business you are applying for. The hiring manager will remember someone who did their homework and can speak intelligently about the company they want to work for.

Your cover letter should be single-spaced, with one-inch margins on all sides. In addition, leave a space between each paragraph throughout the document; 6 pt. is standard. Excellent cover letters include all the following elements:

1. Contact Information

At the top left of your cover letter, list your contact information, including your name, address, phone number, and email address. Leaving a blank line after your email address, add the organization's contact information, including the name or title of the person in charge of reviewing the applications (if you know it) and the organization's name and address.

2. Introduction

After the organization's contact information, leave a blank line, and then begin your introduction with a salutation. If you know the name of the person in charge of reviewing the applications, address your letter to them. Although using Mr. or Mrs. before the person's last name is traditional, if you are uncertain of their gender (or to avoid any potential offense), using their full name or their official title is acceptable.

Your introduction should begin with the subject of your letter, as well as who you are. It may also include how you discovered the opportunity (including the name of the person who recommended it to you, if that person maintains a positive relationship with the organization), why you are interested in it, how your qualifications match those required, and how you will help the organization achieve its goals.

The second paragraph of the letter can include a catchy phrase or sentence that highlights your knowledge and experience related to the role or position, alongside what you intend to contribute to the organization's endeavors. Often, passion tilts the tables in favor of one candidate over another when the two share almost equivalent qualifications.

3. Body

In the next paragraph, explain why you are the best fit for the position. Tie your skills and experiences directly to the requirements of the opportunity you are applying for, with specific references to your accomplishments. Use the information you learned through researching the organization to discern exactly what they are looking for, and use your résumé (see next chapter) to address each requirement in turn. Indicate your interest in using every skill at your disposal to benefit the goals of the organization as a whole and the position in particular.

4. Conclusion

Begin your conclusion by summarizing the key information in the body of your letter. Rather than introducing new information, this paragraph should remind the reviewer of your key points and include a call to action. Indicate your gratitude to the reviewer for taking the time to read your letter, and let them know that you look forward to meeting with them in an interview. At the end of your conclusion, tell them that you will call them in one week if you do not hear from them before that time.

5. Signature

End your cover letter with a closing such as "Sincerely," and leave three blank lines before adding your typed signature.

After you have completely written your cover letter text, vertically center the text, leaving the same amount of white space above your header as below your signature. This will create the most visually appealing document possible.

If you will be sending your cover letter by mail, print the letter, then sign it in black or blue ink between your closing and your typed signature.

In summary, when writing your cover letter, remember these five key points:

- Keep it short and sweet.
- Tailor it to the specific opportunity for which you are applying.
- Use your research to demonstrate how your experience and skills are the best fit for the organization.
- Be honest and genuine; doing so will make you seem real and your story seem relatable.
- End by expressing your gratitude, and include a call to action.

See Appendix B for sample cover letters that are sure to impress any reviewer.

"The beginning is the most important part of the work."

— Plato, Greek philosopher and founder of the Academy in Athens

Chapter 4:
An Amazing Résumé

The secret to landing an interview lies in your résumé. Your résumé is the tool you will use to convey your professional history, based on which, a reviewer will decide whether to set up an interview. To create an attention-getting résumé, you must make it concise, consistent, and easy to read. This chapter guides you through the necessary steps of writing a résumé that will land you interview callbacks.

Choose your preferred type of résumé. Résumés come in four basic forms:

- Chronological résumés, the most used of the four, list your work history starting with the most recent. Often, they include the objective of your résumé and career summary, both placed before your work experiences. The easiest type of résumé to compile, they also allow you to emphasize your work history, thereby raising your chances of holding your potential employer's attention.
- Functional résumés focus on your experiences, as opposed to the order in which you achieved them. They are suitable when changing professions or when applying to a job for which you lack directly related job history.
- Combination résumés are ideal if you intend to emphasize your acquired skills rather than your work history, especially when your work history does not paint the appropriate picture.
- Targeted résumés, on the other hand, focus explicitly on the specific job opening. Therefore, these résumés only highlight your skills and experiences that relate to the job opening.

Be sure to choose the type that most closely matches your situation.

Maintain font type and size consistency. Legibility should be among your primary goals. An appropriate font type and size is one that is neat and leaves enough white space for the résumé to remain easy on the eyes. Do not overuse features such as italics, bold, and underlining. Restrict your usage of bold type to section headings, and italics for quantifiable achievements.

Review assorted résumé samples. In addition to learning which kinds of résumés fit which job types, you will also gain valuable knowledge regarding the kind of information you will need to include in your résumé. However, don't borrow directly from the résumés you have reviewed. Customize yours so that it appropriately and concisely reflects your skills and abilities, and aligns with the job for which you are applying.

Adopt a template. Use a template as a starting point for your résumé. Carefully add your information to the template, and then tweak the content to personalize it. Ensure that the resulting résumé highlights your skills in a unique way.

Utilize prominent résumé keywords. Companies often utilize recruitment software to screen candidates. To increase your visibility, include specific keywords related to the job on your résumé. To achieve this, match your qualifications with the requirements provided in the job description. In addition to getting your résumé selected for further review, these keywords will highlight your skills and experiences, thus showing what an ideal candidate you are for the job.

Seek professional advice. Drafting a professional résumé is not an easy task. Before sending one out to a prospective employer, seek professional advice on how to craft a winning résumé. One such source could be a college career counselor if you are still a student, while another is right on your screen — this book.

Edit and proof your résumé. You are not only seeking a job or internship; you are also revealing some very personal information to someone who could help you grow in your career. You do not want to start with silly, easily avoidable grammar mistakes and style inconsistencies. Therefore, engage a friend, or even a career counselor, to read through your résumé, identifying and correcting any mistakes you might have made.

You can find sample résumés in Appendix C.

"You are who you surround yourself with."

— Selena Gomez, American singer, actress, and producer

Chapter 5:
Your Network

Now that you have drafted your résumé and cover letter, you can use them to network. Prepare and decide what you want before reaching out to friends, alumni, or other connections. Remember that the first impression is everything!

Know Yourself

Take the time to learn about yourself. What are your interests, values, strengths, skills, talents, goals, and dreams? You should be able to answer the following questions comfortably:

- What interests me the most, personally and professionally?
- What are my strengths and weaknesses?
- What are my talents?
- Why am I interested in this organization?
- What will I bring to the organization that makes me unique?
- What are my goals in the future? Immediate goals? Monthly, quarterly, and annual goals?
- What is my purpose in life?
- What do I want to achieve before I die?
- What legacy do I want to leave in this world?

Informational Interviews

Once you know yourself and what you are looking for, start setting up some informational interviews. Remember: There is a fine line between asking someone for an informational interview and asking them for an internship. For an informational interview, it is always best to present yourself as someone interested in the field who would like to hear more about the organizational representative's experiences. People tend to be more receptive toward discussing their experiences than toward talking with someone who is only looking for a position in the organization.

For informational interviews, contact your university's career office for information on how to reach out to alumni. Also, reach out to your connections on LinkedIn, your professors, friends, and family. In addition, do not hesitate to ask other people if they know anyone you should connect with; this is an ideal way to expand your network.

Meeting for informational interviews in person is always most effective. It brings the human element into the interview and will allow you to connect on a deeper level. Remember not to ask for a position. Doing so could make the interviewee uncomfortable.

Every time you meet someone for the first time, treat it like an interview and always give a great first impression. This is important because that person could give you referrals and connect you with other people who could be helpful to you. Therefore, be someone with whom anyone would love to connect. Be thankful, gracious, and always follow up immediately to demonstrate your appreciation of the time they took to speak with you. When you do that, people will know you are reliable and can be trusted, and they would love to connect you with their contacts. However, if you fail to do that, rest assured that the person will see a poor reflection of you.

Be well prepared when you meet with someone, with a solid idea of what you want to get out of the meeting. Be ready to introduce yourself and explain your purpose for the meeting. Don't seem too rehearsed. Act natural, as if you are having a conversation. Take it seriously, yet have fun at the same time.

One of the best abilities that you can possess is knowing how to ask the right questions. The best questions are unique. They are questions you cannot simply find the answer to on a Google search. Show genuine interest in the person, and express curiosity about them and their experiences.

Rule #1: People love to talk about themselves. Therefore, let them do most of the talking. You are not meeting with them just to brag about your awesomeness or how fabulous and accomplished you are. When you *do* speak, ask targeted questions that allow you to maximize the time you spend talking. Shape the conversation or interview to highlight specific issues that you would like to discuss and that would benefit you the most. At the same time, keep an open mind to allow the person to share with you other advice that could be useful to you in your career.

Here are some examples of questions that you could ask:

- How did you get to where you are today?
- What do your day-to-day activities look like?
- What projects do you typically work on?
- What advice do you have for me to acquire the necessary experience to get started in this field?
- If you were in my shoes, exactly where I am now, what would you do to get ahead of the game and try to best position yourself for this internship?

Essentially, ask strategic questions to allow the person to think critically and talk about himself or herself, while you benefit from their answers at the same time. After making this great first impression, share your gratitude with the person: "Thank you so much for taking the time out of your busy schedule to meet with me today. I truly appreciate it. Is there anyone that you think I should meet who would share their experiences and advice about this field with me?"

Now, how many young people that you know write a handwritten thank-you note after meeting with someone? Almost none, right? Most millennials would be satisfied to send a thank-you email, at the most. Emails are fine; however, I challenge you to do the old-school version. Take the extra step, go the extra mile, and do what other young people are not doing.

Today, go to the store and purchase an inexpensive package of thank-you cards. Begin developing the habit of sending nice, well-thought-out handwritten thank-you cards. Each person you send one to will forever remember you! Most people are not doing it, so this will help set you apart as special and unique. In everything, always do what other people are not doing.

"Choose a job you love, and you will never have to work a day in your life."

— Confucius, Chinese teacher, politician, and philosopher

Chapter 6:
The Art of the Interview

Congratulations! Your winning cover letter and standout résumé have captivated the hearts and minds of the reviewers, and you have been invited to an interview for the internship, scholarship, or fellowship you seek. Now what?

Here are some principles you can apply to any interview — not only for these types of opportunities, but also for jobs, graduate school admissions, and even just *coffee dates* with potential employers.

During your interview, you must differentiate yourself from the pack. How? First, establish a core mission statement that embodies who you are — what you represent and believe in. Do some soul searching to understand what drives you in life. What makes you unique? This will allow you to connect with your interviewer on a deeper level, painting a picture for them of who you are and what motivates you. Show them that your experience is valuable and that choosing you would greatly benefit their organization.

You can connect with your interviewer by sharing stories. Politicians such as former President Bill Clinton are effective public speakers in large part because of their ability to share stories. This was demonstrated during the second 1992 presidential debate between Clinton and then-President George H. W. Bush, when a woman in the audience asked the candidates, "How has the national debt personally affected each of your lives? And if it hasn't, how can you honestly find a cure for the economic problems of the common people if you have no experience in what's ailing them?"

Bush responded immediately, "I think the national debt affects everybody. Obviously, it has a lot to do with interest rates."

The woman interrupted, "On a personal basis, how has it affected you?"

Bush responded, "Well, I am sure it has. I love my grandchildren. I want to think that they're going to be able to afford an education. I think that's an important part of being a parent." He clearly struggled with his response, but because of the woman's insistence, he was unable to dodge the question altogether.

Bush's evasive answer is exactly what you should NOT give during an interview. Instead, focus on the tenets of the question in such a way that you make the discussion about the interviewer's insight. Do not rush your answer. Think about your response before you speak, and use it to bring the discussion back to your message and your core issues; that way, you will retain control of the interview.

In contrast, when it was his turn to answer (https://www.youtube.com/watch?v=7ffbFvKlWqE), Bill Clinton stood and walked over to the woman. He looked directly in her eyes and stated, "I've been governor of a small state for 12 years," he said. "I'll tell you how it's affected me. Every year, Congress and the president sign laws that make us do more things and give us less money to do it. I see middle-class people whose services have gone down while the wealthy have gotten tax cuts. When people lose their jobs, there is a good chance I know them by their name. If a factory closes, I know the people who ran it."

To produce the *Bill Clinton effect* during your interview:

- Nod your head.
- Repeat words used by the interviewer to show that you approve of their statements.
- Ask interesting questions.
- Direct the flow of the interview.
- Listen well. Information is key.
- Learn as much as you can about the interviewer.

Throughout your interview, always demonstrate the best version of yourself. Conclude by sharing the top three qualities that make you the ideal candidate for the internship.

"Public service must be more than doing a job efficiently and honestly. It must be a complete dedication to the people and to the nation."

— Margaret Chase Smith, former U.S. senator and representative

SECTION 3:
Interning in the Nation's Capital and Beyond

As someone who moved to the United States without speaking a word of English, I faced more challenges than the average young leader does. First, I had to learn how to speak the language, then how to navigate the U.S. academic system, and then how the professional world works. Advancing my career in a new country required making many adjustments.

In the end, I successfully mastered the art of applying for internships and scholarships, receiving priceless opportunities and over $300,000 in funding for my education. I received full scholarships to Georgetown University (for my bachelor's degree) and the University of Oxford (for my master's). Additionally, I interned in both chambers of the U.S. Congress — the U.S. House of Representatives and the U.S. Senate — as well as in the French Ministry of Foreign Affairs & Overseas and the Organization of American States.

In this book, I share the myriad pieces of wisdom and resources I acquired along the way. This section begins with a story from my days as a student at Georgetown University in Washington, D.C. One morning, sometime around Thanksgiving in 2013, I was in my dorm room, reading an amazing article on Lifehacker (https://lifehacker.com/5956035/how-to-meet-anyone-from-steve-wozniak-to-the-president) filled with advice on how to connect with anyone, from the president of Russia to Steve Wozniak, the co-founder of Apple. Here are a few key points made by the author of the article:

- Initiate conversations with strangers.
- Be your authentic self.
- Never give up.

I felt so inspired by the article that I jumped up and put on my nicest suit and bow tie, having decided to put the lessons I had learned in the article into practice immediately.

I was broke, so I took the free Georgetown University shuttle bus, which dropped me off at the law school, just a few blocks from Capitol Hill. I headed to the Hart Senate Office Building. Once past the security check, the first thing I saw was a directory on the wall listing all the senators.

At that time, Senator Harry Reid, a Democrat from Nevada, was the majority leader. I took a deep breath and walked toward his office. Even though it was scary, I felt as fired up as President Obama himself that day. I went into the office of Senator Harry Reid, the most powerful senator in the United States at the time, and asked to speak with the intern coordinator.

Of course, the staff assistant sitting at the front desk asked me if I had a meeting scheduled. I said no and politely introduced myself, saying, "I am Steeve Simbert. I am a student at Georgetown University, and I would love to have the opportunity to speak with your intern coordinator to discuss my strong interest in interning for Senator Harry Reid." The coordinator came out to the front desk and asked smoothly and pleasantly, "So, Steeve, Georgetown does not have school today?" I replied with my thick Haitian-French accent, "Haha, no, we don't!"

We had a wonderful conversation. I had broken the most important rule impressed upon all would-be congressional interns: "Don't call! Don't stop by! Just email your application." Moreover, at the end of the conversation, I had the nerve to ask, "What is the possibility, do you think, that I might be fortunate enough to receive an internship with Senator Reid?" She responded, "Very good!" She told me to email her my schedule and what days of the week I would be available to intern.

Less than two hours after I met with her, I emailed her my schedule and thanked her for taking the time to meet with me. In addition, I sent her a handwritten thank-you note in the mail. My handwriting has always been elegant, and I carefully took my time to write her a very nice note. As I look back on it, I think I put her into a position from which she had to give me an internship! Today, most of my closest friends in Washington, D.C., whose weddings I attend and with whom I celebrate Thanksgiving and Christmas, are former staffers of Senator Reid.

The moral of my story is this: Take the risk! The worst that can happen is that someone will say no. But who cares? Don't take rejections personally. Just view them as an opportunity to try harder and work more creatively. Confront your fears, think outside of the box, and just do it!

According to the National Association of Colleges and Employers (NACE) (http://www.naceweb.org/talent-acquisition/internships/intern-to-full-time-hire-conversion-returning-vs-nonreturning-interns/) and Internships.com (http://www.internships.com/internship-jobs), more than half of all internships result in full-time job offers. No wonder so many students are seeking them! This section presents a rich array of hundreds of internships currently available at government institutions, nonprofit organizations, and private-sector firms.

Many opportunities require just a cover letter and résumé (see previous section) to apply. Some require transcripts and accept only applicants with a GPA of at least 3.0 or 3.5. U.S. citizenship or the ability to work in the United States may be necessary as well.

A Note on Pay

In the past, many internships were unpaid; however, in today's world, most offer some pay or a stipend. The amount of pay ranges from an eye-popping $10,000 per month at Snapchat (according to a 2016 survey) (https://www.theguardian.com/technology/2016/apr/29/tech-intern-wages-snapchat-twitter-apple) to minimum wage or even, in a couple of cases, a stipend of $150 per week or $500 per month. Our listings indicate whether each internship is paid or unpaid, but be sure to visit the webpage in each listing to learn the specific amount, if pay is a factor in your decision about whether to apply. According to NACE, the average intern's hourly wage across all sectors was $18.06.

While the private sector offers a myriad of paid internships, some internships in the government and within nonprofit organizations remain unpaid, or are paid at a minimal level. In these situations, it may be best to think of your internship as a two-way street on which you provide labor in return for skills that can make you a more competitive job candidate, a more knowledgeable employee, and a more effective advocate for change, while also enriching your life.

To compile this section, our team used our knowledge and networks of contacts, backed by original research, trustworthy sources, and reputable rankings by *Forbes* and the business-ranking site Vault, among others.

We want to particularly recognize and give credit to the Congressional Research Service for its 2016 report, "Internships, Fellowships, and Other Work Experience Opportunities in the Federal Government." We also want to recognize *Forbes*, Vault, and all the other websites that were invaluable in our research. We have included links to these and related resources in the appendix, should you wish to explore these topics further.

Part I:
U.S. Government Internships and Fellowships

As we reflect about the state of our nation today, we should always remember that our American story is one of struggle and achievement. It is a story in which patriotic and brilliant men and women have always fiercely debated how our country should move forward.

No person, cause, or idea is bigger than the constantly evolving nation that is the United States of America. The Constitutional Convention teaches us all that America can and will continue being the City on the Hill as long as we always strive for progress and work together to protect a government *of the people, for the people, and by the people.*

In the summer of 1787, delegates convened at the Constitutional Convention in Philadelphia to revise the Articles of Confederation. The Constitutional Convention ultimately created the United States Constitution. The debates and compromises that took place at the Convention set the rules for the founding of our government.

The Convention gave birth to our Constitution as the living symbol of the nation. It also established our three branches of government, which are at the heart and soul of our democracy, and which are emulated worldwide by other nations.

The 55 visionary delegates who convened in Philadelphia, Pennsylvania, in May 1787 to discuss possible improvements to the Articles of Confederation went beyond the scope of their responsibility and created a new form of government. The Convention began with the election of a president, George Washington, and a secretary, William Jackson.

The delegates nominated a three-member committee consisting of Messrs. Wythe, Hamilton, and Pinckney to draft the rules for the Convention. The delegates from Virginia presented a plan for the separation of the three branches of government (the executive, legislative, and judicial) at the Convention.

They determined that the legislative branch of government would consist of two houses rather than one. Further, they concluded that each state should have an equal vote in the upper house and that the number of representatives from each state in the lower house should be determined according to the population of the state.

The ultimate result of the Convention was the United States Constitution, which created a Federal Government, supreme within its sphere of operation, but which reserved substantial powers for the states. The Constitution enumerated the limited powers of the Federal Government and separated them among the three branches in order to protect individual liberty. It established an independent and unelected Federal judiciary to safeguard Federal authority and the rights of the people. The Constitution, as its preamble indicates, sought to *form a more perfect Union* and ensure that citizens of each state could pass freely to others and enjoy the rights of citizens there.

In his famous 1961 inaugural speech, former President John F. Kennedy proclaimed a call to action: "Ask not what your country can do for you; ask what you can do for your country." His words inspired many to pursue careers in public service.

Nearly five decades later, former President Barack Obama inspired a new generation with his own words: "Change will not come if we wait for some other person or some other time. We are the ones we've been waiting for. We are the change that we seek."

As an immigrant to this country, I find it truly extraordinary to observe from an insider's perspective the types of work the government performs. According to a recent Quinnipiac poll, Congress has only a 10 percent approval rating. This seems excessively harsh to me.

Consider this: Politics involves people from all kinds of backgrounds, cultures, traditions, and beliefs. Our governmental system places them all in a room and tells them to decide which path to follow and what is best for our country. Think about it. That's a messy process. Even with your significant other, or with a group of three or four people, you can barely decide which movie you should watch together.

Now imagine combining the 435 people in the U.S. House of Representatives with the 100 senators from across the country. How in the world can you expect them to make decisions expediently while representing the views of their diverse constituents?

Political decision-making is complex. The policymaker's job is to ask, "Should I allocate my hard-working constituents' dollars to build this highway or that much-needed hospital? On the other hand, should I give more money to children with cancer or veterans who have sacrificed their lives to serve our country? Alternatively, perhaps the money should go toward building a park in one neighborhood over another, or to build roads and bridges."

Every cause has advocates who think theirs is the most important project or issue in the world. The policymaker's job is to make those very difficult decisions. No matter what they decide, someone is inevitably unhappy.

These are just a few of the challenges that face policymakers. It is a difficult job that involves many people — complex creatures — each highly confident that they know the best solution, yet each wanting something different.

At its core, despite the conflicts surrounding how to best move the country forward, I believe politics is a noble profession. Politicians go to work every day and try to make decisions that will improve people's lives. It is a truly rewarding profession. In the end, it is worth the fight to make a difference in the lives of underserved people in need of assistance.

This section presents a wide array of internships and fellowships in all three branches of the federal government.

A Note on Internships and Fellowships

What is the difference between an internship and a fellowship? In general, internships are intended for students who are more than a year of study away from earning their degree, whereas fellowships are for graduating seniors or students at the graduate or postgraduate level. This is not a hard-and-fast rule, however, as some fellowships are intended for graduate students. Additionally, fellowships often fund professional development and/or academic research and include a stipend as the only form of payment.

"America will never be destroyed from the outside. If we falter and lose our freedoms, it will be because we destroyed ourselves."

— Abraham Lincoln, former president of the United States

Chapter 7:
Executive Branch — White House

Donald J. Trump is the president of the United States. Whatever your views are about that fact, no one becomes president by mere luck. You may be asking yourself, "What in the world happened?" If so, you are not alone. Thousands of political scientists in America spent their entire lives studying politics, and still, nearly all of them failed to predict this outcome.

When President Trump was elected, I thought, "I spent four years of my life studying politics, yet my teachers were all dead wrong in predicting who has the potential to win the presidency." I thought that maybe I had chosen the wrong major. Maybe I should have studied something more useful and practical, like engineering or math. "What in the world have I done?" I asked myself.

Then I realized that President Trump is a man who had a dream, believed in it, and made it happen. Even with no prior political experience, he succeeded. At that point, I said to myself, "If Donald Trump could become the president of the United States, don't tell me there is any job I'm not qualified for."

When you read some internship or job descriptions, the amount of experience the companies require can be truly daunting. Perhaps just reading the description can convince you not to apply, making you feel you would never receive a call back. That is the wrong attitude. Whenever you face these circumstances, think about President Trump.

The outcome of the 2016 presidential election taught me that it is not about what you studied in school, what college you attended, or whether your parents are wealthy or well connected. Though these factors may help to some extent, they alone will not determine your success. Your success is determined by knowing what you want and being willing to make it happen. Only you have the power to change your destiny. Don't ever let anyone stand between you and your dreams. You try, you fail, you try harder, you learn from your mistakes, and you try again until you succeed.

The White House provides unique opportunities to acquire professional experience while strengthening your leadership skills. This chapter presents three highly prestigious and competitive White House programs for undergraduates, graduate students, and recent graduates.

Insider's Tip: Interested in a White House tour? Book three months in advance through the office of your member of Congress.

White House Internships

The White House offers unpaid internships to undergraduate, graduate, and recently graduated students, as well as veterans, year-round.

http://www.whitehouse.gov/

White House Fellowships

The White House offers full-time, paid fellowships to young men and women who have completed their undergraduate education, allowing them to experience working at the highest level of the federal government for one year.

https://www.whitehouse.gov/get-involved/fellows/

❡ White House Office of Science and Technology Policy (OSTP) Internships

OSTP's unpaid internships offer undergraduate, graduate, and some postgraduate students the opportunity to experience working either in its policy division or on its legal team.

https://www.whitehouse.gov/ostp/internships/

"A dream doesn't become reality through magic; it takes sweat, determination, and hard work."

— Colin Powell, former national security adviser and retired four-star general

Chapter 8:
Executive Branch — Departments and Agencies

Thinking about a career in the federal government? This chapter presents government resources that can help you find your niche, followed by several programs sponsored by outside organizations, and then a host of opportunities available in specific departments and agencies.

Insider's Tip: Young Government Leaders (http://younggov.org/) offers networking, mentoring, and developmental opportunities for young leaders throughout the country.

Federal Government Resources

GO Government

GO Government, a project introduced by the Partnership for Public Service, promotes career opportunities within the federal government. Its website showcases hundreds of internships in U.S. departments and agencies and provides valuable information on the hiring process for young people starting their careers.

http://gogovernment.org/government_careers/students_entry-level_talent.php

Office of Personnel Management (OPM)

OPM manages the federal government's civilian workforce by directing human resources and employee management services. College students, recent graduates, and veterans may be eligible to pursue federal government internships and jobs through the three Pathways Programs, administered by OPM.

The Pathways Programs provide meaningful training and career development for young people who aspire to work in government. They comprise the following three programs, each detailed on OPM's website:

- Internship Program

- Recent Graduates Program
- Presidential Management Fellows Program

Visit OPM's website to learn more about each of these opportunities.

https://www.opm.gov/about-us/careers-at-opm/students-recent-graduates/

USAjobs.gov, OPM's official portal for showcasing jobs at all U.S. agencies, includes links to the three Pathways Programs above and much more.

http://www.usajobs.gov/

Presidential Innovation Fellows

This highly competitive program addresses challenges within the United States, enabling technology leaders to work on a wide variety of innovative projects in various agencies during their 12-month tenure. This paid program offers multiple opportunities to serve citizens through far-reaching or extremely focused efforts. It is aimed toward professionals with a minimum of 10 years of experience in their field.

https://presidentialinnovationfellows.gov/

Nonprofit-Sponsored Programs

American Association for the Advancement of Science (AAAS) Science and Technology Policy Fellowship

The AAAS Science and Technology Fellowship helps engineers and scientists contribute to and learn firsthand about federal policymaking. Fellows come from a broad range of backgrounds, disciplines, and career stages. They receive a stipend of $75,000 to $100,000 for a yearlong assignment in the federal government. AAAS sponsors more than 150 placements in the executive branch, two legislative placements, and one judicial placement. In addition, roughly 30 additional placements in the legislative branch are available through partner societies.

https://www.aaas.org/page/stpf/become-st-policy-fellow

Hispanic Association of Colleges and Universities National Internship Program (HNIP)

HNIP is a paid internship that places undergraduate and graduate students in federal agencies, as well as corporations and nonprofit organizations, across the country. About 450 students are placed each year in positions from which they can be recruited by federal agencies and corporations.

https://www.hacu.net/hacu/HNIP.asp

Native American Congressional Internship

The Native American Congressional Internship, offered by the Udall Foundation, allows American Indian and Alaska Native students the opportunity to affect policy and gain experience in the federal legislative and executive branches, including Congress, federal agencies, and the White House. Internships are paid and open to undergraduate, graduate, and law students. Students are provided a stipend of $1,200 to cover housing, transportation, and educational opportunities.

https://www.udall.gov/OurPrograms/Internship/Internship.aspx

Cabinet-Level Departments

Department of Agriculture (USDA)

The USDA helps rural Americans thrive by providing economic opportunities, promoting agriculture production, and preserving natural resources. It offers a variety of internships:

- Internships for Students With Disabilities (https://www.dm.usda.gov/employ/student/seo-internship-disabilities.htm)
- Pathways Programs (https://www.dm.usda.gov/employ/student/seo-pathways-programs.htm)
- Student Volunteer Program (https://www.dm.usda.gov/employ/student/seo-volunteer-program.htm)
- Third-Party Internships (https://www.dm.usda.gov/employ/student/seo-internship-programs.htm)

The USDA offers these full- and part-time internships to students and graduates.

https://www.dm.usda.gov/employ/student/internship.htm

Department of Commerce

The Department of Commerce strives to promote economic growth within the United States. It offers paid and unpaid internships, ranging from the Bureau of Economic Analysis (https://www.bea.gov/jobs/beajobs_internprogram.htm) to the National Institute of Standards and Technology (https://www.nist.gov/careers/internship-program), to students and graduates.

http://hr.commerce.gov/Careers/StudentCareerOpportunities/index.htm

Department of Defense (DOD)

The DOD, the nation's oldest and largest government agency, strives to deter war and protect the United States via the military. Its full- and part-time paid internships provide training and career development to students and graduates at the beginning of their federal service careers.

http://godefense.cpms.osd.mil/internships.aspx

Department of Education (ED)

The ED fosters educational excellence and ensures equal access by promoting student achievement and preparation for global competitiveness. It offers unpaid internships in government and federal education policy, as well as in administration, providing interns with the opportunity to work on a wide range of projects, including legislative affairs, policy analysis, and communications. All students attending a postsecondary school (including two- and four-year colleges, graduate schools, and vocational, technical, and trade schools) are eligible.

https://www2.ed.gov/students/prep/job/intern/index.html

Department of Energy (DOE)

The DOE employs transformative science and technology solutions to address America's energy, environmental, and nuclear challenges. It offers selective paid internships at its labs to students pursuing a postsecondary education.

https://www.energy.gov/student-programs-and-internships

Department of Health and Human Services (HHS)

HHS focuses on improving and protecting the health of Americans by fostering advances in medicine, public health, and social services. It offers a variety of internships to students and recent graduates.

http://www.hhs.gov/about/careers/pathways/index.html

Department of Homeland Security (DHS)

DHS ensures national security in America. It offers a variety of internships, scholarships, and fellowships via the following departments and programs:

Students:

- Health and Science (https://www.dhs.gov/homeland-security-careers/student-and-recent-grads)
- Intelligence and Analysis (https://www.dhs.gov/homeland-security-careers/office-intelligence-and-analysis-internship-program)
- Law Enforcement (https://www.dhs.gov/homeland-security-careers/student-and-recent-grads)
- Legal (https://www.dhs.gov/homeland-security-careers/student-and-recent-grads)
- Pathways Programs (https://www.dhs.gov/homeland-security-careers/student-and-recent-grads)
- Public Affairs (https://www.dhs.gov/homeland-security-careers/public-affairs)
- Secretary's Honors Program (https://www.dhs.gov/homeland-security-careers/secretarys-honors-program)

Recent Graduates:

- Acquisition Professional Career Program (https://www.dhs.gov/homeland-security-careers/acquisition-professional-career-program)
- Presidential Management Fellows (https://www.dhs.gov/homeland-security-careers/presidential-management-fellows-program)
- Secretary's Honors Program (https://www.dhs.gov/homeland-security-careers/secretarys-honors-program)

These internships are available to students and recent graduates.
https://www.dhs.gov/homeland-security-careers/students

Department of the Interior (DOI)

DOI strives to protect natural resources and cultural heritage, provide information regarding those resources, and honor its commitments and responsibilities toward particular groups and communities within America. It offers a variety of internships and fellowships, as well as three Pathways Programs in various offices and bureaus, such as the following:

- Bureau of Land Management (https://www.blm.gov/careers/students-and-grads)
- Bureau of Ocean Energy Management (https://www.boem.gov/Students-and-Recent-Graduates/)
- Bureau of Reclamation (https://www.usbr.gov/)
- Bureau of Safety and Environmental Enforcement (https://www.bsee.gov/what-we-do/administrative-services/human-resources/students-and-grads)
- National Park Service (https://www.nps.gov/aboutus/pathways.htm)
- Office of Surface Mining Reclamation and Enforcement (https://www.osmre.gov/about/getInvolved.shtm)
- U.S. Fish and Wildlife Service (https://www.fws.gov/humancapital/)
- U.S. Geological Survey (https://www2.usgs.gov/humancapital/sw/studentandrecentgrads.html)

These opportunities are available to students and recent graduates.
Pathways Programs: http://www.doi.gov/pathways/index.cfm
Other DOI internships: https://www.doi.gov/ibc/about-us/jobs/student-opportunities

Department of Justice (DOJ)

The DOJ focuses on defending the interests of the American people, enforcing the law, ensuring the public's safety, providing federal leadership in preventing and controlling crime, seeking just punishment for the guilty, and ensuring fair and impartial administration of justice. It offers paid and unpaid internships:

- Attorney General's Honors Program for Entry-Level Attorneys (https://www.justice.gov/legal-careers/entry-level-attorneys)
- Summer Law Intern Program (https://www.justice.gov/legal-careers/summer-law-intern-program)
- Volunteer Legal Intern Opportunities (https://www.justice.gov/legal-careers/volunteer-legal-internships)

These internships are available to law students.

https://www.justice.gov/crt/volunteer-and-paid-student-internships

Department of Labor (DOL)

The DOL fosters, promotes, and develops the welfare of wage earners, job seekers, and retirees; improves working conditions within the United States; advances employment opportunities; and assures work-related benefits and rights. It offers students and recent graduates various internships and the three Pathways Programs for the DOL's departments and offices, such as those offered by the Bureau of Labor Statistics, the Employment & Training Administration, the Mine Safety & Health Administration, the Occupational Safety & Health Administration, and the Office of the Inspector General.

https://www.dol.gov/oasam/programs/internship/

Department of State

The Department of State focuses on the conduct of American diplomacy. It offers various paid and unpaid internships and fellowships:

- Department of State Student Internship Program (https://careers.state.gov/intern/student-internships/)
- Pathways Internship Programs (https://careers.state.gov/work/pathways/internship-programs/)
- Student Programs (https://careers.state.gov/intern/student-programs/)
- Other Student Programs (https://careers.state.gov/intern/other-programs/)

These internships are available to students and recent graduates.

https://careers.state.gov/intern/

Department of Transportation (DOT)

DOT ensures the safety, efficiency, and modernization of the U.S. transportation system. It offers paid and unpaid internships, fellowships, and the three Pathways Programs, including the following:

- Student Transportation Internship Program for Diverse Groups (STIPDG) (http://www.fhwa.dot.gov/education/stipdg.cfm)

- DOT Internships for Law Students (http://www.dot.gov/mission/administrations/general-counsel/jobs-internships)
- DOT Secretarial Internship Program (https://www.transportation.gov/interns)
- DOT Pathways Programs (https://www.transportation.gov/careers/pathways-program)
- DOT Presidential Management Fellows (https://www.transportation.gov/careers/presidential-management-fellows-agency-contacts)

These internships are available to students and recent graduates.
https://www.treasury.gov/careers/hq-careers/Pages/student-employment.aspx

Department of the Treasury

The Treasury strives to maintain a strong economy while creating economic and job opportunities by promoting conditions favorable toward economic growth and stability. In addition to the three Pathways Programs, Treasury offers a Treasury Scholars program to promote racial and gender diversity. All four opportunities can be found on their website.
https://www.treasury.gov/careers/hq-careers/Pages/student-employment.aspx

Department of Veterans Affairs (VA)

The VA serves and honors American veterans. It offers various internships at almost 100 locations under a number of different programs, including the following:

- Graduate Healthcare Administration Training Program: Health System Management Trainees (https://www.vacareers.va.gov/students-trainees/graduate-healthcare-administration-training-program.asp)
- Graduate Healthcare Administration Training Program: Interns and Recent Graduates (https://www.vacareers.va.gov/students-trainees/graduate-healthcare-administration-training-program.asp)
- Technical Career Field Program (https://www.vacareers.va.gov/students-trainees/technical-field.asp)

These internships are available to graduate students, recent graduates, and VA employees.
http://www.vacareers.va.gov/

Agencies

Administrative Conference of the United States (ACUS)

ACUS garners recommendations from both the public and the private sector regarding improvements to the administrative process and procedure. It offers both year-round unpaid internships and ad hoc unpaid fellowships. Law students in their second and third years are encouraged to apply. Tasks are primarily research-based but may vary by position.

https://www.acus.gov/internships-and-research-fellows

Animal and Plant Health Inspection Service (APHIS)

Part of the USDA, APHIS works toward identifying standards for the humane treatment and care of animals within the United States. It offers unpaid externships to full- and part-time college students who maintain at least a 2.5 GPA. Tasks vary by position.

https://www.aphis.usda.gov/aphis/banner/careers/ct_careers_students

Central Intelligence Agency (CIA) Human Resources Directorate

The CIA utilizes high-level technology to research, evaluate, and disseminate information pertaining to national security. It offers full-time, paid internships to undergraduates in fields such as human resource management, human capital management, business administration, psychology, organizational development, public administration, and sociology.

https://www.cia.gov/careers/student-opportunities

Consumer Financial Protection Bureau (CFPB)

The CFPB protects the interests of American consumers. Its four internship programs aim to create and sustain a new generation of leaders, providing them with in-depth knowledge and training.

- **Director's Financial Analyst Program**
  This two-year rotational program aims to increase the efficacy of financial markets.

- **Joseph Story Honors Attorney Program**
  This two-year program is available to law students and recent graduates who want to use their legal and analytical skills to make a difference in the lives of American consumers.

- **Research Assistant Program**
  This program is open to recent graduates in economics, mathematics, statistics, computer science, and behavioral and cognitive research.

- **Summer Internship**

This paid 12-week summer internship offers students on-the-job training while they work on a variety of mission-oriented and operational projects.

These internships are available to students and recent graduates.

https://www.consumerfinance.gov/about-us/careers/students-and-graduates/

Environmental Protection Agency (EPA)

The EPA protects human health and the environment, working to improve American citizens' health and well-being while also ensuring clean air and water throughout the country. It offers various paid and unpaid fellowships, scholarships, and internships to students and recent graduates.

https://www.epa.gov/careers/student-internships

Federal Communications Commission (FCC)

The FCC implements and enforces communication laws and regulations in America. It offers various paid and unpaid internships to students and recent graduates throughout the year. Internship positions update regularly and are available on an ad hoc basis.

https://www.fcc.gov/general/student-internships-fcc

Federal Reserve Board

The Board, the central bank of the United States, promotes the effective operation of the economy and public interest. It is one of the most selective places for students and recent graduates in finance, economics, law, information systems, or accounting to obtain paid and unpaid internships.

https://www.federalreserve.gov/careers-internships.htm

National Aeronautics and Space Administration (NASA)

NASA conducts aeronautical and aerospace research, and retains responsibility for the civilian space program. It offers internships at two locations:

- Armstrong Flight Research Center in California
- Stennis Space Center in Mississippi

Other NASA facilities offer various independent internships and fellowships for students and recent graduates. NASA also participates in the three paid Pathways Programs.

Internships and fellowships: intern.nasa.gov (https://intern.nasa.gov/index.html)

Pathways Programs: nasajobs.nasa.gov (http://nasajobs.nasa.gov/studentopps/Pathways.htm)

National Security Agency (NSA)

The NSA monitors, collects, and processes information regarding foreign intelligence and counterintelligence. It offers students a variety of opportunities, including scholarships, paid internships, and summer programs.

http://www.intelligencecareers.gov/

Smithsonian Institution

The Smithsonian represents a community of learning, featuring the world's largest museum, education complex, and research complex. It offers students and recent graduates various unpaid internships, scholarships, and fellowships within its museums and research institutes. Variable stipends are available to help offset living expenses, depending on the position.

Internships: https://www.smithsonianofi.com/blog/2012/12/26/smithsonian-internships/

Fellowships: https://www.smithsonianofi.com/blog/2012/12/26/smithsonian-fellowships/

United States Agency for International Development (USAID)

USAID promotes and demonstrates democratic values abroad. It offers various types of paid and unpaid internships and fellowships within various departments to students and recent graduates, including within the Bureau for Legislative and Public Affairs, the Office of the General Counsel, and the Office of Transition Initiatives.

Internships: http://www.usaid.gov/work-usaid/careers/student-internships

Fellowships: http://www.usaid.gov/work-usaid/careers/fellows-program

"We need to stand up, go out and vote, talk to our legislators, and get educated."

— David Hogg, young leader, age 18

Chapter 9:
Legislative Branch

This chapter presents a broad sample of the numerous opportunities available to work in a congressional office on Capitol Hill.

Insider's Tip: The Congressional Management Foundation has compiled an excellent 134-page resource, "Congressional Intern Handbook: A Guide for Interns and Newcomers to Capitol Hill," (http://www.congressfoundation.org/storage/documents/CMF_Pubs/cmf-congressional-intern-handbook.pdf.) which you can download at no charge. In addition, for news and updates from the U.S. Embassy, visit https://internationalclubdc.com/.

Internships

Internships are available in the offices of all members of Congress in Washington, D.C., as well as in district, state, and committee offices. These typically unpaid positions are available throughout the year, and are listed on both the House (https://www.house.gov/educators-and-students/college-internships) and Senate (https://www.senate.gov/employment/po/positions.htm) websites.

Fellowships

The fellowships listed in this chapter are sponsored by a range of independent organizations. Some are intended for undergraduate or graduate students, or recent graduates, while others are designed for professionals in a variety of careers.

Air Force Legislative Fellows

The Air Force Legislative Fellows program assures the continued efficacy of the U.S. Air Force and American national security. This fellowship provides qualified field-grade Air Force officers and selected civilians with an extensive education in national security policy through 10- to 18-month tours within the DOD, as well as within other government agencies or distinguished civilian institutions.

http://www.airuniversity.af.mil/AF-Fellows/

American Association for the Advancement of Science (AAAS) Science and Technology Policy Fellowship

The AAAS Science and Technology Fellowship helps engineers and scientists contribute to and learn firsthand about federal policymaking. Fellows come from a broad range of backgrounds, disciplines, and career stages. They receive a stipend of $75,000 to $100,000 for a yearlong assignment in the federal government. AAAS sponsors multiple legislative placements. In addition, roughly 30 additional placements in the legislative branch are available through partner societies.

https://www.aaas.org/program/science-technology-policy-fellowships

American Political Science Association Congressional Fellowship (APSA)

The APSA Congressional Fellowship, a highly selective program, aims to expand public understanding of policymaking and advance the quality of teaching and reporting on American national politics. It offers political scientists, journalists, federal employees, health specialists, and other professionals a nine-month placement on a congressional staff.

https://www.apsanet.org/cfp

Army Congressional Fellowship Program (ACFP)

The ACFP educates selected Army officers and civilians on the importance of the strategic relationship between the Army and Congress. This three-year program includes the pursuit of a master's degree in legislative affairs at George Washington University (GWU), service on the staff of a member of Congress, and the opportunity to assist the Army or joint staff in a legislative liaison duty position.

http://www.nationalguard.mil/Leadership/Joint-Staff/Personal-Staff/Legislative-Liaison/Congressional-Fellowship-Program/

Asian Pacific American Institute for Congressional Studies (APAICS) Fellowship

The APAICS program focuses on developing leadership, building public policy knowledge, and expanding the pipeline for Asian Pacific Americans to pursue public offices at all levels. Available to graduates and young professionals, this fellowship focuses on legislation and public policy, and enables fellows to work as staff members in a congressional office.

http://apaics.org/congressional-fellowship/

Brookings Institution Congressional Fellowships

Brookings provides fellows with a comprehensive understanding of how Congress operates, while also enabling them to gain valuable contacts on Capitol Hill. Applicants must have at least a GS-13 grade level or a minimum of seven years of management experience.

https://www.brookings.edu/fellowships-programs/legis/

Congressional Black Caucus Foundation (CBCF) Fellowships

The CBCF is dedicated to advancing the global African-American and black community by developing young leaders and educating the public. In its 20-month fellowships, African-American and black holders of graduate or professional degrees work with members of Congress and committees, attend leadership development seminars, complete community service projects, and produce policy papers. It offers four fellowship programs:

- Congressional Fellowship (https://cbcfinc.academicworks.com/opportunities/465)
- Congressional Fellowship on Women in Health Sciences Leadership
- Donald M. Payne Foreign Policy Fellowship
- Small Business and Entrepreneurship Fellowship (https://cbcfinc.academicworks.com/opportunities/503)

Fellows are paid an annual salary of $40,000 plus benefits. Typically, the CBCF accepts fewer than 10 percent of those who apply for its nine fellowship positions.
https://www.cbcfinc.org/fellowships/

Congressional Black Caucus Foundation (CBCF) Internships

The Congressional Black Caucus Foundation (CBCF) offers three internship programs. Participants receive housing, a stipend, placement in Congressional Black Caucus member offices or federal agencies (depending on the program), and opportunities to meet and interact with legislators and leaders in all branches of government. Additionally, interns are eligible for scholarships for prestigious public policy graduate programs, and they are actively recruited by executive branch agencies.

- Congressional Internship
- Emerging Leaders Internship (https://cbcfinc.academicworks.com/opportunities/460)
- Communications Internship (https://cbcfinc.academicworks.com/opportunities/461)

https://www.cbcfinc.org/internships/

Congressional Budget Office (CBO)

The CBO provides analyses of issues relating to the congressional budget process. Interns, who work on analysis, budget, and economic policymaking, receive a modest stipend.
https://www.cbo.gov/about/careers/internships

Congressional Hispanic Caucus Institute (CHCI) Congressional Internship

The CHCI provides educational and leadership programs to train the next generation of Hispanic American leaders. The CHCI's internship provides promising undergraduates with the experience of working in a congressional office. All interns are placed in a member of Congress's office and receive a stipend.

https://chci.org/programs/congressional-internship-program/

Congressional Research Service (CRS)

The CRS provides policy and legal analysis to members of Congress. It offers undergraduates, graduate students, and postgraduates various unpaid internship and fellowship opportunities. Fellows receive varying levels of compensation depending on the position.

https://www.loc.gov/crsinfo/

Galloway International Congressional Fellowship (GICF)

The GICF promotes quality journalism in an era when journalism has profoundly changed, regarding both the sources and level of funding available and the myriad of technological advances that have swept the industry. Fellows work on foreign policy issues in Congress.

http://www.gallowayfoundation.org/foundation-programs/#gicf

Government Accountability Office (GAO)

The GAO offers 10- to 16-week long paid internships. After completing 400 hours of service and meeting their degree requirements, interns are offered opportunities to become full-time employees. These internships are available to graduate and undergraduate students.

https://www.gao.gov/careers/student.html

HillVets House Fellowship

HillVets, a network of veterans in Washington, D.C., offers veterans an internship in the House of Representatives. Benefits include a food stipend and four months of housing.

https://www.hillvets.org/hillvets-house/

Library of Congress (LOC)

LOC offers students both paid and unpaid volunteer and internship opportunities. Interns work in various departments, including the following:

- American Folklife Center (http://www.loc.gov/folklife/interns.html)
- Conservation Division (https://www.loc.gov/preservation/outreach/intern/int_cons.html)

- Hispanic Division (https://www.loc.gov/item/internships/hispanic-reading-room-volunteer-internship/)
- Law Library of Congress (http://www.loc.gov/law/opportunities/internships-metadata.php#Law)

Other opportunities include the paid Junior Fellows Summer Intern Program: https://www.loc.gov/item/internships/junior-fellows-program/
https://www.loc.gov/internships-and-fellowships/

Marine Corps Congressional Fellowship Program (CFP)

The CFP enables Marine officers, SNCOs, and civilian Marines to work in Congress for one session. It consists of three components: (1) training and education through the Government Affairs Institute at Georgetown University, (2) working in the office of a senator or member of Congress, and (3) beginning a two-year utilization tour immediately upon completion of the fellowship.
https://www.hqmc.marines.mil/Agencies/Office-of-Legislative-Affairs/Congressional-Fellowship-Program/

National Oceanic and Atmospheric Administration (NOAA) Knauss Marine Policy Fellowship

NOAA's Knauss Marine Policy Fellowship supports highly qualified graduate students interested in water resources such as the Great Lakes, oceans, and coastal resources. The program matches these students with hosts in the legislative and executive branches of government in the Washington, D.C., area for a one-year paid fellowship.
Other NOAA opportunities: https://seagrant.noaa.gov/Funding
https://seagrant.noaa.gov/Knauss

Navy Legislative Fellows Program

The Navy Legislative Fellows program enables Navy officers to broaden their experience and knowledge of Congress. The fellowship entails a one-year full-time assignment in the office of a member of Congress or senator who serves on a defense-related committee.
http://www.public.navy.mil/bupers-npc/officer/detailing/educationplacement/pages/legislativeaffairs.aspx

TechCongress Congressional Innovation Fellowship

TechCongress enables talented technologists to gain firsthand experience in federal policymaking and to help shape the future of tech policy through a one-year fellowship with a member of Congress or congressional committee. Fellows receive a $75,000/year-equivalent stipend.
http://www.techcongress.io/

Women's Congressional Policy Institute (WCPI) Fellowship

The WCPI Fellowship trains potential leaders in public policymaking to examine issues from the perspectives, experiences, and needs of women. It is the only graduate-level fellowship on Capitol Hill that focuses exclusively on women. This fellowship is available to graduate students or those who have recently completed a master's, doctorate, or professional degree with a proven commitment to equity for women. Fellows receive a stipend.

http://www.womenspolicy.org/our-work/congressional-fellows/

Wounded Warrior Program (WWP)

The Wounded Warrior Fellowship, a two-year fellowship within the House of Representatives, helps veterans acquire valuable legislative skills in order to increase their career opportunities.

https://cao.house.gov/wounded-warrior/about-wounded-warrior-program

"To listen well is as powerful a means of communication and influence as to talk well."

— John Marshall, former chief justice of the United States

Chapter 10:
Judicial Branch

Article III of the United States Constitution established the judicial branch of the federal government. The judicial branch consists of the Supreme Court and lower courts, as established by Congress. This chapter presents several prestigious opportunities to work within this segment of the government.

Supreme Court Programs

Judicial Interns

The Supreme Court offers a unique judicial intern program specifically designed for undergraduate and graduate students. The program provides students with useful insights into the inner workings of the Court. Various offices offer unpaid internships, including the following:

- Office of the Administrative Assistant to the Chief Justice (http://govcentral.monster.com/education/articles/1809-supreme-court-internship)
- Office of the Clerk
- Office of the Counselor to the Chief Justice
- Office of the Curator
- Public Information Office
  https://www.supremecourt.gov/jobs/internship/Internship
Program.aspx

Supreme Court Fellows

The Supreme Court offers unique opportunities for exceptional young people to serve the administration of justice at a national level. Placement of fellows within these highly selective programs includes the following:

- Supreme Court (https://www.supremecourt.gov/fellows/fellowships.aspx#SupremeCourt)
- Federal Judicial Center (https://www.supremecourt.gov/fellows/

fellowships.aspx#FJC)
- Administrative Office of the U.S. Courts (https://www.supremecourt.gov/fellows/fellowships.aspx#AO)
- U.S. Sentencing Commission (https://www.supremecourt.gov/fellows/fellowships.aspx#Sentencing)

Selected fellows have the opportunity to earn salaries equivalent to a GS-12 pay scale. https://www.supremecourt.gov/fellows/

Nonprofit-Sponsored Program

American Association for the Advancement of Science (AAAS) Science and Technology Policy Fellowship

The AAAS Science and Technology Fellowship helps engineers and scientists contribute to and learn firsthand about federal policymaking. They receive a stipend of $75,000 to $100,000 for a yearlong assignment in the federal government. AAAS sponsors one judicial placement. It is open to applicants with a minimum of three years of postdoctoral professional experience. Applicants with a J.D. degree or legal experience are preferred.

https://www.aaas.org/program/science-technology-policy-fellowships

Part II:
Nonprofit-Sector Internships

This section presents a wide array of fulfilling and enriching opportunities in the nonprofit sector, from advocacy organizations, trade associations, and political action committees (PACs) to public policy research organizations (think tanks) and international organizations.

Many nonprofit organizations and think tanks offer both internships and fellowships. If you are a graduating senior or a recent graduate, we recommend you consider applying for a fellowship rather than an internship. Fellowships may be more difficult to obtain, due to how competitively they are sought after, but they generally offer higher pay and levels of responsibility. If an organization offers both, we note that in its listing and provide a link to a webpage with full information about the fellowship.

Listings in Part II include Twitter handles when available, allowing you to easily follow and interact with organizations of interest. Following one of these well-connected organizations on Twitter is a convenient way to learn more and discover related groups and issues.

"With fame comes opportunity, but in my opinion it also includes responsibility — to advocate and share, to focus less on glass slippers and more on pushing through glass ceilings, and, if I'm lucky enough, then to inspire."

— Meghan Markle, Duchess of Sussex and former American actress

Chapter 11:
Advocacy Organizations and Foundations

From ending segregation to winning women's right to vote, nearly every wrong ever righted was achieved through advocacy. When the public is engaged, informed, and mobilized around an issue, change can happen. As such, it's a small wonder many young leaders with passion and commitment are drawn to advocacy organizations. Washington, D.C., is home to literally thousands of them, from issue-oriented groups to trade associations to PACs. This chapter presents a curated collection of venerable powerhouses and modern upstarts to give you ideas for your own research. At the end of the chapter is a short section on foundations that offer internships.

Insider's Tip: If bridging the civic divide and supporting young leaders is of interest to you, check out the Bridge Alliance (https://www.bridgealliance.us/ourmembers), a network of 80 modern, innovative groups.

American Civil Liberties Union (ACLU)

The ACLU defends the rights and liberties guaranteed by the Constitution and laws of the United States. Internships are available at many chapters for undergraduate, graduate, and law students, who are encouraged to pursue academic credit. In some cases, interns may receive a stipend, depending on the position and the availability of funds. Law students, for example, may receive a $5,000 stipend for a 10-week, full-time internship.

https://www.aclu.org/careers
Twitter: https://twitter.com/ACLU

^^ American Conservative Union (ACU)

Chaired by Matt Schlapp, the ACU advocates limited government and presents the well-known annual Conservative Political Action Conference (CPAC), which attracts famous speakers (including President Trump in 2018) and thousands of conservatives from across the country. Paid interns may engage with members of Congress, media personalities, and other leaders of the conservative movement. Internships are available to college students and recent graduates.

> https://conservative.org/careers/internship
> Twitter: https://twitter.com/ACUConservative

American Federation of Labor-Congress of Industrial Organizations (AFL-CIO)

The AFL-CIO, the largest federation of unions in the United States, offers a variety of opportunities, from union-specific internships to summer internships for law students. Pay and benefits vary.

> https://aflcio.org/about-us/careers-and-apprenticeships
> Twitter: https://twitter.com/AFLCIO

American Israel Public Affairs Committee (AIPAC)

AIPAC strengthens, protects, and promotes the U.S.-Israel relationship. It offers semester-long and summer internships. The summer internship, called the Diamond Internship, offers interns a stipend in return for their participation. The internship offered during the academic year, the AIPAC Internship, is available only for academic credit. Participants in the AIPAC Internship work 15-20 hours a week on tasks ranging from writing and research to event management.

> https://www.aipac.org/connect/students/intern-at-aipac
> Twitter: https://twitter.com/aipac

^^ Americans for Prosperity

Americans for Prosperity, a grassroots organization based in Arlington, Virginia, promotes free markets, lower taxes, and limited government regulation. Paid internships are available around the country and may involve collecting data or building relationships with prospective community activists. Benefits include learning, workshops, and professional development.

> https://americansforprosperity.org/careers/internship/
> Twitter: https://twitter.com/TexasAFP

^^ The Borgen Project

The Borgen Project, with volunteers in 754 cities, is an innovative national campaign to make poverty a focus of U.S. foreign policy. It offers unpaid internships to undergraduate and graduate students in its Seattle office, as well as part-time telecommute internships in human resources, public relations, journalism, writing, and political affairs. Telecommute interns attend meetings via conference calls and submit regular reports. Internships are offered year-round and are highly selective, with only 12 percent of applicants selected.

Seattle Internships: https://twitter.com/TexasAFP

Telecommute Internships: https://borgenproject.org/telecommu te-internships/

Twitter: https://twitter.com/borgenproject

Citizens United

Headed by David Bossie, Citizens United advocates free enterprise and limited government, and calls itself the nation's premier conservative filmmaker. It offers year-round paid internships to undergraduates and recent graduates. Interns perform a wide range of tasks, including helping manage donor relations, processing policy petitions, and developing databases.

http://www.citizensunited.org/Internship.aspx

Twitter: https://twitter.com/Citizens_United

Environmental Defense Fund (EDF)

The EDF seeks to mitigate climate change and encourage companies to adopt environmentally friendly practices. It offers internships to college students and recent graduates, either for academic credit or for pay, year-round.

https://www.edf.org/jobs/internships-fellowships

Twitter: https://twitter.com/envdefensefund

Everytown for Gun Safety

Founded by former New York City mayor Michael Bloomberg, Everytown for Gun Safety seeks to stop gun violence. It offers paid internships in various departments on an ad hoc basis.

https://everytown.org/job-board/

Twitter: https://twitter.com/everytown

Family Research Council (FRC)

The Christian-based FRC works on issues such as the sanctity of life, marriage and family, religious liberty, education, bioethics, and judicial activism. It offers various internships to undergraduates and graduate students year-round. In addition to fulfilling daily research assignments, interns attend a weekly seminar. They are challenged to defend their policy positions through mock scenarios such as a legislative hearing, TV interview, or city council meeting. They receive a modest bi-weekly stipend.

https://www.frc.org/internships

Twitter: https://twitter.com/FRCdc

FreedomWorks

FreedomWorks advocates limited government and individual liberty. Interns monitor hearings and press conferences on Capitol Hill and at the White House, attend conferences and seminars, and conduct research on policies that promote economic liberty. Internships are offered to individuals interested in free market ideas and public policy. Candidates must be interested in turning ideas generated by think tanks into action and must possess basic computer skills.

http://www.freedomworks.org/about/internships

Twitter: https://twitter.com/FreedomWorks

Human Rights Campaign (HRC)

HRC envisions a world where LGBTQ people are assured equal rights. It offers unpaid summer and fall internships in both Washington, D.C., and the South to undergraduate, graduate, and recently graduated students. Interns can work in communications and marketing, education and outreach, policy and political affairs, or development, or do cross-organizational work. A limited number of need-based scholarships are available to defray interns' living expenses. These scholarships require a separate application, and preference is given to candidates seeking a full-time internship.

https://www.hrc.org/hrc-story/internships

Twitter: https://twitter.com/HRC

Human Rights Watch

Human Rights Watch seeks interns who are passionate about human rights and determined to make an impact on lives around the world. It offers unpaid internships year-round at various HRW offices in the United States and abroad. Responsibilities include monitoring international law developments in targeted countries, researching and drafting papers on issues related to international justice, conducting desk research, planning events, and fundraising. Law, undergraduate, and graduate students are eligible to apply.

https://recruiting.ultipro.com/HUM1004HRW/JobBoard/1f3f0f f9-99fb-4df2-8d3b-d832e12107eb/?q=&o=postedDateDesc&f5=QNQQslAC_ka_ jCGSBvLkhQ

Twitter: https://twitter.com/hrw

NARAL Pro-Choice America

NARAL Pro-Choice America supports reproductive rights and women's health. It offers paid year-round internships to undergraduates with a strong commitment to reproductive health and freedom. Students interested in political processes, nonprofit work, and/or reproductive health are strongly encouraged to apply. Candidates must be committed to NARAL's goal of building a political constituency to protect and promote the rights of all women to exercise the full range of their reproductive choices, including abortion, as well as their rights to a workplace environment in which diversity is valued and supported.

https://www.prochoiceamerica.org/about/jobs/

Twitter: https://twitter.com/NARAL

^^ National Association for the Advancement of Colored People (NAACP)

Founded in 1909, the NAACP is the nation's oldest and largest grassroots-based civil rights organization, with over 2,000 volunteer-run branches nationwide. It offers a variety of internships on an ad hoc basis.

https://www.naacp.org/employment/

Twitter: https://twitter.com/NAACP

National Education Association (NEA)

The NEA represents public schoolteachers and other school support staff. It offers a limited number of paid and unpaid internships to undergraduate, graduate, and recently graduated students, as well as doctoral candidates who are interested in public education policy and education issues. Interns are recruited on a rolling basis until all positions are filled. Unpaid interns are eligible to receive course or program credit for their internship experience.

https://neacareers.silkroad.com/

Twitter: https://twitter.com/neatoday

National Rifle Association (NRA)

The NRA is the primary firearms-education organization in the world and the largest defender of Second Amendment rights in America. It offers summer internships to college students with a background or interest in event planning, graphic design, and marketing. Interns help with administrative duties, compile information packets, and assist with events.

http://careers.nra.org/job-openings.aspx

Twitter: https://twitter.com/NRA

National Right to Life Committee (NRLC)

Founded in 1968, the NRLC is the nation's oldest and largest pro-life organization. It offers 10 internships to students each summer. Interns, who are required to attend weekly seminars, receive a modest stipend to cover their living expenses.

https://www.nrlc.org/site/students/internships/

Twitter: https://twitter.com/nrlc

Natural Resources Defense Council (NRDC)

NRDC, which advocates for the environment, is based in New York City but maintains a Washington, D.C., office as well. It offers paid summer internships in the legal department for law students; and in its administration, communications, and development departments for other students. Responsibilities may include administrative support, scheduling, and research.

https://www.nrdc.org/careers
Twitter: https://twitter.com/nrdc

^^ Our Revolution

Founded by veterans and volunteers of Senator Bernie Sanders' 2016 presidential campaign, Our Revolution seeks to revitalize American democracy, empower progressive leaders, and elevate political consciousness. Paid interns perform organizational work, such as supporting the needs of grassroots groups, or political work, such as analyzing ballot initiatives.

https://corehr.hrcloud.com/OurRevolution#/jobs
Twitter: https://twitter.com/ourrevolution

Planned Parenthood

Planned Parenthood offers low-cost reproductive health services across the United States. A Litigation and Law Fall Internship is available for second- and third-year law students interested in receiving course credit; various other internships are available to students year-round.

https://jobs.lever.co/ppfa
Twitter: https://twitter.com/PPact

Sierra Club

Based in San Francisco, the Sierra Club focuses on environmental preservation and conservation and has chapters located throughout the country. It offers various paid internships on an ad hoc basis.

https://www.sierraclub.org/careers
Twitter: https://twitter.com/sierraclub

Swing Left

Swing Left, a grassroots network of more than 350,000 volunteers working toward Democratic victories in the House, is led by professionals from the tech, media, finance, nonprofit, and art worlds in collaboration with veteran political organizers and strategists. It offers unpaid, part-time, remote fellowships to college students living within 60 miles of a swing district. Fellows receive expert organizational training. Their responsibilities include hosting events on campus, organizing voter outreach programs, and coordinating with local Democratic campaigns.

https://swingleft.org/p/open-positions
Twitter: https://twitter.com/swingleft

U.S. Chamber of Commerce

The U.S. Chamber of Commerce, the largest business organization in the world, offers competitive internships to students year-round. Interns may choose either a salary or academic credit.

https://www.uschamber.com/about/careers/internship-program
Twitter: https://twitter.com/USChamber

Foundations

^^ Eurasia Foundation (EF)

The Eurasia Foundation promotes sustainable, resilient change within communities, providing grants that empower citizens to take responsibility for their own civic and economic prosperity. It offers full- and part-time unpaid internships. Duties include overseeing projects, conducting research, drafting technical documents, and communicating with program participants. Applicants must possess a bachelor's degree or above in international relations or a related field.

    http://www.eurasia.org/CareerOpportunities
    Twitter: https://twitter.com/efnetwork

Ford Foundation

Based in New York City, the Ford Foundation is the second-largest foundation in the world. It seeks to strengthen democratic values, reduce poverty and injustice, promote international cooperation, and advance human achievement. The Ford Foundation offers summer internships to college juniors or seniors in the New York tri-state area. Interns' duties include administration, research, and project-oriented tasks.

    https://www.fordfoundation.org/careers/job-description/?id=4466
    Twitter: https://twitter.com/fordfoundation

Tides Foundation

Based in San Francisco and New York City, the Tides Foundation is committed to building a world of social justice and shared prosperity. Paid interns work in areas such as communications or business development. They receive an introduction to the social impact sector and must complete a project, which they can later discuss with prospective employers.

    https://www.tides.org/careers/
    Twitter: https://twitter.com/TidesCommunity

"Believe in something larger than yourself ...
get involved in the big ideas of your time."

— Barbara Bush, former first lady

Chapter 12:
Public Policy Research Organiza-
tions

Many public policy research institutions offer paid and/or unpaid internships. In addition, some also offer fellowships, which generally provide a higher level of pay and responsibility. Therefore, for your convenience, available fellowships are noted in the listings below.

Insider's Tip: The D.C. Public Affairs + Communications (https://publicaffairsjobs.blogspot.com/2017/01/think-tank-jobs-14.html) blog is must-reading for job seekers in these fields, or for those looking for internships. This special post, devoted entirely to think tanks, provides links to the websites of many of the organizations presented in this chapter (as well as many others), all in one place.

Action Tanks

Action tanks don't just think; they also organize and mobilize. We have included their Twitter handles, where possible, because they tend to be very active on social media.

^^ ⸗ Center for American Progress (CAP)

CAP aims not just to change the conversation, but to change the country as well. It offers a host of full- and part-time paid internships year-round to students at all levels. Each internship position has a special focus, such as energy and the environment, faith, immigration, LGBT issues, poverty, the Spanish language, videos, web technology, and women's health and rights. Its Generation Progress project educates and mobilizes young progressives on issues such as campus sexual assault, climate change, civic engagement, and criminal justice.

Internships: https://www.americanprogress.org/internships/
Generation Progress: http://genprogress.org/
Twitter: https://twitter.com/genprogress

^^ Institute for Policy Studies (IPS)

IPS works to create a more equitable, ecologically sustainable, and peaceful society. Its 10-week Next Leaders summer program offers paid internships that provides interns the opportunity to explore the connection between policy research and grassroots activism. IPS also offers a $39,000 Newman Fellowship in digital communications.

Next Leaders: https://www.ips-dc.org/about/jobs-internships/#nextleaders

Newman Fellowship: https://www.ips-dc.org/about/jobs-internships/#newman

Twitter: https://twitter.com/IPS_DC

^^ New America

New America is pioneering a civic platform that connects a research institute, technology lab, solutions network, media hub, and public forum. It brings together top thinkers, researchers, and agents of change, and offers both internships and fellowships. They offer both unpaid internships and fellowships in various fields related to technology.

https://www.newamerica.org/jobs/

Twitter: https://twitter.com/NewAmerica

^^ Young Invincibles (YI)

Founded by students in 2009, YI mobilizes young people to advance solutions regarding higher education, health care, jobs, and civic engagement. YI is always looking for interns and fellows in law, policy, social entrepreneurship, web and tech, video production, and graphic design. It also offers a paid leadership program called Young Advocates in California and Colorado, which includes on-the-ground organizing and working with policy and communications teams.

Internships: http://younginvincibles.org/who-we-are/work-with-us/job-opportunities/

Young Advocates: http://younginvincibles.org/who-we-are/work-with-us/advocates-2/

Twitter: https://twitter.com/younginvincible

Think Tanks

Most of the leading think tanks presented in this chapter are located in the Washington, D.C., area, but we also include a number of prestigious institutions across the country that offer notable opportunities. We want to particularly recognize and give credit to TheBestSchools (https://thebestschools.org/) for its comprehensive article, "The 50 Most Influential Think Tanks in the United States."

American Enterprise Institute (AEI)

AEI supports the principles and enhances the institutions of American freedom and democratic capitalism. Its unpaid internship provides undergraduates, graduate students, and recent graduates with an opportunity to work directly with some of America's most renowned scholars, economists, political scientists, and foreign policy specialists, conducting research on prominent public policy issues.

http://www.aei.org/internships/

Twitter: https://twitter.com/aspeninstitute

Aspen Institute

The Aspen Institute is dedicated to fostering enlightened leadership, the appreciation of timeless ideas and values, and open-minded dialogue on contemporary issues. Most of its internships are located in Washington, D.C., and generally require applicants to possess at least a bachelor's degree.

https://www.aspeninstitute.org/careers/career-opportunities/

Twitter: https://twitter.com/aspeninstitute

Atlantic Council

The Atlantic Council is a forum for the world's political, business, and intellectual leaders. The council offers talented unpaid interns the opportunity to advance its mission of promoting international security and global economic prosperity. Internships are available to college juniors or above, graduate students, and recent graduates.

http://www.atlanticcouncil.org/careers/employment-internships

Twitter: https://twitter.com/AtlanticCouncil

Bipartisan Policy Center (BPC)

BPC conducts bipartisan research to find common ground. It offers full-time summer internships and part-time unpaid fall and spring internships. Summer interns must be college juniors or above. Fall and spring interns must be currently enrolled in either an undergraduate or graduate program. Summer interns receive a stipend, while fall and spring interns are unpaid.

https://bipartisanpolicy.org/internships/

Twitter: https://twitter.com/BPC_Bipartisan

Brookings Institution

The Brookings Institution conducts research and education in the social sciences, primarily in economics, metropolitan policy, governance, foreign policy, and global economy and development. Its paid, for-credit, and sponsored internships offer undergraduate and graduate students an opportunity to advance their careers in economics, government, foreign policy, and related fields.

https://interns-brookings.icims.com/

Twitter: https://twitter.com/BrookingsInst

Carnegie Council for Ethics in International Affairs (CCEIA)

CCEIA, located in New York City, provides an exciting opportunity for students in international relations. Interns experience the inner workings of an international organization while exploring the dynamics of ethics in international affairs. CCEIA internships are unpaid, although the organization may cover the costs of commuting. Internships are available to undergraduates and graduate students in the New York metro area.

https://www.carnegiecouncil.org/about/jobs
Twitter: https://twitter.com/carnegiecouncil

Carnegie Endowment for International Peace (CEIP)

A nonpartisan think tank, CEIP specializes in foreign policy. It lists available unpaid internships, which focus on a regional area of study (e.g., China, the Middle East), on its employment webpage. In addition, CEIP offers the yearlong James C. Gaither Fellowship to college seniors and recent graduates of participating universities.

Internships: http://carnegieendowment.org/about/employment
Fellowship: http://carnegieendowment.org/about/jr-fellows/
Twitter: https://twitter.com/CarnegieEndow

Cato Institute

Cato Institute offers paid internships to undergraduates, recent graduates, graduate students, law students, and early-career professionals with a strong commitment to individual liberty, limited government, free markets, and peace.

https://intern.cato.org/
Twitter: https://twitter.com/CatoInstitute

Center on Budget and Policy Priorities (CBPP)

CBPP provides full- and part-time paid internships to undergraduate and graduate students (including law students), as well as recent graduates, in areas such as media, health policy, housing policy, food assistance, national budget and tax policy, and welfare reform and income support.

https://www.cbpp.org/careers/intern
Twitter: https://twitter.com/CenterOnBudget

Center for Immigration Studies (CIS)

CIS provides immigration policymakers, the academic community, the news media, and concerned citizens with reliable information about the social, economic, environmental, security, and fiscal consequences of legal and illegal immigration into the United States. It offers unpaid internships to undergraduates, graduate students, and recent college graduates in fields such as public relations, public policy, law, and law enforcement.

https://cis.org/Center-Immigration-Studies-Internship-Program
Twitter: https://twitter.com/wwwCISorg

Center for a New American Security (CNAS)

CNAS develops strong, pragmatic, and principled national security and defense policies that promote and protect American interests and values. Each fall and spring, it offers six to eight paid, six-month Joseph S. Nye Internships in research, external relations, and development. Interns work closely with staff and maintain considerable professional responsibilities such as contributing to the center's research, publications, and events. Selection is very competitive and requirements vary by position, though each candidate should possess a genuine interest in the field.

https://www.cnas.org/careers/internships
Twitter: https://twitter.com/cnasdc

Center for Strategic and International Studies (CSIS)

CSIS focuses on how to sustain American prominence and prosperity as a force for good in the world. It offers year-round full- and part-time paid internships to undergraduates, graduate students, and recent graduates interested in public policy.

https://www.csis.org/programs/about-us/careers-and-internships/internships
Twitter: https://twitter.com/csis

Competitive Enterprise Institute (CEI)

CEI promotes libertarian ideas through analysis, education, advocacy, and coalition building. Its paid and unpaid internships offer students and recent college graduates the opportunity to promote the principles of limited government, free enterprise, and individual liberty.

https://cei.org/jobs
Twitter: https://twitter.com/ceidotorg

Council on Foreign Relations (CFR)

CFR offers selective paid and unpaid internships to undergraduates and graduate students in its New York and Washington, D.C., offices. Internships are available in the executive office, on the CFR.org website, the studies program, publications, communications, the meetings program, the corporate program, and Foreign Affairs publishing. CFR also offers various fellowships.

https://www.cfr.org/career-opportunities/volunteer-internships
Twitter: https://twitter.com/CFR_org

Freedom House

Freedom House vigorously opposes threats to democracy, from dictatorships in Central America to human rights atrocities worldwide. Freedom House offers unpaid internships to undergraduate and graduate students who are fulfilling an academic requirement or receiving academic credit.

https://freedomhouse.org/content/career-opportunities

Twitter: https://twitter.com/freedomhouse

Fund for Peace (FFP)

A leader in the conflict assessment and early warning field, FFP focuses on finding holistic and sustainable solutions to issues stemming from failing states. It works not only to identify conflicts and problems, but also to create practical tools to address any issues found. FFP offers undergraduates, graduate students, and recent graduates full- and part-time internships. Interns receive a stipend.

http://global.fundforpeace.org/internships

Twitter: https://twitter.com/fundforpeace

Heartland Institute

The Heartland Institute, in Arlington Heights, Illinois, is dedicated to free-market social and economic solutions and supports skepticism concerning man-made climate change. It offers internships in graphic design, editorial positions, communications, government relations, and development. Requirements vary, but generally include an interest in public policy and familiarity with computers and the internet. Interns receive a stipend of $150 per week.

https://www.heartland.org/about-us/internships/index.html

Twitter: https://twitter.com/HeartlandInst

Heritage Foundation

Established in 1973, the Heritage Foundation is a well-known conservative research and educational think tank. Its Young Leaders Program offers a 12- to 15-week internship that provides a complete educational program to college juniors and above.

https://www.heritage.org/young-leaders-program/highlights-the-ylp-internship

Twitter: https://twitter.com/heritage

Hoover Institution

The Hoover Institution is associated with Stanford University. Its Washington, D.C., internship offers undergraduate, graduate, and recently graduated students professional growth and practical work experience. Interns participate in meetings and events at the Hoover Institution, regularly attend congressional hearings, and network with lawmakers and scholars.

https://www.hoover.org/internships

Twitter: https://twitter.com/HooverInst

Hudson Institute

Revered as one of the oldest and most respected think tanks in the world, the Hudson Institute challenges conventional thinking, providing innovative and strategic transitions to the future in defense, international relations, culture, and health care. It offers internships on an ad hoc basis, in which interns gain hands-on research opportunities in policy areas.

https://www.hudson.org/about/employment
Twitter: https://twitter.com/HudsonInstitute

Independent Institute

These internships provide participants with hands-on training while encouraging the professional development of the leaders, scholars, and pioneers of tomorrow. Internships are available to undergraduate, graduate, and recently graduated students in a variety of departments, including acquisitions, marketing and communications, and technology. All Learning to Lead internships are unpaid.

http://www.independent.org/students/internships/
Twitter: https://twitter.com/IndependentInst

Inter-American Dialogue

Inter-American Dialogue specializes in policy analysis, exchange, and communication issues in the Western Hemisphere, specifically Latin America. It is committed to the professional development of young leaders from around the world. It offers undergraduate, graduate, or recently graduated students full- or part-time unpaid internships.

https://www.thedialogue.org/careers/
Twitter: https://twitter.com/The_Dialogue

Manhattan Institute for Policy Research (MIPR)

MIPR, a conservative think tank in New York City, seeks to develop and disseminate new ideas that foster greater economic choice and individual responsibility. Its internship offers undergraduates and graduate students the opportunity to work in a range of policy research, communications, and fundraising roles.

https://www.manhattan-institute.org/internships
Twitter: https://twitter.com/ManhattanInst

Middle East Institute (MEI)

Founded in 1946, MEI seeks to promote a better understanding of the Middle East in America, as well as to improve relationships between the two regions. It strives to be an unbiased resource for other groups and individuals. All internships at MEI are unpaid, although they offer fringe benefits such as free language courses, a subscription to *The Middle East* journal, and a $100 per month stipend to cover transportation costs. MEI welcomes applicants from all academic backgrounds.

http://www.mei.edu/internships
Twitter: https://twitter.com/middleeastinst

Migration Policy Institute (MPI)

MPI works with leaders and professionals at the local, state, national, and international levels to address migration and refugee policies. It offers both research and editorial/communication internships to college seniors and above. Participants receive a stipend relative to their workload. Students from minority, immigrant, and refugee backgrounds are encouraged to apply.

https://www.migrationpolicy.org/about/internships
Twitter: https://twitter.com/MigrationPolicy

National Democratic Institute (NDI)

NDI, a nonpartisan, nongovernmental organization, has supported democratic institutions and practices around the world for more than three decades. It seeks to build political and civic organizations, safeguard elections, and promote citizen participation. It offers three- to six-month paid internships to undergraduates, graduate students, and young professionals.

https://www.ndi.org/internships
Twitter: https://twitter.com/ndi

National Endowment for Democracy (NED)

NED focuses on strengthening democratic institutions worldwide. It offers internships to undergraduate and graduate students year-round. The internships are unpaid, although interns may receive college credit for their participation.

https://www.ned.org/about/jobs/
Twitter: https://twitter.com/nedemocracy

Pew Research Center

The Pew Research Center, a nonpartisan fact tank, informs the public about problems, trends, and attitudes in America. The center studies religion, public policy, journalism, media, and the internet. It offers paid internships in related fields to undergraduates and recent graduates with an interest in the field.

https://jobs-prc.icims.com/jobs/intro
Twitter: https://twitter.com/pewresearch

Potomac Institute of Policy Studies (PIPS)

PIPS, in Arlington, Virginia, informs the government on key science and technology issues, particularly regarding defense and national security. It offers unpaid internships year-round to undergraduate and graduate students. It also offers a paid Center for Revolutionary Scientific Thought (CReST) Fellowship. In addition, the associated International Center for Terrorism Studies offers internships as well.

Internships: http://www.potomacinstitute.org/about-us/internships
Fellowship: https://potomacinstitute.bamboohr.com/jobs/view.php?id=1
Twitter: https://twitter.com/PotomacInst

Progressive Policy Institute (PPI)

PPI was the main purveyor of policy innovations to former President Bill Clinton's New Democrats. It offers unpaid internships year-round for students with a genuine interest in public policy and government in specific areas, such as editorial, public affairs, education, and economics.

http://www.progressivepolicy.org/about/jobs/
Twitter: https://twitter.com/ppi

RAND Corporation

RAND provides research and analysis to the U.S. Armed Forces. Its Graduate Student Summer Associate Program allows outstanding students to conduct short-term independent research within the framework of an ongoing RAND project. Applicants should have completed at least two years of graduate work. Participants receive a biweekly stipend.

https://www.rand.org/about/edu_op/fellowships/gsap.html
Twitter: https://twitter.com/RANDCorporation/

Reason Foundation

The Reason Foundation, located in Los Angeles, has become a libertarian powerhouse. It offers internships in policy research, journalism, video production, and fundraising. Internships include a modest stipend.

https://reason.org/internships/
Twitter: https://twitter.com/reason

Resources for the Future (RFF)

A think tank devoted to the improvement and preservation of the environment and natural resources, RFF strives to improve both environmental and economic outcomes. It offers a variety of internships, fellowships, and grants to undergraduate and graduate students. Participants receive stipends based on their educational background and employment.

http://www.rff.org/about/fellowships-internships-and-grants
Twitter: https://twitter.com/RFF_org

Stimson Center

Stimson, which uses analysis and outreach to solve the world's greatest threats to security and prosperity, employs the highest number of women in policy leadership positions of any leading think tank. Its unpaid internship provides a professional and educational experience to individuals with bachelor's degrees in related fields to help

them develop a greater understanding of international peace and security issues.
https://www.stimson.org/internships
Twitter: https://twitter.com/StimsonCenter

Tax Foundation

As America's leading independent tax policy nonprofit, the Tax Foundation works to ensure that tax policy does not stand in the way of success. It supports the belief that the ideal tax code exhibits neutrality, simplicity, stability, and transparency. It offers full- and part-time internships that provide firsthand experience working on projects that affect state and national tax reform debates. Interns receive a stipend based on hours worked.
https://taxfoundation.org/internship-program/
Twitter: https://twitter.com/taxfoundation

Third Way

Founded by former Clinton administration staffers, Third Way seeks to reconcile right- and left-wing politics. It offers a full-time, yearlong fellowship to students interested in bipartisan cooperation. Fellows receive a generous stipend. Additionally, the Third Way Adam Solomon Intern Program offers paid internships to students interested in public policy and government.
https://www.thirdway.org/internships
Twitter: https://twitter.com/ThirdWayTweet

Urban Institute

The Urban Institute, dedicated to studying the nation's urban problems, evaluates initiatives set in motion by LBJ's Great Society laws. Unpaid research assistants contribute objective analysis and expertise to important economic and social policy conversations. Applicants should be enrolled in an undergraduate program focusing on economics, mathematics, sociology, or other related fields.
https://www.urban.org/aboutus/who-we-are/careers
Twitter: https://twitter.com/urbaninstitute

U.S. Institute of Peace (USIP)

USIP is a conflict management think tank created by Congress to resolve or mitigate international conflict without resorting to violence. While it works to prevent violent conflict and preserve lives, it also seeks to reduce government costs and enhance national security. USIP offers students paid, part-time research assistant positions.
https://www.usip.org/about/careers/research-assistant-program
Twitter: https://twitter.com/USIP

Woodrow Wilson International Center for Scholars

The Wilson Center deals primarily with issues of international development, science and technology, security, and international affairs. It offers current, recent, or returning college students a wide range of mostly unpaid internships, and usually employs 80 to 90 interns at a time.

https://www.wilsoncenter.org/internships

Twitter: https://twitter.com/thewilsoncenter

World Resources Institute (WRI)

WRI strives to preserve and provide natural resources for those in need. It seeks to address and resolve wasteful and harmful use of resources and pursue more sustainable options. WRI offers paid internships to students and recent graduates. Intern tasks vary depending on position, but may include research, writing, and analyzing data.

http://www.wri.org/internships-wri

Twitter: https://twitter.com/worldresources

"Not all those who wander are lost."

— J.R.R. Tolkien, writer, poet, and philologist

Chapter 13:
International Organizations

Many international organizations offer internships to help talented students and recent graduates advance in their careers. Some of the internships in this chapter are located in the United States, most often in Washington, D.C., or New York City, while others are abroad. Visit the webpages of the organizations that interest you for full details on the positions available now. Happy browsing!

Insider's Tips:
- Devex.com (https://www.devex.com/jobs/) features the world's largest global development job board, with most jobs located abroad; signing up for its jobs newsletter, emailed weekly, literally opens up a world of possibilities.
- The NGO Job Board (https://ngojobboard.org/), a service of InterAction (see listing below), is a smaller job board that contains U.S. jobs and internships, and allows you to filter for internships only.
- If you do not find your perfect match on either of those job boards, this extensive list (https://www.usip.org/publications/international-organizations) compiled by the U.S. Institute of Peace includes many more organizations.

^^ All Together in Dignity (ATD) Fourth World

ATD Fourth World strives for a world without poverty. With grassroots teams in 34 countries around the world, this organization holds general consultative status at the United Nations. In the United States, Fourth World's interns live together in New York City; Gallup, New Mexico; Dickenson County, Virginia; Boston; and New Orleans. Intern responsibilities focus on community activism, research, and minor construction. Interested parties should begin by volunteering with the organization.

https://4thworldmovement.org/where-we-are/
Twitter: https://twitter.com/atd4thworld_us

^^ Amnesty International

The largest grassroots human rights organization in the world, Amnesty International has 2.8 million supporters, members, and activists in more than 150 countries and territories who campaign to end grave abuses of human rights. Its U.S. offices accept rising college juniors and above year-round. Its unpaid internships, located in New York City, Washington, D.C., Chicago, San Francisco, and Atlanta, focus on issues such as gun violence, women's advocacy, government relations, country-specific groups, and refugee/migrant rights.

https://careers.amnesty.org/
Twitter: https://twitter.com/amnesty

Doctors Without Borders

This organization strives to assist people across the world, bringing medical supplies to those affected by natural disasters, epidemics, conflicts, or exclusion from health care. It offers year-round paid internships in the organization's New York office at $13.50 an hour. Requirements and tasks vary by position.

https://www.doctorswithoutborders.org/careers/work-us-office/office-internships
Twitter: https://twitter.com/MSF_USA

Global Green Growth Institute (GGGI)

GGGI, located in Seoul, South Korea, supports emerging countries that seek to develop rigorous green growth economic development strategies. This internship offers an opportunity to college seniors, graduate students, and doctoral students, allowing them to contribute to analytical work and innovative rethinking on sustainable green growth. Interns receive a stipend of $500 per month.

http://gggi.org/careers/fellowships-and-internships/
Twitter: https://twitter.com/gggi_hq

Greenpeace International

Greenpeace International aims to protect the planet and tackle climate change, deforestation, and ocean pollution. It offers students and recent graduates a small number of internships at its headquarters in Amsterdam, The Netherlands. Participants are provided a stipend to assist with travel expenses.

https://workfor.greenpeace.org/
Twitter: https://twitter.com/greenpeace

InterAction

Located in Washington, D.C., InterAction is the largest alliance of U.S.-based international NGOs and their partners. It offers unpaid internships year-round to anyone with an academic, professional, or volunteer interest in humanitarian issues. Interns are welcome at its meetings on humanitarian and development topics and may engage with key stakeholders and leverage the relationships they build in their future careers.

https://www.interaction.org/about/internship-program
Twitter: https://twitter.com/interactionorg

Inter-American Development Bank (IDB)

IDB, in Washington, D.C., provides solutions to development challenges in Latin America and the Caribbean. It offers undergraduates and graduate students paid two-month internships that teach corporate development and management. It also offers a Research Fellows Program, performing research or other activities in a managerial, administrative, or technical environment, and a Young Professionals Program, an entry-level staff position.

> https://jobs.iadb.org/en/students-recent-graduates/
> Twitter: https://twitter.com/the_IDB

International Committee of the Red Cross (ICRC)

ICRC accepts interns from all over the world to work on humanitarian issues and assist victims of armed conflict and other situations involving violence and war. Internships are based at the ICRC headquarters in Geneva, Switzerland. Pay varies depending on education level.

> https://www.icrc.org/en/who-we-are/jobs
> Twitter: https://twitter.com/icrc

International Criminal Court (ICC)

The ICC offers various types of unpaid internships to current students and recent graduates willing to work in the Netherlands. Through international criminal justice, the court holds those responsible accountable for their crimes and helps prevent crime.

> https://www.icc-cpi.int/jobs/Pages/internships-and-Visiting-Professionals.aspx
> Twitter: https://twitter.com/IntlCrimCourt

International Criminal Police Organization (Interpol)

Interpol enables international police cooperation. It offers internships to current students or recent graduates. Interns, who receive a monthly stipend, gain a greater understanding of how international organizations operate. Most internships are located in France, although other postings are available on an ad hoc basis.

> https://www.interpol.int/Recruitment/Other-recruitment-pages/Internships
> Twitter: https://twitter.com/Interpol

International Energy Agency (IEA)

The IEA examines energy issues, including supply and demand of oil, gas, and coal; renewable energy technologies; electricity markets; energy efficiency; access to energy; and more. IEA offers unpaid internships to postgraduate students currently studying economics or other related fields in its headquarters in Paris, France. Interns receive a modest monthly stipend.

> https://www.iea.org/about/jobs/
> Twitter: https://twitter.com/iea

International Labour Organization (ILO)

The ILO promotes international labor standards, social protection, and work opportunities for all. Its unpaid internship is devoted to advancing opportunities for people to obtain decent and productive work in conditions of freedom, equity, security, and human dignity. Interns without financial support from another institution receive a modest monthly stipend to assist with expenses. Applicants should be willing to work in Switzerland, although other postings are available on an ad hoc basis.

http://www.ilo.org/washington/about-the-office/jobs-and-internships/lang--en/index.htm

Twitter: https://twitter.com/ilo

International Monetary Fund (IMF)

The IMF promotes international financial stability and monetary collaboration. It offers graduate students under the age of 32 and doctoral students under the age of 28 studying macroeconomics or a related field 10- to 12-week paid internships. These internships are based in Washington, D.C.

https://www.imf.org/external/np/adm/rec/job/summint.htm

Twitter: https://twitter.com/IMFNews

International Office on Migration (IOM)

IOM provides international assistance for migrants, and sponsors migration research and policy programs. It accepts hundreds of interns year-round at its Geneva headquarters and in its country offices. Applicants must be college seniors, graduate students, or recent graduates. Interns are assigned tasks based on their skills and interests. These primarily paid internships last two to six months.

https://www.iom.int/internships-iom

Twitter: https://twitter.com/UNmigration

International Renewable Energy Agency (IRENA)

IRENA supports countries in their transition to a future of sustainable energy. Its internship offers undergraduate and graduate students direct exposure to IRENA operations and the opportunity to enhance their educational experience through practical work assignments. Participants receive a monthly stipend to help cover expenses.

https://employment.irena.org/careersection/1/jobdetail.ftl?lang=en&portal=8205020217&job=INT0000

Twitter: https://twitter.com/IRENA

International Rescue Committee (IRC)

The IRC helps people experiencing humanitarian crises recover and regain control of their lives. It offers unpaid summer internships, primarily located at IRC headquarters in Seattle, to college students or recent graduates. Duties vary depending on position but may include administrative tasks, research, and community outreach.

http://www.rescue.org/announcement/2018-summer-internships

Twitter: https://twitter.com/theirc

International Tribunal for the Law of the Sea (ITLOS)

ITLOS arbitrates disputes arising out of the interpretation and application of the UN Convention on the Law of the Sea. It offers 20 unpaid internships, located in Hamburg, Germany, to college juniors and above each year in the legal office, library, linguistic services, and press office.

https://www.itlos.org/en/the-registry/training/internship-progr amme/

Twitter: https://twitter.com/itlos_tidm

North Atlantic Treaty Organization (NATO)

NATO provides collective security to the United States, Canada, and several western European nations while promoting democratic values and peaceful conflict resolution. It offers internships in Brussels to students and recent graduates living in a country that is a NATO member. These internships provide interns with the latest theoretical and technical knowledge regarding NATO countries, offering them the opportunity to learn from the NATO community. Participants receive a monthly stipend, assistance with travel expenses, and 15 days of leave.

https://www.nato.int/cps/ic/natohq/71157.htm

Twitter: https://twitter.com/nato

OPEC Fund for International Development (OFID)

OFID works with developing country partners and the international donor community to stimulate economic growth and alleviate poverty in disadvantaged regions of the world. It offers students an unpaid internship in Austria to build their potential through practical day-to-day work in an international organization.

http://www.ofid.org/ABOUT-US/Internship-Opportunities

Twitter: https://twitter.com/@OFIDnews

Organisation for the Prohibition of Chemical Weapons (OPCW)

OPCW works toward a world free of chemical weapons. It offers three- to six-month internships in the Netherlands to students who are citizens of OPCW member states. These internships expose students to a multicultural working environment and decision-making at an international level. Interns receive a monthly stipend to assist with expenses.

https://www.opcw.org/jobs/internships-at-opcw/

Twitter: https://twitter.com/OPCW

Organization of American States (OAS)

OAS promotes and consolidates representative democracy. Interns acquire experience in an international and multicultural environment, enhancing networking possibilities. Located in Washington, D.C., and OAS member states, these unpaid internships are available to students who have completed at least two years of an undergraduate program.

http://www.oas.org/en/saf/dhr/internships/

Twitter: https://twitter.com/oas_official

Organization for Security and Co-operation in Europe (OSCE)

The OSCE works toward stabilizing peace and democratic values for more than a billion people through political dialogue. It offers unpaid internships in Eastern Europe for graduate students. Nonresident candidates receive a stipend to cover cost-of-living expenses.

https://jobs.osce.org/employment-types/internships

Twitter: https://twitter.com/osce

Oxfam International

Oxfam strives toward ending poverty, hunger, and social injustice around the world. It offers internships to currently enrolled students, who receive college credit or a college-provided stipend.

https://www.oxfam.org/en/work-oxfam

Twitter: https://twitter.com/oxfamamerica

People for the Ethical Treatment of Animals (PETA)

PETA, founded in 1980, establishes and defends the rights of animals. Internships are available to individuals 18 years of age or older with at least one year of professional or volunteer experience. PETA also offers unpaid PETA Foundation Law Internships. Located in Washington, D.C., these internships provide law students with experience in the field.

https://www.peta.org/about-peta/intern-at-peta/

Twitter: https://twitter.com/peta

Permanent Court of Arbitration (PCA)

The PCA consists of a three-part organizational structure: the Administrative Council, overseeing its policies and budgets; the Members of the Court, a panel of independent potential arbitrators; and the International Bureau, its secretariat. The PCA offers unpaid internships to law students and recent graduates. Interns are offered a balance of legal and administrative assignments.

https://pca-cpa.org/en/about/employment/internship-program/

Twitter: https://twitter.com/PCA_CPA

United Nations

The United Nations is dedicated to ensuring peace and security worldwide. Employees work to counter the effects of climate change, alleviate poverty, and defend human rights. The UN offers unpaid internships, based in New York City, to college seniors, graduate students, and recent graduates interested in public policy and diplomacy.

https://careers.un.org/lbw/home.aspx?viewtype=IP

Twitter: https://twitter.com/UN

United Nations Association of the United States of America (UNA-USA)

UNA-USA builds understanding of and support for the ideals and work of the United Nations among the American people. It offers semester-long and part-time unpaid internships to undergraduates, graduate students, and recent graduates year-round.

http://www.unausa.org/about-us/internships

Twitter: https://twitter.com/unausa

United Nations Development Programme (UNDP)

UNDP works to eliminate poverty and reduce economic inequality through sustainable development. It offers unpaid development internships, which are financed by a nominating institution or government, to students and recent graduates. Internships are located either in New York or in UNDP member countries. Requirements include written and spoken proficiency in at least one (preferably two) of the three languages used by UNDP: English, French, and Spanish.

http://www.undp.org/content/undp/en/home/jobs/types-of-opportunities/internships.html

Twitter: https://twitter.com/UNDP/

United Nations Educational, Scientific and Cultural Organization (UNESCO)

UNESCO coordinates international cooperation in education, science, culture, and communication. Unpaid interns gain a practical understanding of the organization's mandate and educational programs while enhancing their knowledge and skills with work relevant to their field of study.

https://en.unesco.org/careers/internships

Twitter: https://twitter.com/unesco/

United Nations Entity for Gender Equality and the Empowerment of Women (UN Women)

UN Women promotes human rights for women. Unpaid interns work in strategic partnership, communications, advocacy, policy, evaluation, human resources, program planning, research and data, or finance. Applicants should be currently enrolled in a master's, post-master's, or doctoral program. Internships are available in the United States, Africa, Europe, South America, or the South Pacific.

> http://www.unwomen.org/en/about-us/employment/internship -programme
>
> Twitter: https://twitter.com/UN_Women

United Nations Environment Programme (UNEP)

The United Nations Environment Programme sets the environmental agenda across the globe and works to assess and address environmental patterns and concerns. It offers unpaid internships at locations around the world.

> https://www.unenvironment.org/work-with-us
>
> Twitter: https://twitter.com/unenvironment

United Nations Framework Convention on Climate Change (UNFCCC)

UNFCCC, an intergovernmental treaty addressing climate change, offers an unpaid internship, enabling students to enhance their educational experience through practical work assignments. Applicants must have completed their undergraduate degree, be working toward their master's degree, and be willing to work in Bonn, Germany.

> http://unfccc.int/secretariat/internship_programme/items/2653.php
>
> Twitter: https://twitter.com/unfccc

United Nations High Commissioner for Refugees (UNHCR)

UNHCR protects forcibly displaced refugees. It offers paid two- to six-month internships that provide experience in field offices to students and recent graduates in fields relevant to UNHCR. Internships are located in Geneva, Switzerland, as well as in regional and country offices.

> http://www.unhcr.org/en-us/internships.html
>
> Twitter: https://twitter.com/Refugees

United Nations Human Rights Office of the High Commissioner (UNHRO) — Geneva

UNHRO in Geneva, Switzerland, protects the human rights that are guaranteed under international law. It offers unpaid internships, located across the world, to outstanding students and recent graduates, increasing their understanding of current human rights issues.

> https://www.ohchr.org/en/aboutus/pages/internshipprogramme.aspx
>
> Twitter: https://twitter.com/unhumanrights

United Nations International Children's Emergency Fund (UNICEF)

UNICEF provides humanitarian and developmental assistance to children and mothers in developing countries. Unpaid interns work in the New York City headquarters. Duties include fundraising, communications, marketing, research, administration, and more. Internships are offered to students enrolled in undergraduate, graduate, or doctoral programs on a space-available basis. Recent graduates may also apply.

> https://www.unicef.org/about/employ/index_internship.html?p=printme
> Twitter: https://twitter.com/unicef

United Nations Population Fund (UNFPA)

UNFPA focuses on reproductive rights and health around the world. It aims to end domestic violence, child marriage, and female genital mutilation, while providing health care and support to women. Unpaid internships with UNFPA are available in New York to recent graduates and students enrolled in graduate programs.

> https://www.unfpa.org/jobs/unfpa-internship-programme
> Twitter: https://twitter.com/unicef

United Nations University (UNU)

UNU, a global think tank and postgraduate teaching organization headquartered in Tokyo, Japan, addresses global problems of human survival, development, and welfare. It offers paid internships to graduate students or recent graduates with a master's degree. Interns work in areas such as graphic design, digital media, and communications. Internships are available in Tokyo; Dresden, Germany; and locations around the world.

> https://unu.edu/about/internship
> Twitter: https://twitter.com/ununiversity

World Bank

The World Bank, based in Washington, D.C., aims to reduce extreme poverty and boost shared prosperity. It offers paid internships to highly motivated students interested in international development.

> http://www.worldbank.org/en/about/careers/programs-and-internships
> Twitter: https://twitter.com/worldbank

World Federation of United Nations Associations (WFUNA)

WFUNA works to strengthen and improve the United Nations. Unpaid interns develop skills and explore new opportunities, taking full advantage of working in a global NGO in New York City or Geneva, Switzerland. Preference is given to those with relevant experience and a valid visa. Some positions require applicants to have an undergraduate degree.

http://www.wfuna.org/internships-at-wfuna

Twitter: https://twitter.com/WFUNA

World Health Organization (WHO)

WHO provides leadership on global health issues. It offers unpaid internships to students, who complete practical assignments over six to 24 weeks. Positions are available worldwide.

http://www.who.int/careers/internships/en/

Twitter: https://twitter.com/WHO

World Trade Organization (WTO)

WTO regulates international trade to ensure that it flows as smoothly, predictably, and freely as possible. It offers three student opportunities:

- China's LDC and Accessions Program (https://www.wto.org/english/thewto_e/vacan_e/iypp_e.htm#China_s)
- WTO Internship (https://www.wto.org/english/thewto_e/vacan_e/iypp_e.htm#WTO_Internship)
- WTO Support Program for Doctoral Studies (https://www.wto.org/english/thewto_e/vacan_e/iypp_e.htm#WTO_Support)

These opportunities are available in Geneva, Switzerland to doctoral, postdoctoral, and recently graduated students.

https://www.wto.org/english/forums_e/students_e/students_e.htm

Twitter: https://twitter.com/WTO

World Vision

World Vision, a Christian humanitarian organization, provides emergency relief and community development services through church-based programs and outreach. It offers unpaid internships to current students who accept the World Vision Statement of Faith and Apostles' Creed. Participants receive a modest stipend to assist with living expenses. Internships may be located in either Washington, D.C., or in the state of Washington.

https://www.worldvision.org/about-us/job-opportunities/intern ships

Twitter: https://twitter.com/WorldVisionUSA

Part III:
Private-Sector Internships

This section presents a diverse array of internships in the private sector, from the media to law school.

When I first arrived in the United States in February 2010, two weeks after the earthquake in Haiti, I knew that this was a once-in-a-lifetime opportunity. To me, coming from a country devastated by an earthquake that had taken the lives of over 200,000 people, America was heaven. After the earthquake, most Haitians would have preferred to walk the streets of any inner city in America than to sip wine in Port-au-Prince. The entire capital city had been ravaged by this cataclysmic natural disaster.

As soon as I landed on the shores of Miami, I felt a burning desire to succeed and maximize every opportunity this country had to offer. I was determined to pursue my American dream. The next day, first thing in the morning, I registered for school at North Miami Beach Senior High School. Because I had moved to Miami during the last semester of 12th grade, I had little time to apply for college and prepare for the SAT. Graduation was only a few months away.

A few weeks after arriving, I began working at Abercrombie & Fitch almost every night after school to cover my living expenses. I was always exhausted from lack of sleep. When I arrived home after work, I still had to complete my homework, so I went to bed very late and woke up early the next morning for school. My twin brother and I were always rushing to catch the bus in the morning.

Many times, we missed the bus. Sometimes, we would fall asleep waiting for the next bus, and the bus driver, failing to recognize two innocent souls at the bus stop waiting to be picked up, would leave without us. We would sleep anywhere, really: on the floor, on the bus, in class, and even at work.

I remember that during my first week of work, I got in trouble because the manager saw me sleeping in the shelves in the back of the store. It is not that I was lazy; I just had way too much on my plate as an independent 18-year-old boy, moving to a new country with limited English, preparing for college, and pursuing my American dream at any cost.

When my dad evicted my brother and me from his house after we had lived with him for a month, a friend allowed us to stay at his place. Although our friend was approximately our age, he was married with three kids at the time. His father stayed in his spare bedroom during the week. My twin brother and I would sleep on the floor whenever his dad came, but on the weekends, we had the twin-size bed to ourselves.

After paying my bills, I would have $26 left to eat for the entire month. Of course, I had to learn how to cook the only dish I could afford — spaghetti and hot dogs. The box of spaghetti cost less than $1, and the package of hot dogs cost $2. I would pack the spaghetti and hot dogs for work, and I would eat it in the morning, in the evening, and at night.

Despite these challenges, America remained my heaven. I still cannot comprehend how my mom cared for my twin brother and me on a $40 monthly salary as an elementary teacher when I was born. America opened my world to new possibilities. I embrace it, I cherish it, and I love it.

To truly mold yourself into the man or woman that you want to be, you must overcome the blows life throws at you, even when you fall down and hit rock bottom on your knees. In my case, I had already overcome the worst kinds of chaos during my adolescent years.

I had been born prematurely, weighing in at about three pounds. Afterward, I was raised in a sort of foster home, in a tiny room provided by a Catholic nun. At 7 years old, my appendix was removed. I spent 22 days in Haitian hospitals, where bugs would land on me all the time, since everyone thought I was going to die anyway.

When the coup for President Aristide took place, my native city was the battleground. It was common for me to attend school in the same building that had borne witness to the burning of someone in front of it the night before.

At age 11, I embraced my mom and kissed her farewell when water invaded my native city and destroyed everything. I prayed in the open air on the rooftop for Jesus to give me a glorifying death by being crushed under the cement. I preferred the immediate, honorable death over that of drowning, since I didn't know how to swim.

After escaping this natural disaster, my home was once again devastated when an earthquake struck the new capital city I had moved to, killing over 200,000 people. Still, God allowed me to live, sparing me from yet another calamity.

Coming from these previous life experiences, the United States truly is heaven. I have never known better. The future only looks brighter to me every day. Instead of running away from your past, you must learn to embrace it. It is a part of who you are. However, you cannot allow it to limit your reality. You have the power to shape your own destiny.

There is a light at the core of every chaotic situation. Sometimes you have to dig to find it, but when you do, you can use it to strengthen yourself and to help you create your ideal future. The more obstacles you face, the stronger you become from this process. You absolutely must view your struggles from a positive perspective in order to create a step-by-step plan of action with which to tackle them. We all face our own crises in our lives. The question is, *how will you use your crises to create your destiny?*

"It took me quite a long time to develop a voice, and now that I have it, I am not going to be silent."

— Madeleine Albright, American diplomat and first female United States secretary of state

Chapter 14:
Media Outlets for Politicos

Throughout our nation's history, the media has played a central role in our political system; in fact, it has often been called the fourth branch of government, or the fourth estate. Today's media is often brash, edgy, and opinionated. This chapter presents some of the freshest and/or loudest voices commonly listened to by public policy professionals in our nation's capital, along with a few old reliables. To help you develop a winning application and prepare for an interview, we have included the outlets' Twitter handles where possible.

Insider's Tip: The innovative website AllSides.com (https://www.allsides.com/) compares how the same news story is portrayed by media on the left, right, and center. Check out the Balanced Search and Balanced Dictionary features as well.

Buzzfeed Politics

Based in New York City, Buzzfeed popularized clickbait articles and published the infamous Steele dossier, chronicling the alleged activities of Donald Trump in Russia. It offers paid internships as well as a paid fellowship/residency program for recent graduates, designed to recruit new talent for permanent positions.

Internships: http://www.buzzfeed.com/

Fellowship/Residency: https://boards.greenhouse.io/bfvideointerns

CNN

With a Washington, D.C., bureau just outside Union Station, CNN is the world's best-known and longest-running cable news network. It is part of the global Turner Broadcasting System, which includes 25 channels, from Adult Swim to TNT, and presents *Full Frontal With Samantha Bee*. CNN's news shows from Washington, D.C., include *The Lead With Jake Tapper* and *The Situation Room With Wolf Blitzer*. Paid interns perform fieldwork, work behind the scenes, and schedule and conduct interviews. Enter the keyword "internship" on the webpage to see internships at CNN and the larger Turner Broadcasting System, both in the United States and around the world.

http://www.turnerjobs.com/
Twitter: https://twitter.com/jaketapper; https://twitter.com/TheLeadCNN; https://twitter.com/CNNSitRoom; https://twitter.com/WolfBlitzer97

Comedy Central

Based in New York City, Comedy Central presents *The Daily Show With Trevor Noah*, a satirical treatment of the day's news. Internships at *The Daily Show* are available year-round to college juniors and above. Interns work with various departments and help with daily tapings.

http://www.cc.com/shows/the-daily-show-with-trevor-noah/internships
Twitter: https://twitter.com/ComedyCentral

Crooked Media

Crooked Media, based in Los Angeles, was founded in 2016 by veterans of the Obama administration. It produces numerous podcasts aimed at a progressive audience, publishes a daily newsletter called "What a Day," and engages in community outreach. Internships are available to self-motivated individuals with an interest in politics. Tasks vary by position but may include data collection, writing, editing social media content, and managing social media accounts.

https://crooked.com/crooked-careers/
Twitter: https://twitter.com/crookedmedia

The Daily Beast (see InterActiveCorps)

Fox News

Fox News, featuring shows such as *Hannity* and *Fox & Friends*, is part of a vast media empire that includes television, radio, and the web. It offers paid internships to college sophomores and above. Interns, known as College Associates, may work at Fox News, Fox Business News, Fox News Radio, or a host of Fox News websites. They gain firsthand experience in journalism, or the corporate or digital aspects of news reporting. They benefit from seminars and can pitch stories. Interns are placed in Los Angeles, New York City, or Washington, D.C., year-round; Atlanta, Chicago, and Miami are additional options in summer.

http://careers.foxnews.com/students
Twitter: https://twitter.com/foxnews

The Hill

The Hill reports on politics and business and maintains the largest print circulation of any Capitol Hill publication, including every congressional office and the White House. Its website features six blogs on specific issues. Working quickly in a fast-paced environment, unpaid interns have the opportunity to break stories and obtain extensive exposure to national politics and Congress.

http://thehill.com/contact/internships

Twitter: https://twitter.com/thehill

InterActiveCorps (IAC)

Based in New York City's Chelsea neighborhood, IAC owns over 150 brands, including *The Daily Beast*, Vimeo, Dictionary.com, OKCupid, and CollegeHumor. It offers paid internships year-round to college students, allowing interns to work in content, data analytics, editorial, and other areas. Many of these internships are intended to recruit new talent for permanent positions at IAC.

http://iac.com/careers/job-listings

The Late Show With Stephen Colbert

Based in New York City, *The Late Show With Stephen Colbert* offers a humorous look at the news, along with Colbert's trademark eclectic blend of guests, which often include not only actors and other entertainers, but also top political figures (former vice president Joe Biden has been a repeat guest), journalists, ballet dancers, and classical or popular musicians. *The Late Show* offers a paid internship to college juniors, seniors, and graduate students interested in learning what it takes to produce a late-night variety show. Interns must be able to work at least three full days per week; they assist in all aspects of the show as needed, in line with their skills and interests.

https://www.cbs.com/shows/the-late-show-with-stephen-colbert/news/1008504/the-late-show-with-stephen-colbert-internship-program/

Twitter: https://twitter.com/colbertlateshow

¶ ^^ Mother Jones Ben Bagdikian Fellowship (see Chapter 18, "U.S. Scholarships and Fellowships")

MSNBC

Based in New York City, MSNBC is a cable news network that features news personalities such as Rachel Maddow and Chris Hayes. It offers paid internships to students enrolled in an associate, bachelor's, or graduate program with sophomore standing or greater (30 credits) who hold a 3.0 or greater GPA and are over the age of 18. Interns assist with all aspects of the news, including news-gathering, production, and marketing.

http://www.nbcunicareers.com/our-career-paths/campus-2-career-internship-program

Twitter: https://twitter.com/workatNBCU

National Public Radio (NPR)

Located near the NoMa-Gallaudet stop on D.C. Metro's Red Line, NPR offers a variety of full-time, paid internships to undergraduate and graduate students interested in radio journalism. Interns help compile news stories, assist with radio production and editing, and help prepare news broadcasts. Internships are offered year-round at the Washington, D.C., headquarters as well as in Culver City, California (NPR West); New York City; Chicago; and Boston. (**Insider's Tip:** Interested in a free tour of NPR's headquarters in D.C.? Sign up here (https://www.npr.org/about-npr/177066727/visit-npr).)

> https://www.npr.org/about-npr/181881227/want-to-be-an-npr-intern
> Twitter: https://twitter.com/NPR

The New York Times

The New York Times, an internationally renowned newspaper, offers paid summer internships in the New York City newsroom to undergraduates and some graduate students, who have decided on a career in writing. It also offers business internships at its New York headquarters to those interested in marketing, advertising, and data analytics.

> https://www.nytco.com/careers/internship-opportunities/
> Twitter: https://twitter.com/nytimes

Politico

Based in Arlington, Virginia, Politico is a website that provides global coverage of politics. It offers competitively paid internships with a benefits package, year-round, to college students and recent graduates in a variety of areas, including video and editorial journalism. Applicants may need to submit a portfolio of work as well as letters of recommendation.

> https://recruiting.ultipro.com/PER1013PCLL/JobBoard/b972ff6a
> -41b7-4e97-9c71-273c2595c77d/?q=intern&o=relevance
> Twitter: https://twitter.com/politicocareers

Slate

Originally headed by former New Republic editor Michael Kinsley, *Slate* covers news, politics, culture, technology, and business. It offers paid internships in editorial, science, illustration, and video year-round — mostly located in its Brooklyn office, but some located in Washington, D.C. Internships are available to anyone. Requirements vary by position.

> http://www.slate.com/articles/news_and_politics/slate_fare/2008
> /04/a_job_for_you_at_slate.html
> Twitter: https://twitter.com/slate

¶ Town Hall Media

Townhall.com is the leading online source for conservative news, opinion, and current events, operating RedState, Human Events, Bearing Arms, and other news sites. It offers editorial internships year-round to motivated self-starters.

https://townhall.com/pages/townhall_jobs
Twitter: https://twitter.com/RedState

Univision

Univision is the leading media company serving Hispanic Americans. Internships for undergraduates are available on an ad hoc basis. Enter the keyword "intern" on the webpage to see opportunities available in the New York office and elsewhere.

https://univision.csod.com/ats/careersite/search.aspx?site=2& c=univision
Twitter: https://twitter.com/ucicareers

Vice News

Based in New York City with bureaus around the world, Vice News is an edgy media company that caters to younger people by providing documentaries and reports from international locations through its YouTube channel. Subject to availability, paid summer internships for interested students run from June to August. Interns must work at least 25 hours per week.

https://boards.greenhouse.io/vice#.Wr1Q7NPwZE7
Twitter: https://twitter.com/vice

Vox Media

Vox is an American news and opinion website based in Washington, D.C., founded in 2014 by *Washington Post* veterans Melissa Bell and Ezra Klein, along with former *Slate* blogger Matthew Yglesias. Paid interns contribute to the organization based on their skills, interests, and experience. Vox offers internships in the summer. Requirements and duties vary but can be viewed on Vox Media's LinkedIn page.

https://www.linkedin.com/company/vox-media-inc-
Twitter: https://twitter.com/voxdotcom

The Washington Post

The Washington Post, Washington, D.C.'s premier media website and newspaper, is owned by Amazon CEO Jeff Bezos. It has adopted the motto "Democracy Dies in Darkness." The recipient of 47 Pulitzer Prizes to date, the *Post* conducts investigative reporting focused on the D.C. region and covers national and international events. It offers paid summer internships to college juniors, seniors, and graduate students. Applicants may be aspiring reporters, photographers, videographers, designers, or producers. Interns can work directly with *Post* journalists and make their way up the ranks, like Leonard Downie Jr., who began at the *Post* as an intern and served as executive editor until 2008.

http://intern.washpost.com/
Twitter: https://twitter.com/washpostjobs

The Wall Street Journal

The Wall Street Journal, based in New York City, is a newspaper that specializes in covering the financial sector. It offers full-time, paid internships in a variety of areas, including reporting, editing, and marketing, available year-round on an ad hoc basis.

> https://www.linkedin.com/company/the-wall-street-journal
> https://twitter.com/WSJ

Washingtonian

The *Washingtonian* is a monthly print magazine as well as a daily news website. It offers paid internships year-round, in which interns work in advertising or in events and marketing. Editorial fellowships are also available.

> https://www.washingtonian.com/jobs/
> Twitter: https://twitter.com/washingtonian

¶ The Young Turks (TYT)

Based in New York City, TYT is the largest online news show in the world, with comScore ratings of #1 in News and Politics on all digital platforms among the millennial audience (ages 18 to 24). Co-host Ana Kasparian was named to the *Forbes* "30 Under 30" media list. Paid internships are available year-round, but most are in summer. Applicants must submit a YouTube video sample, among other items.

> https://tytnetwork.com/careers/tyt-investigates-editorial-internship/
> Twitter: https://twitter.com/TheYoungTurks

"Do what you love, and do it well — that's much more meaningful than any metric."

— Kevin Systrom, CEO of Instagram

Chapter 15:
Leading Companies

The leading companies presented in this chapter represent the pulse of the workforce today, in fields ranging from the cutting-edge — social media, e-commerce, and even space flight — to old school, such as energy and banking. Interning with these companies offers you the opportunity to experience the inner workings of a large company, develop mentors, and increase your network of contacts. Additionally, with amenities ranging from dogs in the office to on-site meditation and yoga, these are often not your parents' corporations.

These internships are all paid, and are located throughout the country. Visit the webpages of the companies that interest you for complete information on the specific internship positions available now, locations, duties, and compensation.

Insider's Tip: They make how much?! Enjoy this post on summer intern stipends at some popular companies: www.theguardian.com.

Adobe

Adobe helps its customers make, manage, measure, and monetize their content across every channel and screen. Paid interns at Adobe, based in San Jose, California, work on exciting technology that is routinely published at top academic conferences and integrated into software that impacts the lives of millions of customers. This internship is available to undergraduates, graduate students, and doctoral students.

https://research.adobe.com/internships/

Airbnb

Airbnb enables people to reserve short-term lodging online. Paid interns ("Airterns") work on challenging engineering projects related to the Airbnb platform and its infrastructure; recent graduates in engineering can apply for a paid 12-week summer internship at Airbnb HQ in San Francisco or in various international locales.

https://www.airbnb.com/careers/university

Amazon

Amazon is the largest internet retailer in the world. Paid interns at Amazon work at company headquarters in Seattle and other locations around the world. Interns play an important role on their teams, and work on high-impact projects critical to customers. These internships are available to undergraduates and above.

https://www.amazon.jobs/en/teams/university-tech-internship

American International Group (AIG)

AIG is a leading global insurance company. Paid internships are available to graduate students, offering tangible, hands-on experience in New York City; Jersey City, Parsippany, and Berkeley Heights, New Jersey; and Houston.

http://www.aig.com/careers/students

Apple

Apple designs, develops, and sells consumer electronics, computer software, and online services. Paid interns work primarily in Apple's Silicon Valley, California, locations and are an integral part of the team, taking their ideas and passion to the next level. These internships are available to undergraduates and graduate students.

https://www.apple.com/jobs/us/students.html

Bank of America (BofA)

BofA, one of the world's leading financial institutions, serves individual consumers, small- and middle-market businesses, and large corporations. Paid interns at BofA hone their skills through structured performance evaluations, training, development, and social opportunities. Paid internships are available to college students and recent graduates (check individual listings on the BoA website for more information about required qualifications) at its headquarters in Charlotte, North Carolina, as well as in Atlanta, New York City, and other locations around the world.

https://campus.bankofamerica.com/campus-recruiting.html

Berkshire Hathaway

Berkshire Hathaway, in Omaha, Nebraska, offers students paid internships in finance, legal issues, marketing, and other fields related to the property management and real estate industry.

https://www.bhhc.com/careers/career-opportunities/internship-opportunities.aspx

BlackRock

BlackRock, a global investment firm based in New York City, is entrusted with the management of more assets than any other company in the world is. Its paid internship provides students with a challenging, meaningful, and supportive experience that replicates as closely as possible the full-time employee experience.

https://careers.blackrock.com/

Blizzard

Blizzard, with offices in both Irvine, California, and Austin, Texas, is a game development and entertainment company. It offers paid internships every summer. These internships, targeted toward college students, last 12 weeks between May and September. Paid interns (Blizzterns) can work in one of many different roles, which change yearly but include game development or business support responsibilities.

https://careers.blizzard.com/en-us/students/internships

Bloomberg L.P.

Bloomberg builds products and solutions for the 21st century. Paid interns contribute to projects while managers offer them constructive feedback and career advice through work seminars, as well as cultural and philanthropic events. While the company is headquartered in New York City, it offers internships throughout the world year-round, based on availability.

https://www.bloomberg.com/careers/internships/

Box

Box provides file sharing and cloud content management. It offers paid 12-week general and software engineering internships to undergraduates, graduate students, and recent graduates at its headquarters in Redwood City, California, as well as in a variety of other U.S. locations listed on its website.

https://www.box.com/careers/university

Capital One Financial Corporation

Capital One, based in McLean, Virginia, offers a broad array of financial products and services to consumers, small businesses, and commercial clients. Paid interns, who must be college or graduate students, are involved in some of the company's most critical business decisions. They work with the best and brightest in a collaborative, team-oriented environment.

https://campus.capitalone.com/intern/

Chase

Chase, one of the oldest financial institutions in the United States, serves customers across the world, including consumers, small businesses, and government clients. It offers various paid internships worldwide to graduate and undergraduate students.

https://careers.jpmorgan.com/careers/US/en/programs

Chevron

Chevron, an energy company based in San Ramon, California, and Houston, Texas, engages in oil and gas exploration, production, refining, marketing, and transportation in more than 180 countries. Its paid internships provide students with an opportunity to expand their knowledge and benefit from valuable on-the-job experience.

http://careers.chevron.com/students-and-graduates/internship-programs

Cisco Systems

Headquartered in San Jose, California, Cisco Systems produces security devices, internet conferencing systems, set-top boxes, and other networking equipment for businesses and government agencies. Paid interns gain valuable experience through meaningful work with account managers and sales engineers, interacting with leaders, collaborating with cross-functional teams, partnering and learning from colleagues and mentors, and receiving ongoing feedback. Interns can work in San Jose or in a variety of international locations depending on internship availability. Internships are offered year-round to undergraduate and graduate students.

http://research.cisco.com/students

Dropbox

Dropbox, in San Francisco, is a popular cloud storage and file-sharing service for individuals and companies. Dropbox offers paid summer internships for undergraduates and graduate students in fields relating to computer science and engineering. Interns can work in software engineering alongside employees, in various locations, depending on internship availability.

https://www.dropbox.com/jobs/teams/eng_university_grads

ESPN

ESPN, based in Bristol, Connecticut, is the world's premier sports communications company. It offers year-round paid internships in New York City, Austin, Charlotte, and Los Angeles to college students enrolled in a degree program. Paid interns write and produce sports content for the network and may work directly with well-known names in the sports communications industry.

https://espncareers.com/college/internships

ExxonMobil

Exxon Mobil, a global provider of energy, offers a dynamic environment in which each internship task contributes to the business, allowing paid interns a taste of a typical starting position within ExxonMobil. Interns work at the corporate headquarters in Irving, Texas, as well as in other locations in Texas and around the world.

http://careers.exxonmobil.com/en/How%20we%20hire/Student-US

Facebook

Facebook, a popular online social network, also owns the social media website Instagram. Facebook offers exciting opportunities for paid interns who want to further its mission of bringing the world closer together. Based in Menlo Park, California, it also has an office in Washington, D.C., as well as in many other locations around the world. Internships at Facebook depend on availability within departments but are typically open to college and graduate students.

https://www.facebook.com/careers/students-and-grads/?teams%5b0%5d=Internship%20-%20Engineering%2C%20Tech%20%26%20Design&teams%5b1%5d=Internship%20-%20Business

General Electric Healthcare (GE)

GE is a leading provider of medical imaging equipment around the world. It offers undergraduate and graduate students internships in its Boston headquarters, as well as in a variety of other locations within the United States and internationally. Paid interns work on challenging projects and can jumpstart their careers while making valuable contacts.

https://www.ge.com/careers/students/internships-co-ops

Google

Google, a multinational technology company, specializes in internet-related services and products. It offers paid internships to undergraduate and graduate students. Interns have many responsibilities and can make a meaningful contribution to their teams. Google's parent company, Alphabet, also owns the video-hosting service YouTube. Although Google's main office is located in Mountain View, California, it has other locations in major U.S. cities including Washington, D.C.; Boston; and New York City.

http://careers.google.com/

Groupon

Groupon, based in Chicago, offers coupons and deals for people looking to save a few bucks. It offers paid summer internships for undergraduate and graduate students, particularly for students with an interest and/or background in software engineering, web design, and marketing. Prospective interns must apply to individual listings on the Groupon website and can work on projects relating to software, design, and other aspects of the website.

https://jobs.groupon.com/

Hulu

Hulu, in Santa Monica, California, provides video streaming services. It offers paid internships, primarily in the summer, to college students. Interns assist with business and marketing operations or software development. Positions are available in Santa Monica, New York City, or other U.S. locations.

https://www.hulu.com/jobs/positions

IBM

IBM is one of the world's foremost software engineering companies, with locations across the United States and worldwide. It offers paid internships year-round to undergraduates and graduate students, providing them the opportunity to work in software engineering, business, or other fields as needed.

https://careers.ibm.com/ListJobs/All/Search/Country/US/Position-Type/Intern

Instagram (see Facebook)

Intel

Intel, which has headquarters in Santa Clara, California, develops and supplies processors for computers from a variety of manufacturers, including Dell, Lenovo, and Apple. It offers paid internships to undergraduates and above, which can lead to full-time employment at Intel. Interns can work in a variety of Intel offices in various locations across the United States., including the company's Washington, D.C., office.

https://jobs.intel.com/ListJobs/ByCustom/Intel-Job-Type/Keyword-Intern/

Intuit

Intuit, a business and financial software company, creates and sells financial accounting, tax preparation software, and related services for small businesses, accountants, and individuals. At Intuit, innovation is key, and its custom-designed program gives paid interns the opportunity, resources, and guidance to discover and constructively channel their inner creativity. Most interns work in the company's Mountain View, California office. Intuit's Washington, D.C., office also accepts interns, but internships in this location are subject to availability and are primarily focused on policy and legal issues.

https://careers.intuit.com/university/student-co-ops

LinkedIn

LinkedIn, based in California's Silicon Valley, enables people to make the connections necessary to succeed professionally. LinkedIn offers paid summer internships to undergraduate, graduate, and MBA students. Interns enjoy free food in the office, gym and fitness classes, and reimbursements for transportation expenses. Paid interns work on technical and design projects related to improving the company's web and mobile platforms or on marketing and business aspects.

http://studentcareers.linkedin.com/internships

MathWorks

MathWorks, the leading developer of mathematical computing software for engineers and scientists, makes paid interns part of the team, assigns them a mentor, and allocates concrete milestones with deliverables and regular feedback on performance. These internships are available worldwide.

https://es.mathworks.com/company/jobs/opportunities/students/interns.html

Mercedes Benz

Mercedes Benz, with U.S. headquarters in Sandy Springs, Georgia, is a luxury car company that offers paid three- to six-month internships. Interns should be in the second semester of their sophomore year in a bachelor's degree program with a commercial, technical, or scientific focus and must have completed a prior internship in consulting or in the automotive industry. German language skills are a plus.

https://www.mbusa.com/en/careers

Microsoft

Microsoft, the worldwide leader in software, services, devices, and solutions, helps individuals and businesses realize their full potential. It allows paid interns the opportunity to thrive on their own terms and push their intelligence to the limit. While Microsoft's headquarters are in Redmond, Washington, interns may work in office locations all over the United States, including the Microsoft Corporation's Washington, D.C., office, which is located near the Friendship Heights Metro station. Requirements vary by position, but applicants should generally have at least an undergraduate or graduate degree.

https://careers.microsoft.com/us/en

Morgan Stanley

Morgan Stanley, with headquarters in New York City, is a leading finance company that handles approximately $2 trillion in wealth management assets for clients. Morgan Stanley offers paid internships to undergraduate, graduate, and doctoral students. Responsibilities vary by position. Positions are available across the world.

https://www.morganstanley.com/people-opportunities/students-graduates/programs

Nike

Nike, with headquarters in Portland, Oregon, is one of the most popular sportswear companies in the world. It offers paid internships in sports, sustainability, fashion, retail, e-commerce, technology, finance, legal issues, and design. Its summer internship program offers students enrolled in a university degree-granting program the opportunity to work in a variety of fields, including technology, legal, finance, merchandising, strategic planning, design, and analytics. Exact intern responsibilities vary due to availability and the company's intern needs. Paid interns have the opportunity to work in a casual environment.

https://jobs.nike.com/university

NVIDIA

NVIDIA, based in Santa Clara, California, awakened the world to the power of computer graphics when it invented the graphics-processing unit. Paid interns are part of the team in nearly all aspects of the business, including company meetings and events. NVIDIA also provides intern-only activities, fostering networking.

https://www.nvidia.com/en-us/about-nvidia/university-recruiting/

Oracle

Oracle Corporation, a computer technology company based in Redwood City, California, provides cloud computing and enterprise software solutions. Oracle offers full-time internships to undergraduate and graduate students, including diversity internships and an injured veteran internship program. Paid interns work in a variety of areas, including software development, consulting, and finance. Exact intern responsibilities vary by internship availability.

http://www.oracle.com/oms/campus/na/career-opportunities/index.html

Palantir

Palantir Technologies, headquartered in Palo Alto, California, has a Washington, D.C., office in Georgetown. It offers full-time, paid internships to those with an undergraduate or graduate degree. Internship locations and responsibilities vary by availability.

https://www.palantir.com/students/internships/

Pandora Media

Pandora Media, with headquarters in Oakland, California, is an internet-based music streaming service. It offers paid summer Road Crew internships to college students in all aspects of the business operations, including software, marketing, product, sales, and other departments. Interns work collaboratively to forward the mission of Pandora.

https://www.pandora.com/careers/universityrecruiting

Patagonia

Outdoor-wear firm Patagonia offers 12-week paid summer internships to students in areas from product development to finance to material sciences to marketing. Interns gain valuable work experience and exposure to Patagonia's unique corporate culture at its headquarters in Ventura, California, or in two other locations.

https://www.patagonia.com/internship-program.html

Pinterest

Pinterest, based in San Francisco, is a popular social media website used by over 200 million people each month. Pinterest offers paid internships to students and recent graduates on an ad hoc basis.

https://careers.pinterest.com/careers/interns-and-new-grads

Qualcomm

Qualcomm, based in San Diego, designs and markets wireless telecommunications products and services. In addition to its San Diego location, Qualcomm also maintains an office in Washington, D.C. It offers three-month internships to undergraduates and graduate students. Interns participate in lecture series, lab tours, peer discussions, competitions, and more. Upon completion of these internships, participants may be offered a full- or part-time job with the company.

https://www.qualcomm.com/company/careers/interns

Quora

Quora, in Mountain View, California, is a question-and-answer website. It offers data scientist internships to undergraduate, graduate, and doctoral students, or those demonstrating years of experience in the required field. Interns work closely with engineers, product designers, and product managers to devise appropriate measurements and metrics, design randomized controlled experiments, build visualizations, and other similar tasks.

https://www.quora.com/careers

Salesforce

Salesforce, a leading customer relationship management (CRM) platform, connects companies to customers. Paid interns work in the Salesforce headquarters in San Francisco and around the country to develop strong bonds with mentors who tutor them and help develop their core values.

https://salesforce.wd1.myworkdayjobs.com/External_Career_Site

Snapchat

Snapchat, owned by Snap Inc., is a social media service based out of Venice, California, near Los Angeles. It offers a variety of internships year-round on an ad hoc basis.

https://www.snap.com/en-US/jobs/

SpaceX

SpaceX, in Hawthorne, California, is a commercial aerospace company with interplanetary ambitions. It offers year-round paid internships to undergraduates, graduate students, and recent graduates. Interns can work on engineering projects related to space flight or in the company's business operations.

http://www.spacex.com/university

Square

Square, in San Francisco, is a financial and mobile payment company. Square offers paid internships year-round to undergraduate and graduate students with relevant experience in software engineering or finance. Paid interns can work with Square's employees to develop and implement a project based on their relevant skills and experience.

https://squareup.com/careers/university

Starbucks

Starbucks, with headquarters in Seattle, helps millions wake up and smell the coffee. It offers paid, part- and occasionally full-time summer internships to undergraduate and graduate students. Paid interns work on high-impact projects with well-defined objectives, and receive professional development training and mentorship. Starbucks interns also receive a free pound of coffee each week and discounted food from Starbucks, throughout their internship experience.

https://www.starbucks.com/careers/university-recruiting/internships

Stripe

Based in San Francisco, Stripe builds and supports APIs for financial transactions. It offers various paid internships to students approaching the end of their graduate or doctoral programs. Tasks vary by position.

https://stripe.com/jobs#openings

Tesla

Tesla, located in Palo Alto, California, builds and manufactures electric cars. Tesla offers paid internships year-round to undergraduates and recent graduates with a relevant academic background. Interns have the opportunity to work on many projects based on their interests and experience in automotive design, manufacturing, sales, and other aspects of company operations.

https://www.tesla.com/careers/students

Twitch

Twitch, a popular game streaming company based in San Francisco, allows users to chat with streamers while watching them play a wide variety of games. It offers various paid internships on an ad hoc basis.

https://jobs.lever.co/twitch

Twitter

Twitter, based in San Francisco, is a popular social media service. It offers paid summer internships to students. Interns have the opportunity to work on software projects to improve Twitter or to work in non-software roles such as project management or business operations.

https://careers.twitter.com/en/university.html

Uber

Uber, in San Francisco, is a ridesharing company that enables people to get around quickly and easily by hiring drivers (similar in many ways to a taxi company). It offers paid internships to students approaching the end of their studies and to those with experience in the field. Requirements vary by position. Positions are available worldwide on an ad hoc basis.

https://www.uber.com/careers/

VMware

VMware, the industry-leading virtualization software company, empowers organizations to innovate and thrive by streamlining IT operations. It offers students paid internships, providing them the opportunity to challenge themselves, build relationships with the best and brightest in the industry, and prove that teamwork can result in a remarkable product. Many of these internships are located in Europe.

https://careers.vmware.com/search-jobs/L?orgIds=1567&a
c=44358&alp=ALL&alt=0&ascf=%5b%7b%22Key%22:%22job_
status%22,%22Value%22:%22Internship%22%7d%5d&

Walt Disney Company

Walt Disney Company, headquartered in Burbank, California, is perhaps the world's most successful entertainment and media company, and includes not only Walt Disney Parks and Resorts such as Disney World, but also ESPN, ABC, Marvel, Lucasfilm, and many other Disney enterprises. The Walt Disney Company offers paid internships year-round to college and graduate students. Paid interns can work on a variety of projects in one of the Walt Disney Company's many subsidiaries.

https://jobs.disneycareers.com/professional-internships

Workday

Workday, headquartered in Pleasanton, California with a DC-area location in McLean, Virginia, is an on-demand financial and human-capital management software vendor. Paid interns design and create applications and product enhancements. The intern relationship is a two-way street — in return for hard work, Workday offers development opportunities beyond the work itself. Requirements vary by position.

https://www.workday.com/en-us/company/careers/university-recruiting.html

Yelp

Yelp, headquartered in San Francisco with a Washington, D.C., office, provides users a web and mobile platform for reviews of businesses and services. It offers various paid internships to students year-round. Interns play an integral part in supporting activities designed to rally the Yelp community, both online and offline. Interns gain practical experience and develop a rich network of personal and professional contacts.

https://www.yelp.com/careers/home

YouTube (see Google entry)

"For me life is continuously being hungry. The meaning of life is not simply to exist, to survive, but to move ahead, to go up, to achieve, to conquer."

—Arnold Schwarzenegger, former governor of California

Chapter 16:
Political and Business Consulting Firms

This chapter presents a smattering of leading political and business consulting firms in Washington, D.C. They handle everything from strategic communications to offering politicians advice on their political campaigns. Many work with companies as well.

Political Consulting

FP1 Strategies

FP1 Strategies works with Republican candidates and conservative causes, as well as private-sector clients. It offers both paid and unpaid internships year-round on an ad hoc basis.

https://fp1-strategies.workable.com/

^^ Fenton Communications (see Chapter 18, "U.S. Scholarships and Fellowships")

Ferguson Group

The 30-year-old, bipartisan Ferguson Group specializes in representing local governments before Congress and the administration. It offers paid internships to those with a college degree, research experience, and an interest in government relations. Interns assist lobbyists on projects, research legislation, monitor Congress, and assist with public relations.

http://www.thefergusongroup.com/About-TFG/TFG-Careers

Lake Research Partners

Headed by leading Democratic strategist Celinda Lake, Lake Research Partners is one of the most respected polling firms in the country, known for cutting-edge research on issues including the economy, health care, and the environment, with clients including the AFL-CIO, the Sierra Club, and Planned Parenthood. Paid interns interested in opinion polling and strategic research for progressive causes and candidates work in Washington, D.C., or Berkeley, California. Internships are offered year-round.

http://www.lakeresearch.com/index.php/the-lrp-team/11-site-info/74-employment-opportunities

Precision Strategies

Precision Strategies, founded by three of the young engineers involved in former President Barack Obama's 2012 reelection victory, utilizes data-driven tools to reach targeted audiences and move them to action. It offers various paid internships on an ad hoc basis in digital strategy, web development, design, video, digital advertising, communications, and campaign management and mobilization in two cities: Washington, D.C., and New York City.

http://www.precisionstrategies.com/work-with-us/

^^ Rethink Media

ReThink Media strengthens the communications capacity of think tanks, experts, and advocacy groups in three areas: Money in Politics and Fair Courts; Peace and Security; and Security and Rights. It offers paid internships to undergraduates and graduate students in traditional and digital media, as well as in communications, journalism, design and data visualization, media and public opinion, website management and tech support, and nonprofit management. Interns work in Washington, D.C., or Berkeley, California.

https://rethinkmedia.org/careers/interns

Business Consulting

Accenture

Accenture provides services in strategy, consulting, digital, technology, and operations. It offers paid summer internships to currently enrolled students in locations across the United States, in which interns gain exposure to the roles and responsibilities of a beginner analyst or consultant while working on client engagement.

https://www.accenture.com/us-en/careers/find-your-fit-students-graduates-undergraduate-summer-internships

A.T. Kearney

A.T. Kearney is one of the top management consulting firms in the world. Its 10-week summer consultant program involves participants in all phases of the consulting process, offering interns the opportunity to contribute ideas, opinions, and new information.

https://www.atkearney.com/personalized-programs/article?/a/summer-consultant-program-article

Bain & Company

Bain & Company, one of the world's leading management consulting firms, offers an unparalleled internship to undergraduates, providing successful candidates with wide exposure to the consulting industry and business strategy. Internships are available worldwide on an ad hoc basis.

http://www.bain.com/careers/roles/sa.aspx

Booz Allen Hamilton

Booz Allen Hamilton, a management and information technology consulting firm, offers internships in a number of areas, including software engineering, network security, malware analysis, information security, intelligence analysis, systems engineering, reverse engineering, cloud computing, decision analytics, and organizational efficiency. Internships are available to undergraduate and graduate students across the United States.

https://careers.boozallen.com/en-US/page/graduation-students?utm_medium=Web&utm_source=BoozAllenCom&utm_campaign=FindYourFitLink&utm_content=Graduating%20Students%20%26%20Internships

Boston Consulting Group (BCG)

BCG, a global management-consulting firm with headquarters in Boston, offers paid internships to students from many disciplines and backgrounds, providing them with the opportunity to experience the life of a consultant. Interns work on client projects and obtain mentorship from BCG consultants.

https://www.bcg.com/en-us/careers/path/internships/default1.aspx

Brattle Group

The Brattle Group provides consulting and expert testimony in economics, finance, and regulation to corporations, law firms, and governments around the world. It offers a summer internship to students, providing successful candidates the opportunity to apply economic concepts from the classroom to a professional services environment.

http://www.brattle.com/careers

Capgemini

Capgemini provides an array of integrated services, combining top-of-the-line technology with extensive private-sector experience. It offers college juniors and seniors an eight-week paid internship at its offices in Mumbai, India, providing a unique study-abroad program and consideration for a job upon graduation.

https://www.capgemini.com/careers/career-paths/students/

Deloitte Consulting LLP

Deloitte, with headquarters in New York City and locations all over the United States, provides auditing, consulting, and risk and financial advisory services. It offers students paid internships during the summer, working on a variety of projects.

http://www2.deloitte.com/us/en/careers/students.html

Ernst & Young LLP (EY) Consulting Practice

EY provides assurance, tax, transaction, and advisory services. It is one of the Big Four accounting firms, with more than 250,000 employees in 700 offices, in around 150 countries in the world. Its interns are exposed to a variety of responsibilities, working on tasks that include collecting data, completing analyses, preparing presentations, and more. Positions are available for students working toward undergraduate and graduate degrees, in locations across the globe.

https://www.ey.com/us/en/careers/students/your-role-here/students---programs---internships

Grant Thornton LLP

Grant Thornton LLP's business consulting and technology services help clients adjust their organizations for optimal performance, accomplish business objectives, and transform their value to become agile, forward-thinking organizations that are ready for whatever the future may bring. It offers internships across the United States to those with undergraduate or graduate degrees in accounting or other fields relevant to the position.

https://www.grantthornton.com/careers/for-students.aspx

Huron Consulting Group

Huron, a worldwide professional services firm, offers internships on an ad hoc basis, allowing students the opportunity to gain basic consulting skills while working on projects in team environments. Projects may include informational interviews, video blogs, and community service. Positions are available across the United States.

https://huron.jobs/

IBM Global Services

IBM Global Services, the professional services branch of IBM, offers its 12-week Extreme Blue internship to college seniors, graduates, and postgraduates worldwide majoring in technical and business fields. Interns identify a business problem, develop a solution, and turn it into a product. Positions are available worldwide.

http://www-01.ibm.com/employment/us/extremeblue/

Klynveld Peat Marwick Goerdeler (KPMG) LLP

KPMG, one of the biggest professional service companies, is also one of the Big Four accounting firms. Interns at KPMG learn business skills, find a mentor, build personal networks, and gain real-world experience before graduation. Positions are available to students worldwide on an ad hoc basis.

https://home.kpmg.com/ca/en/home/careers/students/under graduate/summer-internship-program.html

L.E.K. Consulting

L.E.K. offers its clients strategy, mergers and acquisitions, marketing and sales, and strategy activation consulting. It offers its eight- to 10-week summer consultant program to undergraduate students. This program demands a high level of responsibility for guiding and managing the case team, including structuring analyses, identifying critical issues, and solving cases. Positions are available worldwide.

https://www.lek.com/join-lek/apply/internships

Lockheed Martin Corporation

Lockheed Martin, a global security firm, designs and manufactures advanced technology systems and products. It offers paid internships to students studying engineering, math, physics, and business disciplines. Positions are available across the United States.

https://www.lockheedmartin.com/en-us/index.html

McKinsey & Company

McKinsey, a global management consulting firm, supports private-, public-, and social-sector institutions. It offers competitive internships to students, challenging them to master teamwork and find solutions to difficult problems. Positions are available worldwide on an ad hoc basis.

https://www.mckinsey.com/careers/students

Mercer LLC

Mercer, an international investment consulting firm, offers paid internships in the United States and Poland to college students graduating within one calendar year. Interns develop analytical and communication skills while fulfilling client needs.

https://www.mercer.us/mercer-careers.html

Oliver Wyman

Oliver Wyman advises firms in about a dozen specific industries, including automotive, aviation, aerospace and defense, and financial services. It offers paid internships lasting up to 12 weeks to undergraduates, depending on business needs and location.

http://www.oliverwyman.com/careers/entry-level.html#TheWorkWeDo

Oracle Consulting

Oracle provides strategy and analysis, business process optimization, product implementation, enhancements, upgrades, and ongoing managed services. It offers a variety of internships worldwide to students, during which an experienced manager or mentor guides and advises interns.

http://www.oracle.com/oms/campus/na/career-opportunities/index.html

PricewaterhouseCoopers Advisory Services LLC (PwC)

PwC, a multinational professional service network, offers audit and assurance, tax, and consulting services. PwC's paid internships allow interns to more fully understand the professional service industry, build relationships with partners, and participate in in-person and virtual training designed to develop leadership and technical skills.

https://www.pwc.com/us/en/careers/entry-level.html

Putnam Associates

Putnam Associates is a strategy consulting firm serving pharmaceutical, biotechnology, diagnostics, medical device, and other related clients in the health care industry. It offers paid internships to undergraduate and graduate students, in which interns learn about the most difficult challenges faced by pharmaceutical companies, as well as the specific changes affecting the health care marketplace.

https://www.putassoc.com/careers/join-us/

"The intersection of law, politics, and technology is going to force a lot of good thinking."

— Bill Gates, American business magnate, philanthropist, and founder of Microsoft

Chapter 17:
Top Law Firms

Most of the firms in this chapter have offices in more than one major city, each of which offers internships.

Boies Schiller Flexner LLP (BSF)

As one of the nation's premier litigation shops, Boies maintains heavy-hitter clients like Microsoft, the U.S. Department of Justice, and more. It offers its May-September summer associate program to law students and provides associates with professional opportunities, close mentoring, and training. Associates draft briefs and prepare for oral arguments, hearings, and depositions, among other duties. BSF's college campus visits are noted on its on-campus schedule. Offices are located in major U.S. cities, including New York, Las Vegas, and Washington, D.C., as well as in London, England.

https://www.bsfllp.com/careers/overview.html

Cleary Gottlieb Steen & Hamilton LLP

Cleary, an integrated global partnership, has offices around the world. Its summer associate program provides law students an opportunity to receive a monthlong introduction to the firm's law practice. U.S. offices are located in New York and Washington, D.C.

https://www.clearygottlieb.com/locations/washington-dc/legal-landing-page/careers-interior-pages/summer-associate-program

Covington & Burling LLP

Covington & Burling consistently ranks among the top law firms in the world. It offers 10 placements in each of its two-week summer programs. U.S. offices are located in Los Angeles, New York, and San Francisco. Applicants must have completed their undergraduate studies.

https://www.cov.com/en/careers/lawyers/summer-associates

Cravath, Swaine & Moore LLP

Cravath, one of the nation's preeminent law firms for almost 200 years, strives to undertake the most challenging cases, the most significant business transactions, and the most critical disputes available. Its summer internship actually begins before the summer does, and the recruitment period varies by department. U.S. offices are located in New York, although there may also be opportunities at their London office. Applicants should be prepared to submit transcripts from their undergraduate work and from law school.

> https://www.cravath.com/summerprogram/

Davis Polk & Wardwell LLP

Davis Polk, founded in New York City more than 160 years ago, maintains a highly regarded litigation practice, including a top-notch white-collar criminal defense team. Its summer internship provides students with an all-encompassing experience of work and life at one of the world's top-rated firms. U.S. offices are located in California, New York, and Washington, D.C.

> https://careers.davispolk.com/us-summer-program

Debevoise & Plimpton LLP

Debevoise & Plimpton ranks as one of New York's most powerful law firms, representing high-profile clients in transactions and disputes in established and emerging markets around the world. It offers students summer internships to provide them with training and development, as well as the opportunity to work on the same types of assignments as those completed by long-term employees. U.S. offices are located in New York and Washington, D.C.

> https://www.debevoise.com/careers

Gibson, Dunn & Crutcher LLP

Founded in Los Angeles in 1890, Gibson employs more than 1,200 attorneys in 20 offices spanning the globe. It offers students a summer program, through which the most intelligent, creative, and personable legal talent in the world can become a part of the firm. U.S. offices are located in California, Colorado, Texas, New York, and Washington, D.C.

> https://www.gibsondunn.com/careers/law-students/

Jones Day

A heavy-hitter with a hand in most major areas of law and with internationally recognized prowess in litigation, Jones Day retains offices in 19 countries. Each summer, it welcomes interns who work on the same types of assignments as those completed by long-term employees, while exploring their career options in law. U.S. offices are located in California, Florida, Georgia, Illinois, Michigan, Minnesota, Ohio, Pennsylvania, Texas, New York, and Washington, D.C. Applicants should have completed their first or second year of law school.

http://www.jonesdaycareers.com/unitedstates/welcome-to-jones-day-us/welcome-to-jones-day-us

Kirkland & Ellis LLP

In 1909, fresh-faced attorneys Stuart Shepard and Robert McCormick struck up a partnership in Chicago, laying the foundation for the growth of one of the world's most successful law firms. Its summer internship focuses on formal training and development, and offers a realistic glimpse of a future as a lawyer. U.S. offices are located in Boston, Chicago, Houston, Los Angeles, New York, Palo Alto, San Francisco, and Washington, D.C.

https://www.kirkland.com/sitecontent.cfm?contentID=243

Latham & Watkins LLP

Latham & Watkins, one of the world's largest law firms, in partnership with Sponsors for Educational Opportunity (SEO), provides talented underrepresented students the opportunity to intern at the firm. U.S. offices are located in New York and Washington, D.C.

https://www.lwcareers.com/en/offices/united-states/how-to-apply.html

Morrison & Foerster LLP (MoFo)

Established in San Francisco in 1973, MoFo is renowned for its expertise in intellectual property, finance, life sciences, technology, and litigation with a long reach across the Pacific Rim and, more recently, into Europe. MoFo's summer program allows interns to work in collaboration. U.S. offices are located in Denver, Los Angeles, New York, Virginia, Palo Alto, San Diego, San Francisco, and Washington, D.C. Applicants should have completed at least one year of law school.

https://careers.mofo.com/law-students/

Paul Hastings LLP

Paul Hastings has grown from a mid-market U.S. firm into an international outfit with strengths in employment, tax, and business law, with prominent clients in more than 80 countries. Its summer program offers excellent learning and working opportunities for law students. U.S. offices are located in Atlanta, Chicago, Houston, Los Angeles, New York, Orange County, Palo Alto, San Diego, San Francisco, and Washington, D.C.

http://www.paulhastings.com/careers/law-students/summer-associate-program

Paul, Weiss, Rifkind, Wharton & Garrison LLP

For decades, Paul, Weiss has defended some of the world's largest financial institutions and companies. Its summer program offers excellent learning and working opportunities in various areas of law. U.S. offices are located in New York and Washington, D.C.

https://www.paulweiss.com/careers/lawyers/summers

Ropes & Gray

Known for its corporate and asset management work, this law firm has adapted to law's accelerated globalization by bolstering its practice. Its summer program provides students with excellent learning, training, and hands-on opportunities. U.S. offices are located in Boston, Chicago, San Francisco, Silicon Valley, New York, and Washington, D.C.

https://www.ropesgray.com/en/legalhiring/Career-Opportunities/First-Year-Associates/Summer-Program

Sidley Austin LLP

Sidley Austin, one of the largest U.S. law firms, traces its roots back to the 1866 founding of its predecessor firm, Williams & Thompson, in Chicago. It offers summer opportunities in which interns choose their own assignments and create a workflow that best suits their professional interests. U.S. offices are located in Boston, Chicago, Dallas, Houston, Los Angeles, New York, Palo Alto, San Francisco, and Washington, D.C.

https://www.sidleycareers.com/en/northamerica/summer-program?tab=your-career-begins-here

Simpson Thacher & Bartlett LLP

Simpson, a Wall Street institution, houses elite teams in M&A, banking, capital markets, and litigation. Every fall presents an opportunity for exceptional law students to experience both the firm's day-to-day work and the broader culture of the law. U.S. offices are located in Houston, Los Angeles, Palo Alto, New York, and Washington, D.C.

https://www.stblaw.com/your-career/summer-program

Skadden, Arps, Slate, Meagher & Flom LLP and Affiliates

Skadden consistently ranks in the AmLaw 100 as a highly profitable law firm, having reported $1 billion in annual revenue. Every fall, it accepts students for its internships in all departments. U.S. offices are located in Boston, Chicago, Houston, Los Angeles, New York, Palo Alto, Washington, D.C, and Wilmington.

https://www.skadden.com/careers/attorneys/carve-your-path

Sullivan & Cromwell LLP

Sullivan & Cromwell, ranked in the AmLaw 100 since the 1980s, offers talented students the opportunity to spend 12 weeks learning the practice of law. U.S. offices are located in Los Angeles, New York, Palo Alto, and Washington, D.C.

https://careers.sullcrom.com/summer-program

Wachtell, Lipton, Rosen & Katz

This New York firm still operates out of a single Manhattan office. Every summer, it accepts just a handful of interns, offering them a close look at the work of associates.

http://www.wlrk.com/summerassociates/

Weil, Gotshal & Manges LLP

A powerhouse in restructuring, M&A, private equity, and litigation, Weil has long been one of the world's leading law firms. Every summer, it offers internships to rising first-year law students and above at all 20 of its offices across the United States and around the world.

https://careers.weil.com/Summer_Associate_Program#Summer ProgramLocations

White & Case LLP

Founded at the dawn of the 20th century, White & Case has grown from its New York beginnings to become a truly global law firm. Its summer internship allows students the opportunity to acquire hands-on experience working on the same types of assignments as those completed by long-term employees. U.S. offices are located in Boston, Los Angeles, Miami, New York, Silicon Valley, and Washington D.C.

https://www.whitecase.com/careers

Williams & Connolly LLP

A relatively small firm, Williams & Connolly has resisted globalization and continues to hold its own against firms 10 times its size. Every summer, the firm offers internships to outstanding law students, who receive hands-on experience working on the same types of assignments as those completed by long-term employees. Its U.S. office is located in Washington, D.C.

https://www.wc.com/Careers/Summer-Associates

WilmerHale

WilmerHale is renowned for its intellectual property trial practice, securities enforcement, and white-collar work. Its paralegal internship exposes interns to a variety of practice areas, business functions, and the same types of assignments as those completed by long-term employees throughout the firm. U.S. offices are located in Boston, Dayton, Denver, Los Angeles, New York, Palo Alto, and Washington, D.C. College juniors and seniors interested in becoming lawyers are encouraged to apply.

https://wilmerhalecareers.silkroad.com/wilmerhaleext/Home/Internship.html

"Live as if you were to die tomorrow. Learn as if you were to live forever."

— Mahatma Gandhi, leader of the Indian independence movement

SECTION 4:
Financing Your College and Graduate Education

College tuition is expensive these days. As a young leader focused on your studies, you can easily obtain scholarships and fellowships that will fully fund the cost of college. Taking out loans for college and graduate school may seem like the easiest path right now, but paying them back can present a challenge later. The scholarships and fellowships presented in the following chapters can help you avoid having to assume debt that could take decades to repay.

During my educational career, I was blessed with the opportunity to study at Georgetown University on a full scholarship. Georgetown is the place to study if you are into politics. Attending Georgetown also allowed me to remain in Washington, D.C., my favorite city. To me, it is the center of the world. Nevertheless, at times, even I need to take a break from it.

In this spirit, I took a break and went abroad to study at the University of Cape Town (UCT) with my brilliant black brothers and sisters in Africa. I thought I would be surrounded by mostly black students from across the continent, studying at the mecca of higher education in Africa. I was dead wrong.

I was pleasantly surprised to find that the university was extremely diverse, with people from around the world. I was always mesmerized when I went to the school's cafeteria and saw this amalgamation of representation, as if it was the United Nations. To some of my activist black friends, on the other hand, the population of black students should unapologetically mirror the demographics of the country, 79 percent blacks, 4 percent colored (South Africa's term for those of mixed racial background), and 9 percent white.

My worldview might have been affected by my experiences. In my native city in Haiti, my twin brother and I were the only light-skinned boys in class. There was a complete lack of diversity. In America, at Georgetown, I was this immigrant guy who was always trying to adapt to my new society, and often, I was the only black guy in class, representing the views of the entire black race. Clearly, I was not qualified to represent the experience of African-Americans, who were born in America; however, at times, I was the only black guy around.

My strategy in life is very simple: Wherever I go, I adapt. If I hadn't adapted, I would have never progressed. First, I had to learn how to speak English. Then, I had to learn how to write English. Then, I had to learn how to fit in at Georgetown and in Washington, D.C. Then, I had to learn how to excel and thrive.

When I took a break to study at UCT, I wanted to experience different cultures and people. However, I also thought that studying abroad would provide a perfect opportunity to leave my comfort zone, sipping cheap wine from Stellenbosch, partnering with a joyful 65-year-old colored woman for ballroom dancing, and enjoying the local cuisine. I also thought it would be an ideal opportunity to study for the GRE and apply for graduate school.

During this time, my nerdy computer friend insisted that I submit my application to Oxford. Of course, I had never thought of applying to Oxford before. I thought it was for Rhodes Scholars, nerdy geniuses like Einstein, and brilliant mathematicians like Stephen Hawking. My politician self, who embraces chaos and challenges, loves submitting all kinds of applications. Therefore, I applied to Oxford at the last minute, just before the application was due for the Master of Public Policy.

In fact, when I was filling out my application, the form asked me to choose which college I wanted to attend. I was puzzled by this question. Not only did I not know anything about the different colleges in Oxford, I did not know anyone who had attended Oxford.

So, with all odds against me, I chose the option that says any college. In my mind, I was thinking that if I chose a college, it might decrease my chances of acceptance. Therefore, I was perfectly fine with anything they were willing to give me.

To make a long story short, when I returned to Georgetown for the next academic semester, I received a plethora of rejections, but I was accepted into Oxford around late April. Now, I was broke. A young, single immigrant with no girlfriend and few close family members in the United States, but with a new-found, burning desire to attend Oxford. For me, it was truly simple. It was a matter of life or death. No one in the entire world could come between me and Oxford.

When you have a dream, you have to protect it by all means necessary. If I was decent enough to get into Oxford, I should be creative enough to find a way to get a scholarship. I immediately reached out to everyone I knew. I even sent letters to the rich and famous in Hollywood, whom I had never met, asking for help.

Once, the sister of Warren Buffett responded to a letter I had sent to him. She mailed me a very nice handwritten note and a book about investing. My strategy has always been: In life, you can get anything you want simply by ASKING. Therefore, I asked all kinds of people for help. The worst thing they can say is "no." Don't take it personally.

Then, I remembered that I had received a request to set up a meeting about the Chevening Scholarship. At the time, I had not anticipated being accepted into Oxford, so I had never responded to their email. However, when Oxford accepted my application, I went back to read more about their email.

There was only one issue; I had applied to the Chevening Scholarship, which is the equivalent of the Fulbright Scholarship for the U.S. government, as a Haitian citizen. I was still a Haitian citizen with an American permanent citizenship; unfortunately, the email stated that all applicants were required to be interviewed in their home country.

I called the people in charge of the Chevening Scholarship at the British Consulate in Haiti. I smoothly introduced myself, "I am Steeve, and I kindly would like to share with you my situation, and-"

The lady at the consulate interrupted me with, "Oh my God, Steeve! It is you! I remember you! I remember reading your personal statement! It was so inspirational!" She was Haitian, of course! My people!

I was smiling from my heart, knowing something nice would come out of this. I know how to connect with my people. At the end of the conversation, I asked her, "What do you think? What advice do you have for me? What would you recommend me to do? Should I come to Haiti for the interview?"

She responded, "Yes, Steeve! You should come."

I asked, "Really?"

She continued, "Just between me and you only, my boss loves your application!"

I decided to go to Haiti the next week, borrowed some money from the bank, and booked an airplane ticket. A friend picked me up and dropped me off at the British Consulate. I left that interview feeling as if I had nailed it.

I called the Haitian lady working at the British Consulate that same afternoon and asked how she thought I had done, as she had been a part of the panel. She responded that I had failed miserably. Heartbroken, I asked, "Why?" She said I had failed to explain how I was going to make an impact in Haiti based on my work experience in Haiti.

I felt that it was an impossible mission. I did not have experience working professionally in Haiti. I had been involved by working here in the United States with Haitian-American leaders. In my interview, I had focused on the role of the Haitian Diaspora to help Haiti, but that was not enough for them. They wanted someone with a proven record of accomplishment working in Haiti who also planned to live and work there after graduation.

Upon my return to the United States the next day, I contacted Oxford and told them I had not received the Chevening Scholarship. I immediately started a fundraising campaign. Within three days, I had raised almost $8,000. I needed to prove to Oxford that I was willing to do anything necessary to attend their program.

I continually updated Oxford about my progress with fundraising money to pay for my education. University administrators love that. They want someone who is determined to attend their school, even if they don't have the financial means to. They would rather help a person who is trying their best than someone who is not trying and simply waiting for the university to offer them a full scholarship.

A few weeks later, the Chevening Scholarship contacted me and put me on the waiting list. I was confused. I immediately wrote a lengthy three-page letter explaining to them why they should accept me. Then, they sent me an email stating they were not in a position to award me the Chevening Scholarship, and they put me down as a reserve candidate.

A few weeks later, the Oxford Blavatnik School of Government awarded me a full tuition scholarship. In fact, I think I was one of the first students in my group to whom the Blavatnik School of Government awarded their first full tuition scholarship.

A few days after that, the Chevening Scholarship awarded me a full tuition scholarship plus a living expenses stipend to study at the University of Oxford. For various reasons, I ended up accepting the Oxford scholarship, and declining the Chevening Scholarship.

The moral of this story is: Think of your dream university or internship institution as an investor and give them the right reasons to invest in you. You can best accomplish this by sharing your purpose and vision with them. The best way to convince them to believe in you is by connecting with them through your story, your leadership potential, and your intellectual curiosity.

Paint the picture for them so they can see clearly who you could become in the future. You must convince them that, by investing in you, they will be the school that helped you change the world, and that the wisest investment they can make is in YOU!

In these chapters, each listing indicates:

- the amount of the award
- which types of students are eligible
- for large programs, how many awards are granted each year

We use icons to indicate:

** An especially prestigious award

$$ An award of $25,000 or more, or a tuition waiver for two years or more

^^ An award that emphasizes activism at the local level/ grassroots, whether conservative or progressive; working with the disadvantaged; and/or social entrepreneurship

What is the difference between a scholarship and a fellowship? In general, scholarships are intended for students who are more than a year of study away from earning their degree, whereas fellowships are for graduating seniors or students at the graduate or postgraduate level. Fellowships often fund professional development and/or academic research. This is not a hard-and-fast rule, however; in fact, a number of scholarships, such as the Rhodes Scholarship, the Marshall Scholarship, and the Schwarzman Scholarship, are intended for graduate students.

Note: Some awards require U.S. citizenship, so those without U.S. citizenship should check requirements carefully. For instance, permanent residents may not be eligible for some awards, and non-citizens may be required to have a work visa.

"Education is the most powerful weapon that you can use to change the world."

— Nelson Mandela, former president of South Africa and Nobel Peace Prize winner

Chapter 18:
U.S. Scholarships and Fellowships

Insider's Tip: The www.ProFellow.com website offers a wealth of additional fellowships to explore.

Abba P. Schwartz Research Fellowship

The Schwartz Fellowship supports a scholar's research in the production of substantial work on immigration, naturalization, or refugee policy. Recipients are awarded up to $3,100.

https://www.jfklibrary.org/Research/Research-Grants-and-Fellowships/Abba-P-Schwartz.aspx

Alliance for Catholic Education (ACE) Program

ACE Teaching Fellows is a two-year program in which college graduates and aspiring teachers are trained in a free Master of Education program at the University of Notre Dame. Fellows are also offered the opportunity to teach in some of the country's most under-resourced Catholic schools.

https://ace.nd.edu/teach/prospective-applicants/how-to-apply

American Hotel Lodging Educational Foundation (AHLEF) Scholarships

AHLEF offers a plethora of scholarships for students, from college freshman to graduate students. Scholarships are based on financial need, experience in the hotel and lodging industry, work experience, academic and extracurricular record, and personal qualities.

https://www.ahlef.org/Scholarships/

American Library Association (ALA) David H. Clift Scholarship

The American Library Association (ALA) offers the David H. Clift Scholarship, awarded to a student pursuing a master's degree in an ALA-accredited program. Recipients are awarded up to $3,000.

http://www.ala.org/awardsgrants/david-h-clift-scholarship

American Psychological Association (APA) Scholarships

The APA aims to advance the creation, communication, and application of psychological knowledge to benefit society and improve people's lives. It offers numerous scholarships to undergraduate, graduate, pre-doctoral, and postdoctoral students engaged in psychology research. Scholarship amounts and criteria vary widely.

http://www.apa.org/about/awards/index.aspx

** Beinecke Scholarship

This program supports highly motivated students pursuing a graduate education in the arts, humanities, or social sciences. Scholarship recipients receive $4,000 before entering their graduate program and a further $30,000 while finishing graduate school. The Beinecke African Scholarship Program, which aims to assist African students studying wildlife conservation or ecology, is also available.

http://fdnweb.org/beinecke/

Belfer Center for Science and International Affairs

The Belfer Center, at Harvard University in Cambridge, Massachusetts, focuses on global arms control and nuclear threat reduction. It offers fellowships during the academic year to pre-doctoral and postdoctoral students interested in conducting research in science and international affairs. Some of these fellowships provide fellows a stipend, while others are unpaid.

https://www.belfercenter.org/fellowships

Buzzfeed Fellowship/Residency

Based in New York City, Buzzfeed popularized clickbait articles and published the infamous Steele dossier. It offers a fellowship/residency program to recent graduates, enabling them to work alongside the company's staff. These positions are intended to recruit new talent who can obtain permanent positions at BuzzFeed on completion of the fellowship.

https://boards.greenhouse.io/bfvideointerns

** Carnegie Endowment for International Peace (CEIP) James C. Gaither Fellowships

CEIP offers 12 to 14 one-year fellowships to uniquely qualified graduating college seniors and recent graduates, providing them with the opportunity to work as research assistants. Notable alumni include Senator Jeff Merkley, author and former UN ambassador Samantha Power, and journalist George Stephanopoulos.

http://carnegieendowment.org/about/jr-fellows/

** $$ Charlotte W. Newcombe Doctoral Dissertation Fellowships

The Newcombe Fellowships, administered by the Woodrow Wilson Center, are offered to doctoral students writing a doctoral dissertation in the humanities or social sciences, with a focus on ethical or religious values. At least 20 recipients per year are awarded a one-year, nonrenewable grant of $25,000; a tuition waiver is also requested. Fellows have gone on to lead museums and archives, nonprofit organizations, and government agencies, and have won the MacArthur Fellowship, the Pulitzer Prize, and the Guggenheim Fellowship.

https://woodrow.org/fellowships/newcombe/

Center for LGBTQ Studies (CLAGS) Fellowship

Housed at the City University of New York, CLAGS was founded in 1991 as the first university-based research center in the United States dedicated to the study of issues of vital concern to LGBTQ communities. The CLAGS Fellowship is granted to a graduate student, an academic, or an independent scholar for work on a dissertation or a first or second book manuscript. Recipients are awarded up to $2,000.

http://clags.org/fellowships-and-awards3/#clagsfellowship

Claremont Institute

The Claremont Institute, located in Claremont, California, backs a limited and accountable government that respects natural law and private property, promotes a stable family life, and maintains a strong national defense. It offers one- to two-week fellowships to young professionals and speechwriters working in the public sector. Fellows receive an honorarium, a stipend for travel expenses, and lodging for the event. Fellows participate in seminars, symposia, and workshops.

https://www.claremont.org/page/fellowships/

College Art Association (CAA) Professional Development Fellowship

The CAA's Professional Development Fellowship is offered as funding to artists and art historians pursuing graduate degrees. Successful candidates are awarded $5,000. They receive free registration to the CAA Annual Conference, as well as a one-year CAA membership.

http://www.collegeart.org/programs/fellowships

^^ Davis Putter Scholarship Fund

This need-based scholarship grants up to $10,000 to students involved progressive movements to bring social justice to their communities. Early recipients of the award, founded in 1961, worked for civil rights, against McCarthyism, and for peace in Vietnam; recent grantees have been active against racism, sexism, and homophobia, and for economic justice and peace.

http://www.davisputter.org/

$$ Dolores Zohrab Liebmann Fellowships

This fellowship supports graduate students in the humanities, social sciences, or natural sciences (including law, medicine, engineering, architecture, and other formal professional training) who have an outstanding undergraduate record, demonstrate financial need, and are attending a designated college or university. It also supports publications focusing on Armenian studies, history, and literature of the 19th century or earlier. Awards are $18,000 plus a tuition waiver.

http://fdnweb.org/liebmann/

Dwight David Eisenhower Transportation Fellowship (DDETFP)

The DDETFP awards 150 to 200 fellowships per year to students pursuing degrees in transportation-related disciplines. Award amounts vary.

https://www.fhwa.dot.gov/innovativeprograms/centers/workforce_dev/post_ secondary_education.aspx

^^ Echoing Green Global Fellowships

Echoing Green funds innovators, instigators, pioneers, and rebels in the social impact space, favoring startups in their first two years. It scouts emerging talent in social entrepreneurship around the world, awarding 30 fellowships each year to emerging leaders with innovative solutions. It particularly encourages applications from racial and ethnic minorities, women, LGBTQ communities, and people in currently underrepresented U.S. cities, including Baltimore, Atlanta, Oakland, Detroit, Louisville, Milwaukee, Kansas City, and Miami. Note: These fellowships do not fund academic scholarship or research.

https://www.echoinggreen.org/fellowship

** Elie Wiesel Prize in Ethics

The Elie Wiesel Foundation for Humanity offers college juniors and above an award for the best essay related to ethics. Awards are $5,000 for first place, $2,500 for second place, $1,500 for third place, and two honorable mentions of $500 each.

http://eliewieselfoundation.org/prize-ethics/contest/http:// eliewieselfoundation.org/prize-ethics/contest/

Empire State Fellows Program

The Empire State Fellows Program is a two-year, full-time leadership training program. Under the program, fellows experience working directly with top New York State policymakers.

https://www.dos.ny.gov/newnyleaders/fellows_app.html

^^ Fenton Fellowships

Progressive strategists for social change since 1982, Fenton Communications develops ideas and brands that engage audiences, from grassroots campaigns (e.g., climate change, right to marry) to corporate social action (e.g., Avon, Ben & Jerry's, Toyota). Fenton Fellowships in social change, digital social change, and design social change are offered in Washington, D.C., New York City, Los Angeles, and San Francisco to both students and graduates, who are mentored as they work alongside staff and receive training in digital communications, media monitoring, messaging, pitching, and research.

https://fenton.com/fenton-fellowship/

Foster G. McGaw Graduate Student Scholarship

This $5,000 scholarship provides financial support to health care management graduate students to help offset tuition costs, student loans, and expenses.

https://www.ache.org/Faculty_Students/mcgaw_scholarship.cfm

Fund for Theological Education

The Fund for Theological Education Partnership for Excellence represents an ecumenical effort to identify, inspire, and nurture outstanding college undergraduates and first-year seminary students pursuing vocations in ministry and theological scholarship.

http://fteleaders.org/pages/undergrad

Government Finance Officers Association (GFOA) Scholarships

GFOA offers five separate scholarships to students and professionals in accounting and finance, including the Greathouse Scholarship ($15,000), which supports students preparing for a career in government finance, and the Minorities in Government Finance Scholarship ($10,000), which recognizes outstanding minority students.

http://www.gfoa.org/scholarships

Graduate School Test (GMAT, GRE, MCAT) Waivers

These programs offer reduction certificates or fee waivers for the GMAT, GRE, and MCAT to students with financial difficulty.

GRE: http://www.ets.org/gre/subject/about/fees/reduction/

GMAT: http://www.gmac.com/gmat/prepare-candidates-for-the-exam-classroom/
assist-candidates-with-gmat-exam-fees/gmat-fee-waivers.aspx

MCAT: https://www.aamc.org/students/applying/fap/eligibility/

HACU Southwest Travel Scholarship

This scholarship offers up to four free airline trips to undergraduates and graduate students traveling to or from college. Applicants must prove financial need.

https://www.hacu.net/hacu/Lanzate.asp

** Harry S. Truman Scholarship Foundation

The Harry S. Truman Scholarship Foundation offers scholarships to up to 65 students per year, from all majors. Applicants must be college juniors (or have senior-level standing in their third year of college), possess superior academic ability, maintain a strong record of service and leadership, and intend to pursue a career in public service.

http://www.truman.gov

Harvey Fellows Program

This program helps Christians pursue leadership positions in fields where they are underrepresented. It offers scholarships to Christian graduate students to encourage them to combine their faith and work to improve society.

http://msfdn.org/harveyfellows/overview/

** $$ Herbert Scoville Jr. Peace Fellowship

This six- to nine-month, highly competitive fellowship offers recent graduates the opportunity to work on peace and security issues at a participating nonprofit organization in Washington, D.C. Fellows receive $3,100 per month and health insurance, plus travel expenses to Washington and $1,000 for professional development to attend relevant conferences, meetings, or a language or policy course. The program arranges meetings for fellows with policy experts and social networking events with alumni. Fellows also receive mentoring from a board member and a former fellow. Fewer than 3 percent of applicants are selected.

http://scoville.org/apply/application-information/

Hertog Advanced Institutes

Hertog Advanced Institutes offers exceptional students and professionals an opportunity to engage in serious discussion of a topic in public policy or political theory. Potential applicants include those pursuing study or careers in public policy, including national security and economics, academia, journalism, law, business, and the military.

https://hertogfoundation.org/our-programs

^^ Inter-American Foundation (IAF) Grassroots Development Ph.D. Fellowship Program

IAF Fellows examine the efforts of the rural and urban poor to improve their lives, their methods of organization and production, and the policies and programs designed to alleviate their poverty. The program supports doctoral candidates from U.S. universities who conduct dissertation research in Latin America and the Caribbean. Recipients are awarded up to $3,000.

https://www.iie.org/Programs/IAF-Grassroots-Development-Fellowship-Program

^^ $$ Institute for Policy Studies (IPS) Newman Fellowship

IPS, a multi-issue progressive think tank, works to create a more equitable, ecologically sustainable, and peaceful society. It offers a yearlong, $39,000 Newman Fellowship in digital communications, which is extendable to 24 months. Fellows help bring IPS's work to online supporters. Applicants must submit graphic design and other samples.

https://ips-dc.org/newman-fellowship/

Intercollegiate Studies Institute (ISI) Collegiate Network Journalism Fellowship

The ISI Collegiate Network Journalism Fellowship is awarded annually to up to 15 students. Awards from this conservative organization range from $5,000 to $15,000 each and are intended to recognize exceptional individuals who will help uphold the principles of Western civilization and American liberty.

https://get.isi.org/journalism-internships-fellowships/

Intercollegiate Studies Institute (ISI) Graduate Fellowship

The ISI Graduate Fellowship is awarded to graduating seniors who have demonstrated passion, dedication, a high capacity for self-direction, and originality in pursuit of a goal that will strengthen civil society. Awards range from $5,000 to $15,000.

https://home.isi.org/students/fellowships

Islamic Scholarship Fund

Applicants for this scholarship must be an active member of the Muslim community.

https://islamicscholarshipfund.org/scholarships/

** $$ Jack Kent Cooke Foundation (JKCF) Undergraduate Transfer Scholarship

The JKCF Undergraduate Transfer Scholarship is the largest private U.S. scholarship for community college students seeking to complete their bachelor's degree at a four-

year college. Up to 85 scholars receive up to $40,000 per year for up to three years, ongoing advising, and a pathway to JKCF's $50,000 per year Graduate Scholarship.
https://www.jkcf.org/our-scholarships/undergraduate-transfer-scholarship/

** Jacob K. Javits Fellowships

Javits Fellowships provide financial support to graduate and doctoral students in the arts, humanities, or social sciences fields.
https://www2.ed.gov/programs/jacobjavits/index.html

** $$ Knight-Hennessy Scholars Program, Stanford University

The Knight-Hennessy program offers 100 students around the world up to three years of fully funded support, for use at any graduate program at Stanford University. This opportunity helps students develop as global leaders through mentorship and experiential learning initiatives.
https://knight-hennessy.stanford.edu/program/funding

Kosciuszko Foundation Scholarship

Kosciuszko Foundation tuition scholarships support American students of Polish descent for graduate studies.
https://www.thekf.org/kf/scholarships/about/

Kroc Institute Visiting Research Fellows Program

The Kroc Institute Visiting Research Fellows Program brings outstanding scholars focused on peace research to the University of Notre Dame during each academic year. It supports scholars working on peace processes, peace building in the context of armed conflict, and post-conflict transformation.
https://kroc.nd.edu/research/grants-and-fellowships/apply-for-visiting-research-fellowships/

Littleton-Griswold Research Grant for Research in U.S. Legal History

The American Historical Association offers the Littleton-Griswold Research Grant to students conducting research in U.S. legal history. Recipients are awarded up to $1,000.
https://www.historians.org/awards-and-grants/grants-and-fellowships/littleton-griswold-research-grant

Marjorie Kovler Research Fellowship

The Marjorie Kovler Research Fellowship supports a scholar in the production of a substantial work related to foreign intelligence and the presidency. Recipients are awarded up to $2,500.

https://www.jfklibrary.org/Research/Research-Grants-and-Fellowships/
Marjorie-Kovler.aspx

$$ Mellon/ACLS Dissertation Completion Fellowships

The $30,000 Mellon/ACLS Dissertation Completion Fellowships encourage timely completion of the participating student's doctoral program. Applicants must be prepared to complete their dissertations within their fellowship tenure.

https://www.acls.org/programs/dcf/

** ^^ ¶ Mother Jones Ben Bagdikian Fellowship

The grandmother of investigative reporting, the progressive nonprofit magazine *Mother Jones* offers the six-month Ben Bagdikian Fellowship, considered one of the best in the industry and renowned for its impressive alumni list. Fellows perform hands-on research and fact checking, and can pitch online and print content. There are five different fellowships, based variously in San Francisco, New York, and Washington, D.C.: editorial, online editorial, social media, digital media (application requires video samples), and strategic communications.

https://www.motherjones.com/jobs/fellowships/

National Bureau of Economic Research (NBER) Fellowships

NBER, located near Boston, conducts unbiased economic research and disseminates it to policymakers, business professionals, and the academic community. It offers fellowships in related fields.

http://www.nber.org/jobs/

National Italian-American Foundation

The National Italian-American Foundation awards scholarships to outstanding students who are either Italian-American or of any ethnic background majoring or minoring in the Italian language, studies, Italian-American studies, or a related field.

https://www.niaf.org/programs/scholarships-overview/

^^ New America Fellowships

New America is a think and action tank: a civic platform that connects a research institute, technology lab, solutions network, media hub, and public forum. It offers fellowships including the Learning Sciences Exchange, a two-year fellowship focused on child development; TechCongress, a one-year Congressional Innovation Fellowship with a member of Congress or congressional committee; the New America California Fellowship; and the Millennial Public Policy Fellowship.

https://www.newamerica.org/fellows/

^^ Organizing for Action (OFA)

OFA, a community-organizing project founded in 2013, works toward creating a more tolerant, just, and fair America. The OFA Fellowship program offers participants a chance to develop and refine their skills in community engagement and outreach. Fellows research and identify challenges in the community, develop plans for addressing those challenges, and set those plans in motion.

https://www.ofa.us/get-trained/fellowship/

Open Society Foundations (OSF) Fellowship

OSF offers a fellowship to individuals pursuing innovative and unconventional approaches to fundamental open-society challenges. The amount awarded varies. OSF invites proposals that are responding to a specific proposition or that are relevant to its work. Applicants are currently invited to address new and radical approaches to fight economic inequality.

https://www.opensocietyfoundations.org/grants/open-society-fellowship

** $$ Paul and Daisy Soros Fellowship for New Americans

The Paul and Daisy Soros Fellowship for New Americans provides scholarships and fellowships to immigrants and children of immigrants in America. Each fellow receives up to $90,000 in financial support over two years.

http://www.pdsoros.org

POSCO Visiting Fellowship

The POSCO Visiting Fellowship promotes research on Korean topics. Fellows, who remain in residence at the East-West Center in Honolulu for up to two months, are provided a stipend, as well as airfare between their home base and Honolulu, where they undertake research and write upon an agreed topic. Fellows are required to prepare a high-quality paper for publication in academic journals or in book format.

https://www.eastwestcenter.org/research/visiting-fellow-programs/posco-visiting-fellowship-program

Potomac Institute of Policy Studies (PIPS) CReST Fellowship

PIPS offers a six-month Center for Revolutionary Scientific Thought (CReST) Fellowship that allows fellows to gain hands-on experience in science and technology policy and think innovatively about how science and society intersect in our daily lives. A technical Ph.D. is preferred.

https://potomacinstitute.bamboohr.com/jobs/view.php?id=1

^^ Projects for Peace

Projects for Peace provides up to 100 awards of $10,000 to undergraduates at Davis United World College Scholars Program partner schools (and a few other institutions) to design grassroots summer projects that promote peace and address the root causes of conflict among parties. Projects are encouraged that focus on conflict resolution, reconciliation, building understanding of and breaking down barriers that cause conflict, and finding solutions for resolving conflict and maintaining peace.

http://www.davisprojectsforpeace.org

Resources for the Future (RFF) Fellowships and Grants

A think tank devoted to the improvement and preservation of the environment and natural resources, RFF strives to improve both environmental and economic outcomes. It offers a variety of fellowships and grants.

http://www.rff.org/about/fellowships-internships-and-grants

^^ Roothbert Fund Scholarships

The Roothbert Fund's $2,000 to $3,000 scholarships (renewable for one year) support approximately 20 undergraduates and graduates per year with financial need who are guided by spiritual motives, with preference given to those seeking careers in education. The fund aims to build fellowship among current and former grant recipients, who are encouraged to meet at twice-yearly retreats at Pendle Hill, a Quaker center. The scholarships are open to residents of certain states (Maine, New Hampshire, Vermont, Rhode Island, Massachusetts, Connecticut, New York, New Jersey, Pennsylvania, Ohio, Delaware, Maryland, Washington, D.C., Virginia, West Virginia, and North Carolina). Applicants are required to attend an interview in March, typically held in New York, New Haven, Philadelphia, or Washington, D.C. The fund is not able to pay for travel expenses.

http://www.roothbertfund.org/scholarshipsprogram.php

Russell Sage Foundation (RSF) Grants and Fellowships

Located in New York City, RSF is a preeminent institution for research in the social sciences. It promotes the improvement of social and living conditions in the United States and offers a variety of grants and fellowships: Investigator-initiated Research Project Grants, Visiting Scholars Program, Visiting Journalist Program, Visiting Researchers, Small Grants Program in Behavioral Economics, and RSF Journal.

https://www.russellsage.org/how-to-apply

Smithsonian Institution Scholarships and Fellowships

The Smithsonian represents a community of learning, featuring the world's largest museum, education complex, and research complex. It offers students and recent graduates scholarships and fellowships within its museums and research institutes.

https://www.smithsonianofi.com/fellowship-opportunities/smithsonian-institution-fellowship-program/

** $$ Spencer Foundations Dissertation Fellowships for Research Related to Education

The Spencer Foundation Dissertation Fellowships for Research Related to Education are open to doctoral candidates, specifically those performing research in the field of education. The program grants 35 fellowships of $27,500.

https://www.spencer.org/dissertation-fellowships-1

** $$ Thomas R. Pickering Graduate Foreign Affairs Fellowship

This highly selective program provides up to $40,000 per year for two years of graduate study in foreign affairs, plus mentoring and professional development help to prepare fellows to enter the Foreign Service.

https://woodrow.org/fellowships/pickering/

Tillman Military Scholars

The Pat Tillman Foundation aims to invest in active and veteran military service members and their spouses through educational scholarships, building a diverse community of leaders committed to service to others. Tillman Scholars receive an average award of $10,000.

http://pattillmanfoundation.org/apply-to-be-a-scholar/

** Udall Undergraduate Scholarship

The Udall Foundation offers 50 fellowships each year of up to $7,000 to college sophomores and juniors for leadership, public service, and commitment to issues related to Native American nations or the environment. Alumni have gone on to perform public health work in Central America, become Fulbright Scholars, and hold positions in state government and the U.S. Department of the Interior.

https://www.udall.gov/ourprograms/scholarship/scholarship.aspx

United States Institute of Peace (USIP) Jennings Randolph Peace Dissertation Program

This program awards 10-month, $20,000 nonresidential Peace Scholar Dissertation Fellowships to 12 students per year who are writing doctoral dissertations on international security, conflict, and peace.

https://www.usip.org/grants-fellowships/fellowships/jennings-randolph-peace-dissertation-program-introduction

USA TODAY All-USA College Academic Award

The *USA TODAY* All-USA College Academic Award is given among the first, second, and third teams. The top 20 students will be featured in the newspaper and awarded $2,500. Criteria include grades, academic rigor, leadership, activities and, most important, an essay describing the student's most outstanding intellectual endeavor as an undergraduate.

http://www.allusanomination.com

Vivian Lefsky Hort Memorial Fellowship

The Vivian Lefsky Hort Memorial Fellowship is an award for graduate, doctoral, or postdoctoral research in Eastern European Jewish music, art, and theater, and in Yiddish literature. Recipients are awarded up to $6,500.

https://www.petersons.com/scholarship/vivian-lefsky-hort-memorial-fellowship-111_151730.aspx

World Politics and Statecraft Fellowship

The World Politics and Statecraft Fellowship supports doctoral dissertation research on American foreign policy, international relations, international security, strategic studies, area studies, and diplomatic and military history. The program awards 20 $7,500 fellowships.

https://www.srf.org/programs/international-security-foreign-policy/world-politics-statecraft-fellowship/

"Feminism is not just about women; it's about letting all people lead fuller lives."

— Jane Fonda, American actress and political activist

Chapter 19:
Women's Scholarships and Fellowships

This chapter presents a broad sample of the available opportunities for women.

Insider's Tip: This website lists additional opportunities for women: www.collegescholarships.org.

Accounting & Financial Women's Alliance (AFWA) Foundation Paula Zanni Award

The AFWA offers scholarships to women seeking undergraduate and master's degrees in the fields of finance and accounting, including a diversity-focused undergraduate scholarship open to minority women. The amount awarded may vary each year.

https://www.afwa.org/scholarships/

Alliance for Women in Media Foundation (AWMF) for Empowering America Scholarship

The AWMF for Empowering America Scholarship is available to female undergraduate or graduate students pursuing any degree, with media-career students especially encouraged to apply. AWMF provides one $3,000 scholarship and one $2,000 scholarship.

https://allwomeninmedia.org/app/uploads/2018/02/2018-Empowering-America-Scholarship-Application.pdf

American Academy of Chefs (AAC/ACF) Scholarship

The ACF and AAC offer annual scholarships to female college students and professional chefs seeking to further their education in the culinary field. Recipients are awarded up to $2,500.

https://www.acfchefs.org/ACF/Partnerships/AAC/ACF/Partnerships/AAC/

American Association of University Women (AAUW) Career Development Grants

AAUW offers Career Development Grants to women looking to advance their careers with a postgraduate degree, certification program, or specialized training. Awards range from $2,000 to $12,000.

https://www.aauw.org/what-we-do/educational-funding-and-awards/career-development-grants/

American Association of University Women (AAUW) Dissertation Fellowships

AAUW Dissertation Fellowships provide women pursuing a doctorate in their final year with $20,000.

www.aauw.org

American Association of University Women (AAUW) International Fellowships

The AAUW International Fellowships help non-permanent U.S. resident women pursue higher education. Recipients are awarded $18,000 at the master's level, $20,000 at the doctoral level, and $30,000 at the postdoctoral level.

https://www.aauw.org/what-we-do/educational-funding-and-awards/american-fellowships/af-dissertation-application/

$$ American Association of University Women (AAUW) Postdoctoral Research Leave Fellowship

The AAUW Postdoctoral Research Leave Fellowship assists women in obtaining tenure through a year of research. Recipients are awarded $30,000.

https://www.aauw.org/what-we-do/educational-funding-and-awards/international-fellowships/

American Association of University Women (AAUW) Selected Professions Fellowships

The AAUW offers these fellowships to women pursuing a master's in architecture, computer and information sciences, engineering, or mathematics and statistics, and to women of color pursuing an MBA (second year), law degree (third year), or doctorate in medicine (fourth year). Recipients are awarded $5,000 to $18,000.

https://www.aauw.org/what-we-do/educational-funding-and-awards/american-fellowships/af-postdoctoral-research-application/

American Planning Association (APA) Judith McManus Price Scholarship

The APA scholarship supports minority women who are graduate students in urban planning and who can prove financial need. Recipients are awarded from $2,000 to $4,000.

https://www.aauw.org/what-we-do/educational-funding-and-awards/selected-professions-fellowships/

American Water Works Association (AWWA) Holly A. Cornell Scholarship

AWWA offers the Holly A. Cornell Scholarship, funded by CH2M Hill. This award, a one-time grant of $7,500, assists female or minority graduate students pursuing a master's degree in water supply and treatment.

https://www.planning.org/foundation/scholarships/

Armenian International Women's Association (AIWA) Scholarship

The AIWA scholarship assists women in financial need who are of Armenian descent and college juniors or above. Recipients are awarded up to $2,000.

https://www.awwa.org/membership/get-involved/student-center/awwa-scholarships.aspx

Asian Women in Business (AWIB) Scholarship

The AWIB scholarship encourages, assists, and promotes exceptional Asian female students who have demonstrated scholarship, leadership, community service, and entrepreneurship. Recipients are awarded up to $2,500, subject to fund availability.

http://aiwainternational.org/content.aspx

Association of Romanian Orthodox Ladies' Auxiliaries in America (ARFORA) Undergraduate Scholarship for Women

The ARFORA Scholarship, worth $1,000, is awarded to female undergraduates.

http://www.awib.org/index.cfm?fuseaction=Page.ViewPage&PageID=811

Association of Women Contractors (AWC) Scholarship

The AWC Scholarship assists females entering construction-related careers through the academic track or through an apprenticeship. Recipients are awarded up to $2,000.

http://roea.org/arforaundergrad.html

Automotive Women's Alliance Foundation (AWAF) Education Scholarships

AWAF offers scholarships to women with a passion for the automotive industry. Recipients are awarded up to $2,500.

https://awcmn.org/programs/scholarship/

$$ Campbell Fellowship for Women Scholar-Practitioners from Developing Nations

The Campbell Fellowship assists female postdoctoral social scientists from developing countries whose work addresses women's economic and social empowerment in their country. Recipients are awarded $4,500 each month for six months.

http://awafoundation.org/Scholarships

Center for Women in Government and Civil Society at Rockefeller College (CWGCS) Fellowship on Women & Public Policy

The CWGCS fellowship is available to female graduate students to encourage advocacy and public service. The fellowship awards a $10,000 stipend and tuition assistance.

https://www.afterschoolafrica.com/556/campbell-fellowship-for-women-scholar/

Conchita Poncini Jimenez International Human Rights Fellowship

The Organization for Women in Science for the Developing World offers this fellowship for research by female students on preventing violence and promoting human rights. Awards vary each year.

https://www.albany.edu/womeningov/

$$ Earth Institute and Lamont-Doherty Earth Observatory (EI/LDEO) Marie Tharp Fellowship

The EI/LDEO awards the Marie Tharp Fellowship to outstanding female scientists, enabling them to perform research at Columbia University. Recipients are awarded up to $25,000.

https://owsd.net/conchita-poncini-jimenez-human-rights-fellowship

Educational Foundation for Women in Accounting (EFWA)

The EFWA offers two graduate scholarships and one postgraduate scholarship to women pursuing a professional degree in accounting:

- **Institute of Management Accounts:** $1,000 to female graduate students, along with a CMA Learning System kit and a one-year IMA student membership

- **Moss Adams Foundation:** $1,000 to minority women pursuing a master's in accounting
- **Laurels Fund:** $1,000-$5,000 to women pursuing a doctorate in accounting http://earth.columbia.edu/articles/view/2723

Financial Women of San Francisco (FWSF) Scholarship

The FWSF Scholarship Fund provides graduate and undergraduate scholarships to San Francisco Bay Area women pursuing careers in finance and financial services. Undergraduate recipients are awarded $10,000 while graduate recipients are awarded $15,000.

http://www.efwa.org/scholarships.php

Foreign Policy Interrupted (FPI) Fellowship

The FPI Fellowship targets female students, diversifying voices and opinions on foreign policy. Fellows are matched with an editor and/or producer to develop their expertise in print and/or on-camera appearances.

http://www.financialwomensf.org/

Graduate Women International Awards

The Graduate Women International Awards offers fellowships and grants on an ad hoc basis to women who seek to conduct postgraduate study and research anywhere in the world.

http://www.fpinterrupted.com/fellowship-program/

Hegg Hoffet Fund

The Hegg Hoffet Fund provides small grants to women forced to flee their homelands due to war, political unrest, persecution, or other emergencies. This enables women who have suffered hardship to continue their education or professional training despite adverse circumstances.

http://www.graduatewomen.org/what-we-do/grants-fellowships/international-awards/

** ^^ International Women's Media Foundation (IWMF) Elizabeth Neuffer Fellowship

The IWMF's Neuffer Fellowship supports female journalists with three years of experience or more who focus on human rights and social justice. Fellows conduct research, pursue coursework at MIT's Center for International Studies, and complete journalism internships at *The Boston Globe* and *The New York Times*.

http://www.graduatewomen.org/what-we-do/grants-fellowships/hegg-hoffet/

Jane M. Klausman Women in Business Scholarship

Zonta International offers $2,000 and $8,000 scholarships to women studying business management at the graduate and master's level.

https://www.zonta.org/Global-Impact/Education/Women-in-Business-Scholarship

Judy Wendland-Young College Scholarship

This scholarship, granted by the Jewish Federation of the East Bay (California) and the Jewish Community Foundation, is available to women over 35 who have not previously attended a four-year college. Recipients are awarded up to $20,000 for their first year of college.

https://www.jfed.org/financial-aid/

National Collegiate Athletic Association (NCAA) Ethnic Minority and Women's Enhancement Graduate Scholarship

The NCAA's Ethnic Minority and Women's Enhancement Graduate Scholarship increases opportunities for minorities and female college students pursuing careers in a sports-related field. The NCAA awards scholarships of $7,000 to 13 ethnic minorities and 13 females with provisional admissions for graduate studies.

http://www.ncaa.org/about/resources/ncaa-scholarships-and-grants

National Federation of Republican Women (NFRW) Betty Rendel Scholarship

The NFRW's Rendel Scholarship supports women in political science, government, and economics. Three female undergraduates with at least two years of completed coursework are awarded $1,000.

http://www.nfrw.org/rendel

National Federation of Republican Women (NFRW) National Pathfinder Scholarship

The NFRW's National Pathfinder Scholarship aims to increase the number of women involved in the political process. Scholarships of $2,500 each are awarded to three college sophomores and above.

http://www.nfrw.org/pathfinder

Philanthropic Educational Organization (P.E.O.) International Peace Scholarship

P.E.O. awards up to $12,500 to female graduate students in Canada or the United States through its International Peace Scholarship.

https://www.peointernational.org/about-peo-international-peace-scholarship-ips

SR Education Group Scholarship

SR Education Group offers a scholarship of $2,000 to female students who prove financial need.

https://www.sreducationgroup.org/scholarships

Women in Aviation International (WAI) Scholarship

WAI supports women seeking careers in aviation. It offers scholarships to active members; amounts vary.

https://www.wai.org/education/scholarships

Women in Defense (WID) Horizons Scholarship

The WID scholarship supports women pursuing a career in national security or defense. Recipients are awarded $1,000.

http://www.womenindefense.net/horizons

Women in Transportation (WTS) Scholarships

The WTS Foundation offers several scholarships to women pursuing careers in transportation. Recipients are awarded up to $10,000.

https://www.wtsinternational.org/education/scholarships/

** Women's Congressional Policy Institute (WCPI) Congressional Fellowship

The WCPI Fellowship is designed to train potential leaders in public policymaking to examine issues from the perspectives, experiences, and needs of women. This program is the only graduate-level fellowship on Capitol Hill that exclusively focuses on women.

http://www.womenspolicy.org/our-work/congressional-fellows/

Woodrow Wilson Dissertation Fellowship in Women's Studies

The Woodrow Wilson Women's Studies Fellowships are open to doctoral candidates who exhibit strong evidence of commitment to women's issues and scholarship on women. Ten recipients are awarded $5,000.

https://woodrow.org/fellowships/womens-studies/

"If there is no struggle, there is no progress."

— Frederick Douglass, social reformer, abolitionist, and statesman

Chapter 20:
Diversity Scholarships and Fellowships

This chapter presents scholarships and fellowships for members of historically underrepresented groups (typically African-Americans, Hispanic Americans, and Native Americans/Alaska Natives), as well as recent immigrants and their children. Diversity scholarships specifically for law and STEM students can be found in this chapter.

One day at St. Thomas University in Miami, the Congressional Hispanic Caucus came to deliver a presentation about the opportunity to intern in the U.S. Congress. I am not Hispanic, but I am one of those people who applies for everything — Asian scholarships, African-American scholarships, Hispanic scholarships, everything. If there were a Caucasian scholarship, I would have applied for it too.

Then I realized that if there was a Congressional Hispanic Caucus, there must be a black one too. I Googled it and found that I was right. I, of course, applied to both internships. Fortunately, and unfortunately, I didn't get the Hispanic internship, but I *was* offered the opportunity to intern in the U.S. Congress through the Congressional Black Caucus Foundation.

The next semester, I made my way to Washington, D.C. Until then, all I had seen of the United States was Miami. I had been living in North Miami — near Little Haiti. Almost everyone I knew was an immigrant; if they were not an immigrant, their parents were. I thought Washington, D.C., would be like Miami. I was wrong. Washington, D.C., was completely different from Miami, and I was fascinated by it.

Washington, D.C., consists of a lot of ambitious young people wearing suits. However, what truly impressed me about these young Washingtonians was their passion for public service. "If you want to change the world, you have to be in Washington, D.C.," I thought idealistically. Washington, D.C., was love at first sight. I knew instantaneously that there would be no going back to Miami for me.

Two days later, my friend whom I had met at the Clinton Global Initiative University gave me the nicest tour of Georgetown University. Given that I had mostly attended Catholic schools in the past, it was perfect.

Gaining admission to a school is one thing; paying for it is another. In my case, I have never worried about the *how* when submitting applications. However, when I have received acceptance letters, they have inevitably included a deadline to make a payment to reserve my space. Therefore, the next challenge after obtaining acceptance is deciding what to do in order to make those payments.

In my case, the CBCF program had paid for my living expenses, provided me a stipend, and even paid for the three graduate courses I was taking at night at The George Washington Graduate School of Political Management. I was living the American dream.

Unfortunately, I knew it would end soon unless I took further action. Therefore, from the time I arrived in Washington D.C., I started preparing my next career step. Life is like a staircase that you climb step by step. You should not give yourself any option to go back down.

At the same time, mastering each step as you climb it is vital. Make certain to build a strong foundation so that you can rise exponentially when new doors open. You don't want to jump up more steps than you can handle at one time because you will inevitably pay for the consequences. However, you always need to challenge yourself, as there are continually new skills you can learn to improve yourself.

So there I was, living the life, right up to the moment my CBCF internship in our nation's capital ended. In preparation for the termination of my internship, I had applied to the most prestigious programs in Washington, D.C. The rule for me was simple: The more prestigious and selective the programs were, the more money they must have. Therefore, they could also afford to pay for my living expenses.

Because I didn't have a home to return to in the United States, I usually lived on the school's campus. Then, for the summer, I would have to leave campus and find a place to stay. It can be mentally challenging when you have a vision for yourself, but find yourself stuck because of financial difficulties, especially when your family is unable to provide for you. What do you do?

I was rejected by all the programs I had applied for. I didn't want to be homeless. At the last minute, a friend who I had met at the Clinton Global Initiative University offered me a fellowship in Hong Kong. I went to the Chinese embassy, but they didn't grant me the visa.

In desperation, I contacted various people. As luck would have it, one of my mentors from Miami was hosting a one-week business camp in the Dominican Republic. Since my other plans hadn't worked out, I thought it would be a perfect opportunity to learn Spanish. I told him I would be happy to volunteer at his camp if he could give me a place to live. He agreed but told me I would have to pay for my airplane ticket.

In my free time, I was volunteering for a close advisor to the Haitian president at the time. She paid for a one-way plane ticket for me to go to the Dominican Republic. My mentor allowed me to share a hotel room with someone who was also volunteering at the camp for a week. I then managed to find someone at the camp who would allow me to stay with him for two weeks if I offered my service to his foundation. I agreed!

I flew to the Dominican Republic, a country I had never visited before, with only $50 and a determination to learn Spanish. After three weeks of living in Santo Domingo, I still had no source of income. I took the bus, crossed the border, and went to my native city of Gonaïves in Haiti. When I arrived there, I asked friends and family members to pitch in.

After a few days, I raised enough money to continue my adventure, and I returned to the Dominican Republic. Upon my return, I stayed in the inner cities of Santiago with an old school friend from Haiti. I took summer Spanish classes with fellow Haitian university students who had just come from Haiti and were learning Spanish.

In the midst of these experiences and uncertainties, by some divine intervention, I was awarded a full scholarship at Georgetown through the Georgetown Scholarship Program (GSP). However, I was still stuck in the Dominican Republic, and I did not have enough money to pay for an airplane ticket to start school at Georgetown.

During the summer, GSP connected me with a GSP student mentor to guide me on my transition. Luckily, she was working part-time at the Georgetown Financial Aid office. She taught me about the various opportunities and scholarships that the financial aid office provided. After I told GSP about my situation, GSP paid for my flight to D.C., sent a student to pick me up from the airport, and gave me a bedding set, as well as other essentials.

GSP made it possible for me to attend and thrive at Georgetown. Most GSP students are the first in their families to attend college. The program helps students break down barriers to achievement and navigate successfully through an environment with which many may be unfamiliar.

GSP provides a family-like support community through face-to-face interactions, mentoring, financial support, events, and networking opportunities. While over 70 percent of GSP students are first-generation college-bound, GSP maintains a 96.4 percent graduation rate versus the much lower rate of 30 percent among first-generation college students nationally.

The moral of this story is: You will face all kinds of uncertainty in life, but you should not allow those uncertainties to limit you in the pursuit of your education or dreams. The universe works its magic in strange ways. It is like a perfect equation in which everything works out exactly at the last minute.

Even when it does not, know that there is a bigger plan for you. Some doors were not meant to be opened. Never lose hope — just take it slowly, one step at a time. Try your best, believe in yourself, and believe in your potential.

Albert W. Dent Graduate Student Scholarship

This scholarship assists minority students in health care management graduate programs with tuition, student loans, and expenses. Recipients are awarded up to $5,000.

https://www.ache.org/Faculty_Students/dent_scholarship.cfm

American Water Works Association (AWWA) Holly A. Cornell Scholarship

AWWA offers the Holly A. Cornell Scholarship, funded by CH2M Hill. The award, a one-time grant of $7,500, assists female or minority graduate students pursuing a master's degree in water supply and treatment.

https://www.awwa.org/membership/get-involved/student-center/awwa-scholarships.aspx

** Benjamin A. Gilman International Scholarship

The U.S. Department of State offers the Gilman Scholarship to undergraduates receiving Pell Grant funding to study abroad. More than 2,900 recipients are awarded up to $5,000. By supporting undergraduates with high financial need, the program extends travel opportunities to students who have been historically underrepresented in education abroad. Applicants studying a critical need language while abroad in a country in which the language is predominantly spoken can apply for a supplemental award of up to $3,000.

http://www.gilmanscholarship.org/

** Congressional Hispanic Caucus Institute (CHCI) Graduate Fellowship

CHCI offers a paid, nine-month graduate fellowship in higher education, secondary education, health, housing, law, or STEM to aspiring Hispanic American leaders with a master's or law degree. Placements include the White House, the U.S. Congress, government agencies, advocacy organizations, and trade associations.

https://chci.org/programs/graduate-fellowship-program/

** Congressional Hispanic Caucus Institute (CHCI) Public Policy Fellowship

This prestigious, paid nine-month fellowship opens doors for talented young Hispanic Americans in public policy. Fellows enjoy significant exposure to leaders in congressional offices, federal agencies, advocacy organizations, government-related institutes, and more.

https://chci.org/programs/public-policy-fellowship-program/

Congressional Hispanic Caucus Institute (CHCI) Scholar/ Intern Programs

CHCI offers two scholar-intern programs, providing Hispanic American students with a scholarship plus an internship. Its CHCI-United Health Foundation program awards $5,000 per year plus a $1,000 stipend, while its CHCI-SHRM program awards $2,500 plus an hourly internship.

https://chci.org/programs/chci-scholar-intern-programs/

Consortium for Graduate Study in Management (CGSM)

CGSM recruits African-American, Hispanic American, and Native American MBA students for merit-based fellowships for graduate study leading to a master's degree in business. These fellowships provide full tuition and mandatory fees for two years of full-time study.

https://cgsm.org/

** Ford Foundation Fellowships

The Ford Foundation offers a variety of fellowships to increase diversity in college and university faculties, maximize the educational benefits of diversity, and increase the number of professors who focus on diversity-related subjects.

http://sites.nationalacademies.org/PGA/FordFellowships/index.htm

Hispanic Scholarship Fund (HSF) College Scholarship

The HSF provides scholarships of $500 to $5,000, as well as support services, to exceptional Hispanic American undergraduates and graduate students.

http://www.hsf.net/

Institute for International Public Policy (IIPP) Fellowship

IIPP provides underrepresented minority college students with summer policy institutes, study abroad, intensive language training, internships, graduate study, and student services.

https://www2.ed.gov/programs/iegpsiipp/index.html

JAMAS Future Hispanic Leaders Scholarship

This JAMAS Capital Management scholarship provides $2,500 to Hispanic American students.

https://jamascapital.com/future-hispanic-leaders-scholarship/

** Public Policy and International Affairs (PPIA) Fellowships

PPIA promotes the inclusion and full participation of underrepresented groups in public service. It provides undergraduates with an intensive seven-week Junior Summer Institute (JSI) before their senior year, including mentoring and career development in the field.

https://www.ppiaprogram.org/ppia/what-we-do/junior-summer
-institutes/

** $$ Rangel Graduate Fellowship

The Rangel Graduate Fellowship prepares outstanding young people for careers in the foreign service sector of the Department of State, in which interns help formulate,

157

represent, and implement United States foreign policy. This program, which highly encourages applicants from women, those with financial need, and minority groups historically underrepresented in the Foreign Service, offers two-year fellowships of up to $37,500 annually.

https://www.rangelprogram.org/graduate-fellowship-program/

** $$ Ron Brown Scholar Program

The Ron Brown Scholar Program honors the legacy of Ronald H. Brown through a selective scholarship for community-minded and intellectually gifted African-Americans. Scholars receive four-year scholarships totaling $40,000 ($10,000 each year). The program also includes an alumni association.

http://www.ronbrown.org/

Southern Regional Education Board Dissertation Award

The Southern Regional Education Board works to improve public education at every level, providing educators with professional development, proven practices, and curricula. It offers a $20,000 award to doctoral students in certain Southern states; preference is given to members of historically underrepresented groups in STEM.

https://www.sreb.org/general-information/dissertation-award

UNCF/Merck Undergraduate Science Research Scholarship

The UNCF/Merck Undergraduate Science Research Scholarship is available to African-American students in life sciences, physical sciences, or engineering.

https://scholarships.uncf.org/?_ga=2.19815288.1136844044.
1532393805-1900244888.1532393805

"The way in which you carry yourself, even when seated at a desk, matters."

— Ivanka Trump, American businesswoman and assistant to the president

Chapter 21:
Scholarships and Fellowships for Study Abroad

While attending Georgetown, I wanted to complete a study abroad program at the best political science university in France, Sciences Po Paris. Since most Americans may not have heard of Sciences Po, the simplest way to demonstrate the importance of the school is to say that seven out of the past eight French presidents attended Sciences Po.

I had always dreamed of visiting Europe. Studying in Paris at Sciences Po intimidated me, but at the core of my being, I have always aimed to achieve dreams that frighten me. If your dreams do not scare you, then you are not aiming high enough! Dream bigger!

Studying abroad provides an exciting opportunity to broaden your perspective. As for myself, I wanted to study with the brilliant political minds of Europe, and especially to study with the future French and European leaders.

It is interesting to me that, a few centuries ago, the grandparents of my classmates made decisions that determined the fate of my native country and of my forefathers. France colonized Haiti and arguably left the scar of colonization that still plagues the country today. Yet, I attended school with these political elite who glorified the legacy of Napoleon and Charles de Gaulle, as if they had created a golden age for mankind.

I really don't care about Napoleon, but I had to study him, as well as the French culture and history. Although you might sometimes question why you are studying certain subjects in school, maintain an open mind toward different opportunities as they present themselves. This set of experiences will make you unique and give you an edge over other people.

Your experiences may challenge your preconceived notions. In addition, they will enable you to spend three-fourths of your time appreciating the argument of the other side. That way, you will be even more effective when countering your opponents' arguments in the future and you can look at everything from a more practical point of view.

I have been criticized, particularly by my political activist friends, for being a sellout. However, I believe it is important to be able to relate to a variety of people who may or may not share my political views.

I have always seen myself as a person with a global perspective who can appreciate different people and different cultures, allowing me to consider all sides before I make a final decision. I always consider the consequences of my actions, and I am willing to deal with them, regardless of the outcome. Never make a decision based on an emotion.

Always think critically for yourself and consider the various outcomes and interpretations of your decisions. That way, you will never have regrets after standing by your decision, even if you made the wrong one. Instead, simply appreciate the lessons you learn along the way.

I took the requisite French classes at Georgetown in order to attend Sciences Po. However, unlike most people who study abroad to enjoy the culture and focus on school, I managed to find a way to secure an internship at the French Ministry of Foreign Affairs & Overseas. I knew someone who knew someone who knew another person, and I connected the dots.

I believe in the six degrees of separation notion, and the idea that I could connect with anyone from around the world simply by asking the right person, who could then refer me to various people, culminating in me connecting with the right person.

Here is how to use the six degrees of separation to your advantage: When someone is kind and gracious enough to introduce you to someone else, follow up immediately. Always be nice, humble, and grateful for the opportunity. Always respect the person's time. Part of respecting their time involves always knowing exactly what you need help with. That way, you can help guide the person to help you in the best way possible.

Every time you meet with someone, make sure to leave a good impression. If the person is impressed by you and trusts you, they will be happy to connect you with someone else they know. Employing these strategies helped me secure the French Ministries internship.

Some people say it is best not to plan your career, while others recommend rigidly planning. I think you should do a little bit of both. Focus on what you are doing and make sure to do an excellent job, but, at the same time, if an opportunity presents itself, jump on it. In my life, I have definitely planned many of my greatest internships; however, when any amazing opportunity has presented itself, I have always taken advantage of it.

Prior to attending Sciences Po for the fall academic semester, I was taking classes full time at Georgetown and interning in the office of Senator Harry Reid. I had carefully planned to complete the first part of my summer vacation at Florida State University College of Law Summer for Undergraduates and left a day early for the second half of my summer at Princeton University, Woodrow Wilson School of Public, and International Affairs. While I was at Princeton, I also prepared for my study abroad at Sciences Po.

When I arrived at Sciences Po Paris, I quickly learned that it was a very elitist school. Some of the students thought they were the best minds of France. I am not impressed easily, so I minded my own business. I was interning with the majority leader of the U.S. Senate, so I was not going to allow any college student to think they were superior to me. I never gave anyone the opportunity to put me down.

Let me explain myself. I was in a new country, studying within a new education system, and everything was spoken in French. In addition, I was one of the very few black people in my classes, and on top of that, I was an exchange student.

The simplest way I can describe it is, imagine that you are a white Western student who moves to Nairobi, Kenya to attend university, surrounded by almost all black students. What would you do? How would you feel when the black teacher asks you a question in class?

If you were the only white student in class, and you get the answer wrong, what would the black students think of you? Would you feel that you have to represent the entire white race, if you were the only white student? This is the daily reality of minorities in top Western academic institutions.

My approach has always been to adapt, wherever I go. I never take criticisms personally. I just go about living my life. I had an incredible time studying at Sciences Po Paris learning about the French political system, history, and culture. In addition, I always wore my suits to school, and at times, after my classes had ended, I would go to my internship at the French Ministry of Foreign Affairs & Overseas.

It was interesting to witness what the French people and French politicians think of Sciences Po. There is some type of hypocrisy that exists, in which politicians criticize the very school they attended. French citizens take personal pride in criticizing every problem with the French political system, blaming them on Sciences Po.

My colleague at the French Ministry of Foreign Affairs & Overseas would openly criticize the French political system. Once, we were eating dinner at the Ministry of Agriculture, and he was determined to convince everyone at the table that there was no hope for France and that the grand vision of General Charles de Gaulle was doomed. For him, the only thing that was failing the French was one elitist institution, which was depriving the great French citizens of their inalienable rights to *liberté, égalité, fraternité* (liberty, equality, and fraternity).

He shamed them regarding their so-called superiority, claiming that their lives and careers had been handed to them by their aristocratic and bourgeois family. Indeed, hope to him was slim, and he felt that a sort of cultural revolution was necessary for France to progress and lead the world. He further criticized, saying that Sciences Po graduates would not even take the public train transportation in Paris.

Surprisingly, he had the courage to question other people from across the table to concur with his bold statements. One gentleman in particular, who had been observing his proclamation for thirty minutes, took the liberty to respond, "*Monsieur, je suis un ancien de Sciences Po. Je suis d'accord avec tout ce que vous avez dit sur Sciences Po. Mais la seule chose que je ne suis pas d'accord, c'est que j'utilise les transports publics.*" In English, this means, "Mister, I am an alumnus of Sciences Po. I agree with everything you said about Sciences Po. But the only thing I disagree with is, I use the public transportation."

The moral of the story is, studying abroad provides an ideal opportunity to work outside your comfort zone. It will help broaden your perspective and allow you to be more open-minded toward different people and cultures.

However, keep your goal in mind, and try to connect how that study abroad fits into your larger life's mission and your career goal. Later, you will want to be able to articulate to potential employers how that study abroad fits into the larger picture, and how it can help you in the workplace.

$$Adelaide Scholarships International

The University of Adelaide offers a full-tuition scholarship to a limited number of postgraduate students from countries outside of Australia and New Zealand. The scholarship is awarded for two years for a master's degree and three years for a doctoral degree, which includes tuition, annual living allowance, and health insurance.

http://www.adelaide.edu.au/

** American India Foundation (AIF) William J. Clinton Fellowship

The AIF William J. Clinton Fellowship for Service in India is a 10-month volunteer program that pairs young U.S. professionals with bachelor's degrees with Indian NGOs and social enterprises, to help create effective projects that are replicable, scalable, and sustainable. Candidates must be flexible and adaptable, and possess exceptional ability to build meaningful relationships across cultures. A sensitivity and ability to work with vulnerable communities, as well as the humility and passion to learn by doing, is essential. Although proficiency in an Indian language is not required to apply, it is highly desirable. AIF provides a round-trip ticket to India, insurance, and a monthly living stipend, which covers basic living expenses such as rent, meals, incidentals, and local transportation related to a Fellow's project. Fellows should expect to live modestly.

https://aif.org/fellowship/fellowship-application/

American-Scandinavian Foundation (ASF) Fellowships

ASF provides individuals with fellowships of up to $23,000 to pursue research or study for a year on a specific, specialized project in one or more Scandinavian countries. It gives priority to graduate-level candidates for dissertation-related study or research. All applicants must have some proficiency in at least one Scandinavian language.

http://www.amscan.org/fellowships-and-grants/

American School of Classical Studies at Athens (ASCSA) Summer Sessions Scholarships

The ASCSA offers scholarships to students of literature/English, anthropology, archaeology, museum studies, Near and Middle East studies, classics, history, philosophy, religion, humanities, architecture, or art history, who have completed at least one year of graduate school. Recipients are awarded up to $5,000.

http://www.ascsa.edu.gr/index.php/programs/ss-scholarships

American Research Institute in Turkey (ARIT) Summer Fellowships

ARIT offers 15 fellowships to advanced students for participation in their summer program in intensive advanced Turkish, at Boğaziçi University in Istanbul. The fellowship covers the cost of airfare, application and tuition fees, and a stipend for maintenance costs. Applicants must be faculty or a college student.

http://ccat.sas.upenn.edu/ARIT/ARITSummerLanguageProgram.html

** Anna Sobol Levy Foundation Fellowships

The Anna Sobol Levy Foundation enables students to pursue a master's degree in English at the prestigious IDC Herzliya's International School near Tel Aviv, Israel. Recipients must be U.S. citizens under 30 with at least a bachelor's degree in political science, international relations, economics, geography, military studies, history, or similar fields. The fellowship covers tuition costs up to $16,000.

http://www.annasobollevyfoundation.org/

Archaeology of Portugal Fellowship (APF)

APF assists projects pertaining to the archaeology of Portugal. Such projects include, but are not limited to, research projects, colloquia, symposia, publication, and travel for research or academic meetings. Recipients are awarded up to $8,000.

https://www.archaeological.org/grants/702

Bayer Foundation Fellowship

The Bayer Foundation aims to support the next generation of researchers and teachers. To this end, it offers tailored financial support in the form of fellowships granted to students and young professionals who would like to pursue a project in Germany.

http://www.bayer-foundations.com/en/international-fellowship.aspx

Belgian American Educational Foundation (BAEF) Study and Research Fellowships

BAEF encourages fellowships for advanced study or research during one academic year at a Belgian university. Applicants must be registered in a graduate program toward a doctorate or equivalent degree in the United States, plan to register in a graduate program (master's or doctorate) in Belgium, or currently hold a master's, doctorate, or equivalent degree. Fellowship stipends are $28,000 for masters and doctoral students and $32,000 for post-doctorates.

http://www.baef.be/documents/fellowships-for-us-citizens/study-res-fellow.-for-us-citizen-.xml?lang=en

** Benjamin A. Gilman International Scholarship

The U.S. Department of State offers the Gilman Scholarship to undergraduates receiving Pell Grant funding to study abroad. More than 2,900 recipients are awarded up to $5,000. By supporting undergraduates with high financial need, the program extends travel opportunities to students who have been historically underrepresented in education abroad. Applicants studying a critical need language while abroad in a country in which the language is predominantly spoken can apply for a supplemental award of up to $3,000.

http://www.gilmanscholarship.org/

Blakemore Freeman Fellowships

The Blakemore Foundation offers students Freeman Fellowships, provided for one academic year of full-time, intensive language study at the advanced level in East or Southeast Asia in any approved language programs. Applicants must demonstrate their commitment to helping make an impact in Asia. The program covers tuition costs plus a stipend for living expenses, travel costs, and educational expenses.

http://www.blakemorefoundation.org/

** ^^ Bonderman Graduate Travel Fellowship

Bonderman Graduate Travel Fellowships grant $23,000 to University of Washington graduate students, college seniors with a 3.60 GPA or better, and college seniors in the Honors Program to travel independently for eight months, exploring six or more less westernized/developed countries in two or more major regions of the world. This fellowship is not for research projects, formal study at a foreign university, or internships abroad.

http://bonderman.uw.edu/

Bridging Scholarship for Study in Japan

The U.S.-Japan Bridging Foundation offers America's young people the opportunity to study abroad in Japan, and to prepare for a future in global leadership. Scholarships are awarded up to the amount of $5,000.

https://www.bridgingfoundation.org/scholarship-program

** British Chevening Scholarships

British Chevening Scholarships enable non-U.K. students to study in the United Kingdom. Approximately 600 new scholarships are awarded each year for postgraduate studies and research.

http://www.chevening.org/

Center for Arabic Study Abroad (CASA) Fellowships

CASA Fellowships, administered by Harvard University, fund study at the American University in Cairo, Egypt, or the Qasid Arabic Institute in Amman, Jordan, for undergraduates, graduate students, and holders of either a bachelor's or a master's degree. Applicants must have fluency in Arabic and at least three years of formal Arabic instruction.

http://projects.iq.harvard.edu/casa_at_harvard

Chinese Government Scholarships

This scholarship, established by the Ministry of Education of P.R. China to enable international students and scholars to study or research at universities in China, provides full or partial tuition and a monthly stipend; amounts vary by position. For further information, contact the nearest Chinese embassy and/or sign up on the website to receive a list of available scholarships.

http://ee.china-embassy.org/eng/tzygg/t1531011.htm

** Churchill Scholarship

The Churchill Scholarship offers financial support of approximately $60,000 (depending on the current exchange rate) to American students for a year of graduate study in mathematics, science, or engineering at the University of Cambridge, based at Churchill College.

http://www.winstonchurchillfoundation.org/scholarship.html

CIMI Doctoral Fellowships

CIMI offers a three-year support grant for up to six students working toward a doctorate. Research areas should be developed within the activities at the Institut de Mathématiques de Toulouse (IMT) and the Institut de Recherche en Informatique de Toulouse (IRIT) in France.

http://www.cimi.univ-toulouse.fr/en/doctoral-fellowships

CIMI Master Fellowships

CIMI provides €600 or €1,000 a month fellowships for students enrolled in a graduate course in mathematics or computer science in one of the programs associated with CIMI (see previous listing). Fellows must reside in Toulouse, France, for the duration of the fellowship.

http://www.cimi.univ-toulouse.fr/en/master-fellowships

Confucius China Studies Program Fellowships

The Confucius China Studies Program offers generous funding to U.S.-based students focusing on China. The Research Ph.D. Fellowship ranges from six months to two years and supports doctoral research in China. The Ph.D. in China Fellowship, which lasts from three to four years, supports students with master's degrees to pursue doctorates in China.

https://www.iie.org/Programs/Confucius-China-Studies-Program

$$ Council on Foreign Relations (CFR) International Affairs Fellowship in Nuclear Security (IAF-NS)

The IAF-NS, sponsored by the Stanton Foundation, offers hands-on experience in the nuclear security policymaking field and places selected fellows in U.S. government positions or international organizations. It is open only to faculty members with tenure or on tenure-track lines at accredited universities, between the ages of 29 and 50. The fellowship, which lasts 12 months, provides a stipend of $125,000.

https://www.cfr.org/fellowships/international-affairs-fellowship
-nuclear-security

Critical Language Scholarship (CLS)

The CLS for Intensive Summer Institutes provides funding to U.S. citizen undergraduate, master's, and doctoral students and recent graduates who want to participate in beginning, intermediate, and advanced-level summer language programs at American Overseas Research Centers and affiliated partners.

http://clscholarship.org/

DAAD Intensive Language Courses in Germany

DAAD (German Academic Exchange) offers grants to attend an intensive language course at leading institutes in Germany. Applications are open to undergraduate and graduate students as well as doctoral candidates in any subject area except German studies, German as a foreign language, and translation courses.

https://www.daad.org/en/find-funding/undergraduate-opportunities/
university-summer-course-grant/

DAAD Study and Internship Program (SIP) in Germany

This program offers students a semester of study abroad at one of the UAS7 universities in Germany. Students must be college sophomores or juniors in engineering, science, life science, business, management, economics, architecture, art, design, journalism, or social work.

http://uas7.org/scholarships/study-a-internship-program.html

DAAD Study Scholarships

These scholarships support highly qualified students of all disciplines to pursue postgraduate studies for 10 months in Germany.

https://students.dartmouth.edu/fellowship-advising/fellowships
/post-graduate-opportunities/daad-study-scholarships

DAAD Study Scholarships in Fine Art, Design/Visual Communication, and Film

DAAD scholarships offer graduates the opportunity to pursue a postgraduate degree or continuing course of study at a state or state-recognized German university of their choice.

https://www.daad.de/deutschland/stipendium/datenbank/en/21148-
scholarship-database/?status=3&origin=32&subjectGrps=G&daad=1&q=&page=2
&detail=57135742

** David L. Boren Scholarships

The National Security Education Program (NSEP) offers Boren Scholarships of $8,000 to support outstanding undergraduates who demonstrate strong motivation for developing expertise in languages, cultures, and world regions less commonly studied by Americans. The scholarships support study abroad for one year or more, with priority given to students who will study abroad for longer periods, and who seek to work in the federal government.

http://www.borenawards.org/

** Davies-Jackson Scholarship

The Davies-Jackson Scholarship provides support for a two-year course of study at St. John's College, Cambridge University, leading to a British B.A. degree (the equivalent of a master's degree in America). Applicants must be among the first generation in their families to graduate from college.

https://www.cic.edu/programs/davies-jackson-scholarship

East Asia and Pacific Summer Institutes for U.S. Graduate Students (EAPSI)

The National Science Foundation's EAPSI Fellowship provides U.S. graduate students in a research-oriented graduate or doctoral program in science and engineering with the opportunity to conduct research at one of the seven host locations in East Asia and the Pacific. Participants receive a stipend of $5,000 and a round-trip ticket to the location.

https://www.nsf.gov/od/oise/eap.jsp

** $$ Endeavour Scholarships and Fellowships

Endeavour Scholarships and Fellowships provide full financial support for international students to undertake a master's or Ph.D. in any field of study in Australia. It also provides a vocational award to pursue an Australian diploma, advanced diploma, or associate degree.

https://internationaleducation.gov.au/Endeavour%20program/Scholarships-and-Fellowships/Pages/default.aspx

$$ ETH Zürich Excellence Master's Scholarship

ETH Zürich, a university in Zürich, Switzerland, offers two scholarship programs, the Excellence Scholarship & Opportunity Program (ESOP) and the Master's Scholarship Program (MSP), to top international students who wish to pursue a master's degree. ESOP covers living and study expenses, as well as a tuition waiver, while the MSP consists of a partial stipend for living and study expenses with a tuition waiver. ETH Zürich's areas of focus are medicine, data, food security, and manufacturing technologies.

https://www.ethz.ch/students/en/studies/financial/scholarships/excellencescholarship.html

Fox International Fellowship

The Fox International Fellowship is a graduate student exchange program between Yale University and 19 world-renowned partner universities. Fellows are doctoral students, graduating master's students, or graduating college seniors.

https://foxfellowship.yale.edu/

Frank Huntington Beebe Fund

The Frank Huntington Beebe Fund awards fellowships to gifted young musicians seeking to pursue their studies abroad. Recipients are awarded up to $22,000.

http://www.beebefund.org/

Freeman Awards for Study in Asia (Freeman-ASIA)

Freeman-ASIA provides scholarships for undergraduates with demonstrated financial need to study abroad in East or Southeast Asia. Summer interns receive up to $3,000. Those participating for a full academic year receive up to $7,000, while those participating for a semester receive up to $5,000.

https://www.iie.org/freeman-asia

Fulbright Critical Language Enhancement Award (CLEA)

CLEA provides an opportunity for U.S. Fulbright grantees to pursue intensive language study in mainland China, Egypt, India, Indonesia, Jordan, Morocco, or Russia. Participants receive a $100 book allowance, tuition costs, and round-trip travel to the host country. Daily expenses must be covered by the participant.

https://us.fulbrightonline.org/critical-language-enhancement-awards

** $$ Fulbright U.S. Student Program

The prestigious Fulbright U.S. Student Program offers grants and stipends to graduating college seniors and recent graduates for research and study. It also offers networking opportunities, and the program has its own alumni association. Fulbrighters have gone on to become Nobel Laureates, win the Pulitzer, and become heads of state. Field-specific awards are also available in the arts, business, journalism and communication, and STEM and public health. Award amounts and benefits vary by program.

U.S. Student Program: https://us.fulbrightonline.org/fulbright-us-student-program
Field-Specific Awards: http://us.fulbrightonline.org/about/types -of-awards/study-research
https://us.fulbrightonline.org/

** $$ Fulbright-Hays Doctoral Dissertation Research Award (DDRA)

The Department of Education manages the Fulbright-Hays DDRA, which supports about 100 graduate students for six to 12 months as they complete their doctoral thesis research in Africa; East, Southeast, and South Asia; the Pacific Islands; the Near East; East Central Europe and Eurasia; or the Western Hemisphere, excluding the United States and its territories. Recipients are awarded $15,000 to $60,000.

http://www.ed.gov/programs/iegpsddrap/index.html

Fulbright Summer Institutes for U.S. Undergraduates

The U.S.-U.K. Fulbright Commission offers special Summer Institutes for U.S. citizens to come to the U.K. Fulbright offers participants the opportunity to experience an exciting academic program at a highly regarded U.K. university while exploring the country's culture, heritage, and history.

http://www.fulbright.org.uk/going-to-the-uk/uk-summer-institutes

Gabr Fellowship

The Gabr Fellowship is designed for emerging leaders in art, science, media, law, social, and business entrepreneurship. Applicants should provide big ideas and maintain a strong interest in transnational dialogue. All applicants must be between ages 24 and 35 and citizens of the United States, Egypt, Great Britain, Jordan, Lebanon, or France.

https://eastwestdialogue.org/fellowship/

** Gates Cambridge Scholarship

The Bill & Melinda Gates Foundation provides scholarships to talented students from outside the United Kingdom, for graduate study at the University of Cambridge.

http://www.gatescambridge.org/

** George J. Mitchell Scholarship

The George J. Mitchell Scholarship supports one year of graduate study in Ireland for 12 students in any discipline. The scholarship covers tuition and accommodation, as well as a stipend for living expenses and travel.

http://www.us-irelandalliance.org/mitchellscholarship

High North Fellowship

The High North Fellowship offers scholarships to students from the United States, Canada, Japan, Russia, and South Korea, providing them the opportunity to study at an institution in northern Norway. The program is intended for undergraduate and graduate students, but it is also open to doctoral students.

http://www.studyinnorway.no/High-North-Scholarship

^^ Hostelling International-USA (HI-USA) Explore the World Travel Scholarships

HI-USA offers over 100 $2,000 Explore the World Travel Scholarships to young people ages 18 to 30 with financial need, who live in certain metropolitan areas.

https://www.hiusa.org/programs/travel-scholarships/explore-the-world

^^ Humanity in Action (HIA) Fellowship

The HIA Fellowship brings together international groups of college students and recent graduates to explore national histories of discrimination and resistance — including racial hierarchies, anti-Semitism, and Islamophobia. It seeks to educate, connect, and inspire future leaders in human rights and social justice.

https://www.humanityinaction.org/programs/14-humanity-in-action-fellowship

IMUSE Fellowship

Every summer, 30 students from China and the United States meet in Beijing for a two-week exchange program. IMUSE Fellows participate in discussions on pertinent issues in Chinese-American relations. All students in an American postsecondary school (including two- and four-year colleges, graduate schools, vocational, technical, and trade schools) are eligible.

http://projectimuse.github.io/

$$ Institute of Current World Affairs (ICWA) Fellowship

The ICWA fellowship nurtures expertise in foreign countries and cultures by supporting a fellow who carries out a self-designed program of independent study abroad for a minimum of two years. Candidates must possess the necessary language skills to carry out their proposed project.

http://www.icwa.org/apply

Inter American Press Association Scholarship

The Inter American Press Association Scholarship enables American graduate students in print journalism to study in Latin America. Recipients are awarded up to $20,000.

https://en.sipiapa.org/contenidos/want-a-scholarship.html

International Innovation Corps (IIC)

IIC offers a unique opportunity for graduates to play an active role in building and implementing innovative solutions to some of India's toughest social problems. This fellowship is open to recent and upcoming college graduates. Each IIC fellow receives a stipend, health insurance, and round-trip airfare to India.

http://www.iic.uchicago.edu/

Japan Exchange and Teaching (JET) Program

JET, with the help of the Japanese Ministry of Foreign Affairs, welcomes college graduates to become involved in foreign language education in Japan. This program promotes citizen exchange programs between Japan and other nations.

http://jetprogramme.org/en/about-jet/

Jewish Service Corps (JSC)

The American Jewish Joint Distribution Committee's JSC offers young Jews the opportunity to actively pursue the value of Jewish responsibility through a yearlong, paid service opportunity overseas.

http://jdcentwine.org/jsc/

** $$ Keasbey Foundation Scholarships

Keasbey offers two scholarships to graduating seniors in all fields, covering one or two years of study at the University of Oxford, Edinburgh, Cambridge, or Aberystwyth. Candidates must display a high level of achievement, leadership ability, and a clearly defined academic interest in pursuing a degree in the United Kingdom.

http://keasbeyfoundation.org/eligibility.php

Killam Fellowships Program

The Killam Fellowships Program provides an opportunity for exceptional undergraduates from universities in Canada and the United States to spend either one semester or a full academic year as an exchange student in the other country. The foundation hosts all new Killam fellows at an orientation program in Ottawa each fall and again at a seminar in Washington, D.C., each spring.

http://www.fulbright.ca/programs/killam-fellowships.html

LGT Impact Fellowship

The LGT Impact Fellowship provides additional know-how and capacity to social enterprises and offers professionals the opportunity to apply their skills in a meaningful way. Candidates must hold an undergraduate degree and at least two years of full-time work experience in diverse business areas such as consulting, finance, operations, data analytics, IT, M&E, sales, product development, or marketing. Fellows work full-time for one year with LGT's portfolio companies or regional investment teams in Africa, Brazil, China, India, the Philippines, or the U.K.

https://www.lgtimpact.com/en/about-us/fellowship/

** Henry Luce Foundation Luce Scholars Program

Luce Scholars provides stipends, language training, and individualized professional placement in Asia each year for 15 to 18 college seniors, graduate students, and young professionals who have had limited exposure to Asia.

http://www.hluce.org/lsprogram.aspx

** Marshall Scholarship

The Marshall Scholarship offers financial support to up to 40 young Americans of high ability to pursue a graduate degree in the United Kingdom. This scholarship aims to strengthen the enduring relationship between the British and American people.

http://www.marshallscholarship.org/

^^ Mickey Leland International Hunger Fellowship

The two-year Mickey Leland International Hunger Fellowship combines field and policy work aimed at poverty alleviation and improving food security. Fellows are placed in organizations working on public health initiatives, nutrition programs, and agricultural development research in Africa, Asia, and Latin America.

https://www.hungercenter.org/fellowships/leland/

Mobility Grant for Norwegian Language and Literature

This grant supports one to three months of study in Norway for graduate and doctoral students studying the Norwegian language or literature. Participants receive a monthly stipend; those working in the northernmost counties receive an extra NOK 100 per month.

https://www.studyinnorway.no/mobility-grants

Monbukagakusho Scholarship (MEXT)

The Japanese Ministry of Education, Culture, Sports, Science, and Technology awards this scholarship to undergraduates majoring or minoring in Japanese or Asian studies to further their study of language and culture.

http://www.us.emb-japan.go.jp/english/html/mext-scholarship-info.html

NORAM Scholarship for Americans to Study in Norway

NORAM scholarships support Americans studying or conducting research in areas of mutual importance to Norway and the United States, to strengthen the ties of friendship between the two countries. The size of the individual grant depends on the research subject, purpose, and intended length of stay in Norway.

https://noram.no/en/scholarship-americans/

$$ Olivia James Traveling Fellowship

The Olivia James Traveling Fellowship is offered to one graduate student, doctoral candidate, or recent Ph.D. recipient per year for studying classics, sculpture, architecture, history, or archaeology in the Mediterranean area. Recipients are awarded up to $25,000.

https://www.archaeological.org/grants/700

POSCO Visiting Fellowship

The POSCO Visiting Fellowship invites outstanding scholars and policymakers to engage in policy-relevant contemporary research on political, security, and economic issues in northeast Asia, as they relate to Korea. POSCO visiting fellows will be required to prepare a quality paper to be published in academic journals or in book format.

https://www.eastwestcenter.org/research/visiting-fellow-programs/posco-visiting-fellowship-program

Princeton in Asia (PiA) Fellowships

PiA aims to increase mutual appreciation and understanding of other cultures. It offers yearlong, service-oriented fellowships in 21 Asian countries in the fields of education, international development, public health, environmental advocacy, journalism, and business, with a majority of fellows working as English teachers at universities and high schools.

https://piaweb.princeton.edu/for-applicants

Qatar Scholarship

The Qatar Scholarship offers intermediate and advanced Arabic-language students from the United States an intensive Arabic language program at Qatar University in Doha for a full academic year.

http://www.qu.edu.qa/students/admission/scholarships

** $$ Rhodes Scholarship

The Rhodes Scholarship brings 32 outstanding students from many countries to the University of Oxford for two years. All educational costs, such as matriculation, tuition, laboratory, and other fees are covered by the Rhodes Trustees to Rhodes Scholars. Notable Rhodes Scholars include former President Bill Clinton, Senator Cory Booker, and journalists Ronan Farrow, Rachel Maddow, and George Stephanopoulos. Benefits include full tuition payment and a stipend of at least £14,276 per year.

http://www.rhodesscholar.org/

** Rotary Foundation Scholarships

Rotary International Scholars serve as ambassadors abroad while studying for one academic year. Preference is given to those with fluency in the language of the host country (non-English-speaking). All class levels are eligible to apply, and 1,000 to 1,100 scholarships are awarded each year. Rotary scholarships are given by individual clubs and are open to all; contact the local club via the website for application information and eligibility requirements.

https://www.rotary.org/en/our-programs/scholarships

Samuel Huntington Public Service Award

This award provides a $15,000 stipend for a graduating senior to pursue public service for one year anywhere in the world. The project can be undertaken by the student acting independently or through an established charitable, educational, government, or public service organization.

https://www.nationalgridus.com/Our-Company/Community-Presence/The-Samuel-Huntington-Public-Service-Award

** Schwarzman Scholars Program

The Schwarzman Scholars program offers an international group of students the opportunity to spend a year at Beijing's Tsinghua University to complete a one-year master's degree in public policy, economics, business, or international relations.

https://www.schwarzmanscholars.org/program/

Scotland's Saltire Scholarships

The Scottish government awards Scotland's Saltire Scholarships to undergraduate seniors who want to pursue full-time master's programs at one of 17 Scottish universities. Up to 50 scholarships are available, each worth £8000.

https://www.scotland.org/study/saltire-scholarships

Sightline Media

Sightline Media Group, based in the Washington, D.C., area, offers editorial fellowships to students interested in becoming journalists who cover defense and federal technology issues. With their main office in Tysons, Virginia, Sightline Media owns MilitaryTimes, DefenseNews, FederalTimes, and other media outlets that cover issues relating to defense, cybersecurity, and the public sector. Applicants must live in the

D.C. area, be able to work 15 hours a week, and have previous experience in journalism or be studying journalism or political science in college.

https://boards.greenhouse.io/sightlinemediagroup?gh_src=cpxe2a1

St. Andrew's Society Scholarship

The St. Andrew's Society of the State of New York Scholarship funds two American students of Scottish heritage to study in Scotland, to promote cultural interchange and goodwill between Scotland and the United States. The candidates must demonstrate financial need, academic achievement, and accomplishments in extracurricular activities.

https://students.dartmouth.edu/fellowship-advising/fellowships
/post-graduate-opportunities/united-kingdom-ireland/st-andrews-society-
scholarships/eligibility

Swedish Scholarships for International Students (SISS)

SISS provides scholarships to international students to pursue full-time, one- or two-year graduate programs. The scholarship covers tuition and fees, living expenses, a one-time travel grant, and insurance.

https://si.se/en/apply/scholarships/swedish-institute-study-scholarships/

Swiss Government Excellence Scholarships for Foreign Scholars and Artists

These research scholarships are available to foreign students from more than 180 countries. They are offered at one of the 10 Swiss cantonal universities, the two Swiss federal institutes of technology, and public teaching and research institutes. They are granted to students who plan to pursue doctoral or postdoctoral research or further studies. A monthly allowance, tuition and fees, health insurance, and a lodging allowance are also included.

https://www.sbfi.admin.ch/sbfi/en/home/bildung/scholarships-and-grants/swiss-
government-excellence-scholarships-for-foreign-scholars-an.html

TEFL Fellowships at the American University in Cairo

Fellowships in teaching English as a foreign language (TEFL) are offered to full-time students who wish to pursue a master's degree in TEFL and to acquire language-teaching experience at The American University in Cairo.

http://www.aucegypt.edu/admissions/fellowships/tefl

^^ Thomas J. Watson Fellowship

The Thomas J. Watson Fellowship offers college graduates of unusual promise a year of independent, purposeful exploration and travel. Fellows remove themselves from the comfort and stability of home, explore the world in pursuit of their passion, and discover along the way their potential for humane and effective participation in the world community.

https://watson.foundation/fellowships/tj

UNESCO/People's Republic of China (The Great Wall) Co-Sponsored Fellowships Program

These fellowships are for advanced studies at undergraduate and postgraduate levels by students in African, Asian, Pacific, Latin American, European, North American, and Arabic member states. The fellowships, tenable at a select number of Chinese universities, last for one year.

http://www.unesco.org/new/en/fellowships/programmes/unescopeoples-republic-of-china-the-great-wall-co-sponsored-fellowships-programme/

$$ United States to Australia Scholarships

These scholarships are for Americans performing research or study in life sciences, medicine, engineering, or mining; preference is given to students in oceanography, marine sciences, and stem cell research. Applicants must arrange for their own placement at an Australian university and have a confirmed placement by the time the scholarships are awarded. The scholarship amounts range from $30,000 to $40,000, and are intended to cover part of the costs for one year of study in Australia.

https://www.americanaustralian.org/page/eduoverview

^^ Volunteers in Asia (VIA) Global Community Fellowship

This fellowship is a 13- to 15-month program for graduating seniors and young or established professionals with a bachelor's degree. Fellows work at NGOs and schools across Asia to support community development and youth education programs.

https://viaprograms.org/category/blog/global-community-fellowship/

University of Masstricht High Potential Scholarships

The University of Masstricht Scholarship Fund offers scholarships to highly qualified students from outside the European Economic Area (EEA) to pursue a graduate or a professional education program at the university, located in the Netherlands. The scholarships cover tuition, living expenses, visa costs, and insurance.

https://www.maastrichtuniversity.nl/support/your-studies-begin/coming-maastricht-university-abroad/scholarships/maastricht-university

University of Sydney International Research Scholarships (USydIS)

The University of Sydney, in Australia, invites highly qualified international postgraduate students to participate in research projects. This scholarship covers tuition and a living allowance for up to three years.

http://sydney.edu.au/scholarships/postgraduate/international-postgraduate-scholarships.shtml#usi

Warwick Chancellor's International Scholarships

Each year, the Warwick Graduate School of the University of Warwick, located in the U.K., grants Chancellor's International Scholarships to 25 outstanding international students in any discipline. The scholarships cover tuition and a living allowance.

https://warwick.ac.uk/services/academicoffice/gsp/scholarship/typesoffunding/chancellorsinternational/

Whitaker International Fellows Program

The Whitaker International Fellows Program awards yearlong grants to students with a bachelor's or master's degree in biomedical engineering (BME) or bioengineering, or a demonstrated commitment to BME to study at an institution abroad within three years of graduation.

https://www.whitaker.org/grants/fellows-scholars

Whitaker International Summer Program

The Whitaker International Summer Program provides funding for U.S. bioengineers and biomedical engineers to add to their existing graduate or doctoral degree overseas by undertaking a self-designed project relevant to their field under the supervision of a mentor.

https://www.whitaker.org/grants/fellows-scholars

Yenching Academy of Peking University

The Yenching Academy of Peking University connects China and the rest of the world through an interdisciplinary graduate program focused on six different areas: literature and culture, history and archaeology, philosophy and religion, politics and international relations, economics and management, and law and society.

http://yenchingacademy.org/program

"If you have some power, then your job is to empower somebody else."

— Toni Morrison, Pulitzer Prize winner

Chapter 22:
Pre-Law Programs and Law School Scholarships

A variety of scholarships for law school students are available. Toward the end, this chapter presents opportunities for students in specific geographic areas and for students who are members of a group historically underrepresented in the legal profession (including special no-cost pre-law programs).

AIPLA Robert C. Watson Award

AIPLA sponsors this annual scholarship, encouraging students to submit articles on subjects relating to intellectual property. Recipients are awarded up to $2,000.

http://www.aipla.org/resources2/programs/Pages/Robert-C.-Watson-Award.aspx

American Association for Justice (AAJ) Trial Advocacy Scholarship

AAJ offers this $3,000 scholarship to students interested and proficient in trial advocacy who wish to represent those injured by negligence or misconduct. Applicants must be AAJ law student members who demonstrate financial need.

https://www.justice.org/what-we-do/enhance-practice-law/professional-recognition-awards-scholarships/scholarships/aaj-trial

American Association for Justice (AAJ) Mike Eidson Scholarship

AAJ's $5,000 scholarship supports a rising third-year (or rising fourth-year in a night program) female student committed to a career as a trial lawyer.

https://www.justice.org/what-we-do/enhance-practice-law/professional-recognition-awards-scholarships/scholarships/mike

Asian Heritage Law School Scholarship

Infinity Law Group LLC offers this annual scholarship of $1,000 to law students of Asian heritage. Applications must include a one- to three-page essay and a copy of an acceptance letter from an accredited law school.

http://www.infinlaw.com/scholarship

Christine Mirzayan Science & Technology Policy Graduate Fellowship

This fellowship provides early-career professionals with a 12-week stay at the National Academies of Sciences, Engineering, and Medicine in Washington, D.C., exposing them to science and technology policy and the role that scientists and engineers play in advising policymakers. It is available to graduate students, recent graduates, and professionals in law, social and behavioral sciences, health and medicine, physical and biological sciences, engineering, business, and public administration.

http://sites.nationalacademies.org/PGA/policyfellows/PGA_044687

Don H. Liu Scholars Program

The Don H. Liu Scholars Program nurtures and supports future Asian-American leaders within the legal profession. It awards $15,000 to law students who intend to practice in the New York City metropolitan private sector following graduation. The program also provides mentorship and helps with internship placement and career development.

http://www.donhliuscholars.org/

Dwyer Williams Dretke Attorneys, PC Scholarship

Dwyer Williams Dretke offers $1,000 to a first-year law student. Applications must include a one- to three-page essay and an acceptance letter from an accredited law school.

https://www.roydwyer.com/scholarship/

$$ Electronic Privacy Information Center (EPIC) Law Fellowship

EPIC, a leading privacy and civil liberties organization, encourages applications from law students, recent graduates, and judicial clerks for its $56,000 annual fellowship.

https://epic.org/epic/jobs.html

Howell & Christmas Visionary Scholarship

The law offices of Howell & Christmas provide a $1,000 scholarship to a talented law student.

https://www.howellandchristmas.com/visionary-scholarship-information/

Iranian American Bar Association (IABA) Scholarship

The IABA Foundation provides scholarships to full-time law students of Iranian heritage committed to the advancement of the Iranian American community. Scholarship amounts vary, depending on funding.

http://iabafoundation.org/scholarship-2/

National Italian-American Bar Association (NIABA) & Sons of Italy Foundation (OSIF) Scholarship

NIABA and OSIF provide one scholarship each year to a law student of Italian descent. Recipients must join NIABA. Scholarship amounts vary, depending on funding.

https://www.osia.org/programs/scholarships/niaba-sif/

Serbian Bar Association of America (SBAA) Scholarship

The SBAA scholarship is offered to Serbian American law students in J.D. or LLM programs. In addition to a variable monetary award, recipients are honored at the SBAA's Scholarship Gala.

http://www.serbbar.org/scholarships/

Regional

Many scholarships for law students are offered by local law firms, legal foundations, or other organizations, and are limited to a particular geographic area and/or type of applicant. The list below presents a small sample of such opportunities, to provide ideas for resources to investigate in your own area.

Alabama Law Foundation Scholarships

The Alabama Law Foundation offers three scholarships for academically outstanding Alabama law students: the Cabaniss Johnston Scholarship ($5,000), the William Verbon Black Scholarship (for full-time students at the University of Alabama School of Law), and the Justice Janie L. Shores Scholarship (for women).

https://www.alabamalawfoundation.org/scholarships/law-school-scholarships/

Association of Black Women Attorneys (ABWA) Ruth Whitehead Whaley Scholarship

The ABWA Ruth Whitehead Whaley Scholarship provides awards to selected law students who demonstrate a commitment to public interest and civil rights, make a difference in their community, and live in New York, New Jersey, or Connecticut. Scholarship amounts vary.

https://abwanewyork.org/scholarships/

New York State Bar Association (NYSBA) Scholarships

NYSBA offers five different scholarships of up to $5,000 and seven fellowships ranging from $5,000 to $7,000 for law students residing in New York.

https://www.nysba.org/fellandschol/

Vietnamese American Bar Association of the Greater Washington, D.C., Area (VABA-DC) Scholarship

VABA-DC offers $2,500 scholarships to law students with a strong commitment to serving the Vietnamese American community, or who have overcome adversity to achieve academic success.

http://www.vabadc.com/programs

Diversity

Pre-Law

These prestigious summer programs help undergraduates from historically underrepresented groups prepare for law school, at no cost.

DiscoverLaw.org Pre-Law Undergraduate Scholars (PLUS) Program

PLUS, a four-week residential program at Duke University, provides undergraduates who have completed their freshman or sophomore year of college with the skills necessary to succeed in law school and the legal profession. Preference is given to students from historically underrepresented groups in the legal profession, first-generation students, students from disadvantaged backgrounds, and students who face other significant barriers. Benefits include housing and test fee waivers, as well as a stipend of $1,000.

https://law.duke.edu/plusprogram/

Florida State University College of Law Donald J. Weidner Summer for Undergraduates

This program was the first of its kind, providing a month of training to rising college sophomores and above to equip them with the mindsets and skill sets necessary for law school. Preference is given to students from historically underrepresented groups.

http://www.law.fsu.edu/academics/summer-for-undergraduates

Training and Recruitment Initiative for Admissions to Leading Law Schools (TRIALS)

TRIALS, a full-scholarship residential program resulting from the partnership of the NYU School of Law, Harvard Law School, and the Advantage Testing Foundation, provides talented students from historically underrepresented groups with the skills necessary to successfully apply to law school. Each year, one of the universities hosts the five-week summer program. Participants receive a $3,000 stipend to cover living expenses and supplies.

https://trials.atfoundation.org/

Scholarships

American Association for Justice (AAJ) Richard D. Hailey Scholarship

AAJ offers this $5,000 scholarship to minority students interested in trial advocacy who wish to represent those injured by negligence or misconduct. Applicants must be AAJ law student members with financial need.

https://www.justice.org/what-we-do/enhance-practice-law/professional-recognition-awards-scholarships/scholarships/richard-d

American Bar Association (ABA) Legal Opportunity Scholarship Fund

The ABA awards $15,000 Legal Opportunity Scholarships to first-year racial and ethnic minority law students. Recipients receive funds over a period of three years.

https://www.americanbar.org/groups/diversity/diversity_pipeline/projects_initiatives/legal_opportunity_scholarship.html

Arent Fox Diversity Scholarship

Arent Fox LLP awards a $20,000 Diversity Scholarship and a summer associate position in its San Francisco office to a second-year law student.

https://www.arentfox.com/careers/diversity

Buckfire & Buckfire, PC Law School Diversity Scholarship

This $2,000 scholarship helps law students with financial need achieve their academic and professional dreams. Members of ethnic, racial, and other minority groups are strongly urged to apply.

https://www.buckfirelaw.com/library/scholarships.cfm

** Congressional Hispanic Caucus Institute (CHCI) Graduate Fellowship

CHCI offers a paid, nine-month graduate fellowship in law, higher education, secondary education, health, housing, or STEM to aspiring Hispanic American leaders with a master's or law degree. Placements include the White House, the U.S. Congress, government agencies, advocacy organizations, and trade associations.

https://chci.org/programs/graduate-fellowship-program/

** $$ Earl Warren Scholarship

This scholarship supports African-American law students committed to fighting for civil rights. Recipients are awarded $30,000 over a three-year period.

http://www.naacpldf.org/earl-warren-scholarship

Law Preview Scholarship

The Law Preview program features a weeklong law school prep course taught by some of the country's leading law professors. Scholarships for the program, sponsored by numerous law firms, are available to upcoming law school students. Participating law schools and law firms include the following:

- Baker & McKenzie: George Washington University (http://www.lawpreview.com/baker-mckenzie)
- Baker Botts: Duke University School of Law, Harvard University (http://www.lawpreview.com/baker-botts)
- King & Spalding (http://www.lawpreview.com/king-spalding): Howard University, New York University
- McGuireWood: Notre Dame, University of Virginia (http://www.lawpreview.com/mcguirewood)
- Paul Hastings: University of Pennsylvania (http://www.lawpreview.com/paul-hastings)
- Vinson & Elkins: University of Texas, New York University, George Washington University (http://www.lawpreview.com/vinson-elkins)
- WilmerHale: Columbia University, Northeastern University, Boston University, UC Berkeley, Georgetown University, or Boston College (http://www.lawpreview.com/wilmerhale)
- Winston & Strawn: University of Chicago Law School (http://www.lawpreview.com/Winston-Strawn)

Criteria vary, but may include being a member of a historically underrepresented group in the legal profession, being a member of the LGBT community, being female, or being the first in one's immediate family to attend college. Scholarship amounts also vary, depending on funding.

https://lawpreview.barbri.com/scholarships/

Lloyd M. Johnson, Jr. (LMJ) Scholarship

The Minority Corporate Counsel Association advocates diversity within the legal profession. It offers the LMJ Scholarship to first-year law students.

https://www.mcca.com/career-center/career-development/scholarship-program/

Mark T. Banner Scholarship

This $10,000 scholarship supports the development of intellectual property lawyers from diverse backgrounds. Those enrolled in law school and interested in pursuing a career in intellectual property law are encouraged to apply. This program is specifically interested in admitting those from historically underrepresented groups.

http://www.linninn.org/

Mexican American Legal Defense and Educational Fund (MALDEF) Scholarship

The MALDEF Law School Scholarship is for full-time law students committed to advancing the civil rights of Hispanic Americans. Recipients are awarded $5,000.

http://maldef.org/leadership/scholarships/index.html

Michigan Auto Law Diversity Scholarship

Michigan Auto Law provides a $2,000 annual scholarship to an ethnic or racial minority law student who demonstrates a strong commitment to diversity issues. Applications must include a typed essay.

https://www.michiganautolaw.com/scholarships/diversity/

National Black Prosecutors Association (NBPA) Scholarships

The NBPA provides scholarships to African-American law students who demonstrate a desire to serve their community. Amounts vary.

http://blackprosecutors.org/donate

Sidley Prelaw Scholarship

The Sidley Prelaw Scholarship offers financial assistance with law school application fees and the cost of the LSAT to diverse, high-performing students with financial need. Recipients are awarded up to $2,500, with a possible second scholarship worth $3,500.

https://www.sidley.com/en/diversitylanding/sidley-prelaw-scholars-program

"Life is short. Do stuff that matters."

— Siqi Chen, CEO of Heyday

Chapter 23:
STEM Scholarships and Fellowships

In addition to offering an exciting field of study, science, technology, engineering, and mathematics — collectively referred to as STEM — can be lucrative. For example, unlike many doctoral humanities programs, most doctoral STEM programs offer a stipend to cover living expenses. STEM students can also apply for the fellowships listed in this chapter to earn extra funding or opportunities to work abroad.

STEM also intersects with the policy world, notably in the fields of health, defense, and agriculture. In fact, the critical thinking skills acquired from an education in STEM are highly prized on Capitol Hill, where you are required to think quickly, stay on your toes, and rapidly digest and synthesize information on a variety of topics.

This chapter and the next present scholarships and fellowships for students in STEM who are interested in the nexus of science and public policy. Washington, D.C., is an excellent place to pursue such an interest. The National Institutes of Health are a short drive away in Bethesda, Maryland, while the National Science Foundation lies just south of Washington in Alexandria, Virginia.

If you are a scientist with an interest in policy, consult the other sections in this book to learn more about opportunities in policy. While you may not be able to work on scientific topics in a government internship, your powers of analysis will be a great asset wherever you choose to take your STEM talents!

For opportunities specifically designed for women and/or historically underrepresented groups in STEM (African-Americans, Hispanic Americans, and Native Americans/Alaska Natives), see the next chapter.

Insider's Tip: ZIntellect's Opportunity Catalog (https://www.zintellect.com/Posting/Catalog) lists STEM-related internships, experiential learning opportunities, academic fellowships, and scholarships funded by government and private sector organizations.

$$ Agency for Healthcare Research and Quality (AHRQ)

AHRQ offers an array of pre- and postdoctoral educational and career development grants and opportunities in health services research training. Awards range up to $40,000.

https://www.ahrq.gov/funding/training-grants/index.html

$$ Albert Einstein Distinguished Educator Fellowship (AEF)

The AEF offers a unique opportunity for accomplished K-12 educators in STEM to work for 11 months at the Department of Energy, the National Science Foundation, NASA, or a congressional office. Successful candidates receive a $7,000 monthly stipend, a travel allowance of up to $5,000, and a number of additional benefits.

https://science.energy.gov/wdts/einstein/

** $$ Alfred P. Sloan Foundation Research Fellowship

These fellowships provide support and recognition to young scientists and research faculty in physics, chemistry, mathematics, neuroscience, economics, computer science, and computational and evolutionary molecular biology. Successful candidates receive $60,000.

https://sloan.org/fellowships/

American Association for the Advancement of Science (AAAS) Entry Point Fellowship

The AAAS Entry Point Fellowship identifies and recruits full-time undergraduate and graduate students with apparent and non-apparent disabilities studying science, engineering, mathematics, computer science, and some fields of business.

https://www.aaas.org/program/entrypoint

American Association for the Advancement of Science (AAAS) Mass Media Science & Engineering Fellowship

This 10-week summer program places STEM students at media organizations and news outlets nationwide. Fellows use their academic training to research, write, and report today's headlines, sharpening their abilities to communicate complex scientific issues to the public.

https://www.aaas.org/page/2018-mass-media-fellows

** $$ American Association for the Advancement of Science (AAAS) Science and Technology Policy Fellowship

The AAAS Science and Technology Fellowship helps engineers and scientists contribute to and learn firsthand about federal policymaking. Fellows come from a broad range of backgrounds, disciplines, and career stages. They receive a stipend of $75,000 to $100,000 for a yearlong assignment in the federal government. AAAS sponsors more than 150 placements in the executive branch, two legislative placements, and one judicial placement. In addition, roughly 30 additional placements in the legislative branch are available through partner societies.

https://www.aaas.org/program/science-technology-policy-fellowships

$$ American Board of Emergency Medicine (ABEM) Fellowship

The ABEM Fellowship provides early-career health science scholars with the opportunity to participate in evidence-based health care or public health studies that improve care of patients. Fellows receive a flexible stipend of $25,000.

https://nam.edu/programs/health-policy-educational-programs-and-fellowships/ nam-fellowship-program/american-board-of-emergency-medicine-fellowship/

American Heart Association (AHA) Undergraduate Student Summer Fellowship

The AHA supports highly promising undergraduates with full-time research fellowships. This 10-week program encourages students to pursue careers in cardiovascular research. Fellows receive $5,000.

http://www.heart.org/HEARTORG/Affiliate/Founders-Affiliate-Local-Research-Opportunities_UCM_315885_Article.jsp#.W1eIlbhOl9M

American Medical Association (AMA) Scholarships and Fellowships

The AMA is the largest association of physicians in America. It provides scholarships and fellowships for medical school, including the $10,000 Physicians of Tomorrow Scholarship, for students entering their final year of medical school, and the Medical Student Section (MSS) Government Relations Advocacy Fellowship, which offers the opportunity to be a full-time paid member of the AMA's federal advocacy team for a year.

https://www.ama-assn.org/content/apply-medical-school-scholarships

$$ American Meteorological Society (AMS) Scholarships and Fellowships

The AMS, the nation's premier scientific and professional organization, promotes and disseminates information about the atmospheric, oceanic, and hydrologic sciences. It offers scholarships of up to $10,000 and fellowships of up to $25,000 to undergraduate and graduate students in meteorology and related fields.

https://www.ametsoc.org/index.cfm/ams/information-for/students/ams-scholarships-and-fellowships/

American Occupational Therapy Foundation (AOTF) Scholarships

The AOTF aims to advance the science of occupational therapy to support people's full participation in meaningful life activities. It offers over 50 scholarships, worth up to $5,000, to full-time occupational therapy students at all levels.

http://www.aotf.org/scholarshipsgrants

American Society of Civil Engineers (ASCE) Arthur S. Tuttle Fellowship

ASCE, America's oldest civil engineering society, has more than 150,000 members. It offers the Arthur S. Tuttle Fellowship to graduate students in civil engineering. Fellows receive up to $2,000.

http://www.asce.org/fellowships/tuttle/

American Water Works Association (AWWA) Hazen and Sawyer Scholarship

AWWA is an international, nonprofit scientific and educational society dedicated to providing total water solutions. It offers the Hazen and Sawyer Scholarship to students seeking a master's degree in water science. Recipients are awarded up to $5,000. AWWA awards over 40 scholarships every year.

https://www.awwa.org/membership/get-involved/student-center/awwa-scholarships.aspx

Amgen Scholars

The Amgen Foundation seeks to advance excellence in science education to inspire the next generation of innovators, and to invest in strengthening communities where Amgen staff members live and work. The Amgen Scholars Program provides hundreds of undergraduate science and engineering students with a hands-on summer research experience. Students can apply to participate at any or all of the 10 host institutions, each of which has its own separate application process:

- California Institute of Technology (http://sfp.caltech.edu/programs/amgen_scholars/application_information)
- Columbia University Barnard College (http://www.columbia.edu/cu/biology/ug/amgen/apply.html)
- Harvard University (https://uraf.harvard.edu/amgen-scholars)
- Massachusetts Institute of Technology (http://uaap.mit.edu/research-exploration/urop/options/amgen-urop-scholars-program)
- National Institutes of Health (https://www.training.nih.gov/amgenscholars)
- Stanford University (https://biosciences.stanford.edu/current-students/diversity/programs-for-students/ssrp-amgen-scholars-program/)
- University of California, Berkeley (https://amgenscholars.berkeley.edu/)
- University of California, Los Angeles (http://www.ugresearchsci.ucla.edu/amgenscholars.htm)
- University of California, San Francisco (https://graduate.ucsf.edu/srtp)
- Washington University in St. Louis (http://dbbs.wustl.edu/UndergraduateResearch/AmgenScholars/Pages/default.aspx)

Applicants must be college sophomores, juniors, or non-graduating seniors interested in pursuing a doctorate, or an M.D.-PhD. Awards vary, ranging up to $6,275.

http://www.amgenscholars.com/

ANS Decommissioning, Decontamination, and Reutilization Division Scholarship

The ANS promotes understanding of nuclear science and technology. Its decommissioning, decontamination, and reutilization division awards a $2,000 scholarship to one graduate student per year in nuclear engineering.

http://www.ans.org/honors/scholarships/ddrd/

Association of American Medical Colleges (AAMC) Fee Assistance Program

The AAMC Fee Assistance Program offers two years of financial assistance to U.S. citizens and residents who want to pursue a medical career, providing funding for taking the Medical College Admission Test (MCAT), applying for medical schools that use the American Medical College Application Service (AMCAS), and more. The program offers reduced fees, free study materials, and other assistance.

https://students-residents.aamc.org/applying-medical-school/applying-medical-school-process/fee-assistance-program/

AVANGRID Scholarships for Master's Studies in the United States

These scholarships cultivate the next generation of professionals in the energy industry. They are open to students pursuing graduate work on sustainable energy, energy efficiency, and climate.

https://www.avangrid.com/wps/portal/avangrid/peopleandtalent/scholarships

** Barry Goldwater Scholarships

The Goldwater Scholarships support full-time rising college juniors who intend to pursue research careers in STEM. Up to 300 recipients are awarded up to $7,500 per year.

https://goldwater.scholarsapply.org/

Boren Awards — Summer STEM Semester

Part of the National Security Education Program, the Boren Scholarship aims to fund the study of less frequently taught languages in regions critical to the United States. The Boren Awards offer up to $8,000 to undergraduates to study STEM overseas for at least eight weeks during the summer.

https://www.borenawards.org/scholarships/thinking-applying/special-initiatives/boren-scholarships-summer-initiative-stem-majors

Christine Mirzayan Science & Technology Policy Graduate Fellowship

This fellowship provides early-career professionals with a 12-week stay at the National Academies of Sciences, Engineering, and Medicine in Washington, D.C., exposing them to science and technology policy and the role that scientists and engineers play in advising policymakers. It is available to graduate students, recent graduates, and professionals in law, social and behavioral sciences, health and medicine, physical and biological sciences, engineering, business, and public administration.

http://sites.nationalacademies.org/PGA/policyfellows/PGA_044687

Distinguished Nurse Scholar-in-Residence Program

The Distinguished Nurse Scholar-in-Residence program is designed to assist outstanding nurse leaders. The program seeks individuals with the capacity and skills to bring issues in nursing to greater public understanding and policy attention.

https://nam.edu/programs/health-policy-educational-programs-and-fellowships/nurse-scholar-in-residence-program/

Foundation of the National Student Nurses Association (FNSNA) Scholarships

Created in 1969, the Foundation of the National Student Nurses Association works to support nursing education. FNSNA offers nursing students a variety of scholarships ranging up to $7,500.

http://www.forevernursing.org/

$$ Greenwall Fellowship in Bioethics

The Greenwall Fellowship in Bioethics enables young investigators to further their careers as future leaders, addressing bioethics issues in clinical care, biomedical research, and public policy. Fellows receive a $25,000 research stipend.

https://nam.edu/programs/health-policy-educational-programs-and-fellowships/nam-fellowship-program/greenwall-fellowship-in-bioethics/

$$ Gulf Research Program

The Gulf Research Program, an independent, science-based program, offers a variety of fellowships and grants to enhance oil system safety and protect human health and the environment in the Gulf of Mexico and U.S. outer continental shelf regions. Fellows receive up to a $75,000 stipend for research-related purposes.

http://nas.edu/gulf/index.html

** $$ Hertz Graduate Fellowships

The Fannie & John Hertz Foundation provides graduate fellowships to students in applied physical and biological sciences, mathematics, and engineering. College seniors wishing to pursue a doctorate, as well as graduate students in the first year of doing so may apply. Awards include a tuition waiver and $32,000 per year, renewable for up to five years. Hertz fellows are also eligible for Hertz-Gates Fellowships in Global Health and Development, which offer internships for two successive summers in the Bill & Melinda Gates Foundation's global health or global development programs.

http://hertzfoundation.org/

IBM Ph.D. Fellowship

This fellowship supports exceptional doctoral students with an interest in solving problems that are fundamental to innovation, including cognitive computing and augmented intelligence, quantum computing, blockchain, data-centric systems, advanced analytics, security, radical cloud innovation, next-generation silicon (and beyond), and brain-inspired devices and infrastructure.

https://www.research.ibm.com/university/awards/phdfellow ship.shtml

International Foundation for Ethical Research (IFER) Fellowship

The IFER Fellowship is awarded to graduate students and other scientists whose projects aim to develop alternatives to the use of animals in scientific research. Recipients are awarded up to $15,000 and up to $2,500 for supplies each year.

https://www.ifer.org/fellowships.php

$$ James C. Puffer, M.D./American Board of Family Medicine (ABFM) Fellowship

This fellowship supports talented scholars in family medicine. Preference is given to candidates with a focus on quality health care or health services. Fellows may designate an institution to receive a $25,000 award.

https://nam.edu/programs/health-policy-educational-programs-and-fellowships/nam-fellowship-program/james-c-puffer-m-d-american-board-of-family-medicine-fellowship/

John and Muriel Landis Scholarship

The American Nuclear Society (ANS) grants the John and Muriel Landis Scholarship to qualified student members of the ANS Student Sections who demonstrate a high commitment to the standards set by the society's constituents. Recipients are awarded up to $5,000.

https://www.ans.org/honors/scholarships/

Knowles Teaching Fellowship

The Knowles Teacher Initiative offers this fellowship to recent graduates who have received a bachelor's or advanced degree in STEM and want to teach high school science or mathematics. The fellowship provides professional and financial support for up to five years through a teacher preparation program.

https://knowlesteachers.org/

Lewis and Clark Fund for Exploration and Field Research in Astrobiology

This American Philosophical Society award supports graduate students (as well as doctoral, postdoctoral, and junior scientists) interested in field studies for their theses or other purposes. Recipients are awarded up to $5,000.

https://www.amphilsoc.org/grants/lewis-and-clark-fund-exploration-and-field-research-astrobiology

$$ National Academy of Medicine (NAM) Fellowship in Osteopathic Medicine

This fellowship enables early-career faculty and future leaders in osteopathic medicine to participate actively in NAM's work. Fellows receive a $25,000 research stipend.

https://nam.edu/programs/health-policy-educational-programs-and-fellowships/nam-fellowship-program/nam-fellowship-in-osteopathic-medicine

National Community Pharmacist Associate (NCPA) Foundation Presidential Scholarships

NCPA supports pharmacy students who exhibit leadership qualities, an interest in pharmacy, involvement in extracurricular activities, and academic achievement. These scholarships award $2,000. Successful candidates will receive up to a $300 travel stipend to cover travel costs to the NCPA Annual Convention.

https://www.ncpafoundation.org/scholarships/presidential.shtml

^^ $$ National Health Service Corps (NHSC) Scholarships

NHSC provides scholarships to students who are committed to primary care. The scholarship covers tuition and other educational costs, and provides a living stipend in exchange for a commitment to work for at least two years at an NHSC-approved site in a medically underserved community. Eligible participants may receive the scholarship for a maximum of four years.

http://www.nhsc.hrsa.gov/

** $$ National Institutes of Health (NIH) Oxford-Cambridge Scholars Program

The NIH, combined with the University of Oxford and Cambridge University, offers a collaborative graduate program in biomedical sciences to students who want to combine their Ph.D. with an M.D. from a U.S. medical school. The program covers tuition and fees, while the stipend, medical benefits, and travel allowance for all four years of the program are funded by the applicable NIH mentor.

https://oxcam.gpp.nih.gov/

** National Institutes of Health (NIH) Undergraduate Scholarship

The NIH Undergraduate Scholarship offers competitive scholarships to students from disadvantaged backgrounds who are committed to careers in biomedical, behavioral, and social science health-related research. This program offers scholarship support of up to $20,000, paid research training at the NIH during the summer, and paid employment and training at the NIH after graduation.

http://www.training.nih.gov/

** National Oceanic and Atmospheric Administration (NOAA) Ernest F. Hollings Undergraduate Scholarship

NOAA offers the Hollings Undergraduate Scholarship to undergraduates in oceanic, environmental, biological, and atmospheric sciences; mathematics; engineering; remote sensing technology; and social sciences, including geography, physics, hydrology, geomatics, and teacher education. Recipients are awarded up to $9,500 for two years of full-time study and a 10-week, full-time, paid internship at a NOAA facility during the summer.

http://www.noaa.gov/office-education/hollings-scholarship

National Physical Science Consortium (NPSC) Graduate Fellowship

The NPSC offers this fellowship to physical science students attending any participating NPSC member university or college. The fellowship aims to increase the number of graduates in fields such as astronomy, chemistry, geoscience, physics, and engineering. Recipients are awarded up to $20,000.

http://www.npsc.org/

National Research Council (NRC) Research Associateships

The NRC offers postdoctoral, graduate, and senior research awards, given for research chosen by the doctoral level of scientists and engineers. Applicants must be working toward a doctorate in the field of science or engineering. Each year, the NRC offers these competitive research awards, which are affiliated with 26 United States federal research agencies and over 100 locations in the United States and abroad. Awardees can conduct independent research full-time at one of the excellent federal research laboratories in the United States and can devote their time to research and to writing manuscripts.

http://sites.nationalacademies.org/pga/rap/

** $$ National Science Foundation (NSF) Graduate Research Fellowship Program (GRFP)

The NSF's GFRP offers 900 to 1,000 awards per year. It supports graduate students and undergraduates involved in study and research leading to graduate or doctoral degrees in STEM or STEM education. Fellows receive a three-year stipend of $34,000 per year, along with a $12,000 cost-of-education allowance for tuition and fees. Past fellows include numerous Nobel Prize winners, former U.S. Secretary of Energy Steven Chu, Google founder Sergey Brin, and Freakonomics co-author Steven Levitt.

http://www.nsfgrfp.org/

O.H. Ammann Research Fellowship in Structural Engineering

The O.H. Ammann Research Fellowship in Structural Engineering is an annual award given for the purpose of encouraging innovation in structural design and construction. Recipients are awarded up to $5,000.

https://www.asce.org/structural-engineering/ammann-research-fellowship/

Richard A. Freund International Scholarship

This $5,000 scholarship assists undergraduates with graduate study of the theory and application of quality control, quality assurance, quality improvement, total quality management, or applied math and sciences with an emphasis on quality.

https://asq.org/about-asq/asq-awards/freundscholar

Tau Beta Pi Graduate Fellowships

Tau Beta Pi, the engineering honor society, offers this $10,000 fellowship to members with excellent academic records in engineering.

https://www.tbp.org/fellowships.cfm

Tylenol Scholarships

Tylenol offers these scholarships to undergraduate and graduate students in a variety of health-related fields with the aim of helping them achieve academic excellence in medicine.

https://www.tylenol.com/news/scholarship

U.S. Department of Defense (DoD) National Defense & Science Engineering Fellowships

The DoD's graduate fellowships aim to increase the number of U.S. citizens trained in science and engineering of military importance. These fellowships are awarded to individuals who have demonstrated ability and special aptitude for advanced training in science and engineering.

http://ndseg.asee.org/

196

U.S. Department of Energy (DOE) Office of Science Graduate Fellowships (SCGF)

The DOE sponsors a variety of fellowships for current and prospective graduate students in the sciences at selected universities.

https://science.energy.gov/wdts/scgf/

** Wenner-Gren Foundation Fellowships

The Wenner-Gren Foundation awards grants and fellowships ranging up to $20,000 for dissertation fieldwork in anthropology. Candidates must be enrolled in a doctoral program.

http://www.wennergren.org/programs

"Nothing in life is to be feared, it is only to be understood."

— Marie Curie, physicist, chemist, and first female winner of a Nobel Prize

Chapter 24:
Women's and Diversity STEM Scholarships and Fellowships

This chapter presents opportunities specifically designed for women and members of historically underrepresented groups in science, technology, engineering, and mathematics (STEM), particularly African-Americans, Hispanic Americans, and Native Americans/Alaska Natives.

Insider's Tip: For networking, as well as additional scholarship opportunities, consider groups such as the Association for Women in Science (https://www.awis.org/), the National Action Council for Minorities in Engineering (http://www.nacme.org/scholarships), and the Society of Women Engineers (http://societyofwomenengineers.swe.org/scholarships).

Women

ABC Humane Wildlife Control & Prevention Academic Scholarship

The ABC Wildlife Academic Scholarship is open to women in STEM. It awards $1,000 to the applicant who submits the top essay, as well as to up to nine other applicants, as funding allows.

https://abcwildlife.com/abc-humane-wildlife-control-prevention-inc-s-academic-scholarship

Adobe Research Women in Technology Scholarship

The Adobe Research Women in Technology Scholarship recognizes outstanding undergraduate female students in computer science, computer engineering, or a closely related technical field. Recipients are awarded $10,000.

https://research.adobe.com/scholarship/

American Indian Science and Engineering Society (AISES) A.T. Anderson Memorial Scholarship

AISES offers this scholarship to female members who are full-time undergraduates or graduate students in mathematics, physical science, science, engineering, technology, or natural resources. Undergraduates are awarded $1,000 per academic year, and graduate students are awarded $2,000 per academic year.

http://www.aises.org/scholarships/at-anderson

American Medical Women's Association (AMWA) Haffizulla Family Scholarship

AMWA offers this scholarship to encourage the involvement of young leaders in disease prevention and national health and wellness. Recipients are awarded up to $1,000.

https://www.amwa-doc.org/students/awards/haffizulla-family-scholarship-application/

American Physical Society (APS) APS/IBM Research Internship for Undergraduate Women

The APS assists undergraduate women, including students who present or identify as trans-women, with sophomore or junior standing. Recipients are awarded up to $2,500.

https://www.aps.org/programs/women/scholarships/ibm/index.cfm

$$ American Physical Society (APS) M. Hildred Blewett Fellowship

The APS M. Hildred Blewett Fellowship enables women to return to careers in physics research after an interruption. Applicants must have completed work toward a doctorate. The fellowship consists of a one-year award of up to $45,000.

https://www.aps.org/programs/women/scholarships/blewett/

American Society of Safety Engineers (ASSE) Scholarship Foundation

This ASSE scholarship supports female students who want to further their education in occupational safety. Awards range from $500 to $15,000.

https://foundation.asse.org/scholarships-and-grants/

Applied Computer Security Associates (ACSA) Scholarships

The ACSA offers scholarships to female undergraduate and graduate students in information security. Awards range up to $10,000.

https://cra.org/cra-w/scholarships-and-awards/scholarships/swsis/

Association for Computing Machinery-W (ACM-W) Scholarships for Attendance at Research Conferences

ACM-W scholarships enable female undergraduate or graduate students pursuing a degree in computer science or a related field to attend research conferences. Awards are $600 for intra-continental conference travel and $1,200 for intercontinental conference travel.

https://women.acm.org/scholarships/

Association of Women Geoscientists (AWG) Chrysalis Scholarship

AWG's Chrysalis Scholarship provides funding to female geoscience graduate students who have overcome great difficulties and who demonstrate financial need. Recipients are awarded up to $2,000.

http://www.awg.org/Awards

Association for Women in Science (AWIS) Educational Awards

AWIS offers female undergraduate and graduate students in STEM awards of $1,000 to $3,000. For the undergraduate scholarship, applicants must be in their second or third year of college and expect to major in science or a related field. For the graduate scholarship, students must have been admitted to candidacy for a Ph.D. in a life or physical science or engineering program.

http://www.awis.org/

BHW Scholarship

The BHW Group, based in Austin, Texas, develops web and mobile apps for businesses. The BHW Scholarship assists female undergraduate and graduate students in STEM. Recipients are awarded up to $3,000.

https://thebhwgroup.com/scholarship

Center for Women in Technology (CWIT) Scholars Program

CWIT strives to increase the representation of women in engineering and information technology. It offers scholarships to female undergraduates in computer science, information systems, business technology administration, engineering, or a related program at the University of Maryland Baltimore County. Recipients are awarded up to $15,000 (in-state students) or $22,000 (out-of-state) per year.

https://cwit.umbc.edu/cwitscholars/

Daughters of the American Revolution (DAR) Medical and Nursing Scholarships

The Daughters of the American Revolution is a women's volunteer organization focused on promoting patriotism and education. To be a member, applicants must prove lineal descent from a veteran of the American Revolution. The DAR offers scholarships to students enrolled in medical or nursing programs. Awards vary depending on financial need.

https://www.dar.org/national-society/scholarships/nursing-medical-scholarships

Entertainment Software Association (ESA) Foundation Scholarship

The ESA Foundation Scholarship assists women and minority students pursuing degrees leading to careers in computer science or video game arts. Recipients are awarded up to $3,000.

http://www.esafoundation.org/scholarship.asp

** Henry Luce Foundation Clare Boothe Luce (CBL) Graduate Fellowship

The CBL Fellowship is one of the single most significant sources of private support for U.S. women in STEM. It supports female undergraduate and graduate students. Awards vary.

http://www.hluce.org/cblprogram.aspx

Intel Corporation Scholarships

Intel is one of the biggest names in technology. While they are best known for their processors, Intel also focuses on innovation and social responsibility. Intel Corporation offers $5,000 scholarships to female students interested in engineering.

https://www.intel.com/content/www/us/en/employee/scholarship.html

$$ L'Oreal U.S.A. For Women in Science Fellowship

The L'Oreal Foundation awards five $60,000 fellowships to encourage the advancement and involvement of women in scientific research and development. One beneficiary is selected from each of five international regions: Latin America and the Caribbean, Africa, North America and Europe, Asia and the Pacific, and the Arab states.

http://www.lorealusa.com/csr-commitments/l'oréal-usa-for-women-in-science-program

Microsoft Dissertation Grant Program

This grant supports historically underrepresented groups, including women and people with disabilities. Applicants must be fourth-year or beyond students or postdoctoral researchers who are performing research that relates to computing topics.

https://www.microsoft.com/en-us/research/academic-program/dissertation-grant/

National Black Nurses Association (NBNA) Scholarship

The National Black Nurses Association began in 1971. It aims to provide a voice for black women working in the nursing profession and improve the health of black communities by strengthening health care programs. NBNA offers scholarships ranging from $1,000 to $6,000 to its members who are in nursing programs.

https://www.nbna.org/content.asp?contentid=82

National Physical Science Consortium (NPSC) Fellowship

NPSC offers generous fellowships, which include a tuition waiver, to graduate students in physical sciences and engineering fields, emphasizing recruitment of a diverse applicant pool. The vast majority of its fellows have been those historically underrepresented in science: minorities, women, or both. Recipients are awarded $20,000 per year for up to six years.

http://www.npsc.org/

Society of Women Engineers (SWE) Ada I. Pressman Memorial Scholarship

The SWE offers this scholarship to female students with a minimum GPA of 3.0 in any engineering program. It awards $5,000, renewable for five years.

http://societyofwomenengineers.swe.org/scholarships

Society of Women Engineers (SWE) Scholarship

The SWE offers this scholarship to female graduate students pursuing degrees in engineering, engineering technology, or computer science. Recipients are awarded up to $10,000.

https://scholarships.swe.org/applications/login.asp

Women Techmakers Scholars Program

This program includes a scholarship, a professional and personal development and training retreat, and an online network where scholars can collaborate with one another. It is open to women in computer science and technology who show leadership qualities and achievements.

https://www.womentechmakers.com/scholars

Diversity

American Chemical Society (ACS) Undergraduate Fellowships

ACS offers fellowships to students from historically underrepresented groups who major in chemistry, biochemistry, chemical engineering, or any chemical-related science. Students must demonstrate financial need and possess academic merit in chemistry.

https://www.acs.org/content/acs/en/funding-and-awards/awards/division/organic/orgn_surf.html

American Meteorological Society (AMS) Minority Scholarships

The AMS offers scholarships to Hispanic, Native American, African-American, and other minority students beginning their freshman year of college. Applicants must plan to study atmospheric, oceanic, or hydrologic sciences. The two-year scholarship offers $3,000 each year for freshman and sophomore years.

https://www.ametsoc.org/index.cfm/ams/information-for/students/ams-scholarships-and-fellowships/ams-minority-scholarships/

$$ Bullitt Foundation Environmental Fellowship

The Bullitt Foundation offers a two-year, $50,000-per-year fellowship to an environmentally knowledgeable graduate student in Washington, Oregon, or British Columbia. It encourages applications from students of color and others who have overcome discrimination or other significant hardships.

http://www.bullitt.org/programs/environmental-fellowship/

Entertainment Software Association (ESA) Foundation Scholarship

The ESA Foundation Scholarship assists women and minority students pursuing degrees leading to careers in computer science or video game arts. Recipients are awarded up to $3,000.

http://www.esafoundation.org/scholarship.asp

GEM Fellowships

The National Gem Consortium offers GEM Fellowships, which provide a paid summer internship, a tuition waiver, and a minimum of $16,000 to underrepresented minority students pursuing a master's in engineering, or a postdoctoral degree in engineering or the natural and physical sciences.

http://www.gemfellowship.org/

$$ Gilbert S. Omenn Fellowship

This fellowship enables talented early-career scholars in biomedical science and population health to promote the linkage of public health and medicine, both scientifically and through practice and policy. The program especially welcomes nominations of underrepresented minority group candidates. Fellows receive a flexible $25,000 research stipend.

https://nam.edu/programs/health-policy-educational-programs-and-fellowships/nam-fellowship-program/gilbert-s-omenn-fellowship/

Indian Health Service Scholarship

The Indian Health Service, dedicated to promoting the physical and mental health and well-being of American Indians and Alaskan Natives, provides health services to approximately 2.2 million people. This program offers three separate scholarships to Native American and Alaska Native undergraduate and graduate students seeking degrees and careers in health care.

https://www.ihs.gov/scholarship/?mobileFormat=0

Microsoft Dissertation Grant Program

This grant supports historically underrepresented groups, including women and people with disabilities. Applicants must be fourth-year or beyond students or postdoctoral researchers who are performing research that relates to computing topics.

https://www.microsoft.com/en-us/research/academic-program/dissertation-grant/

$$ National Academy of Medicine (NAM) Fellowship in Pharmacy

This $25,000 fellowship offers a unique opportunity for talented scholars to further their careers as future leaders in pharmacy. The program especially welcomes nominations of underrepresented minority candidates.

https://nam.edu/programs/health-policy-educational-programs-and-fellowships/nam-fellowship-program/nam-fellowship-in-pharmacy/

** National Physical Science Consortium (NPSC) Fellowship

NPSC offers generous fellowships, which include a tuition waiver, to graduate students in physical sciences and engineering fields, emphasizing recruitment of a diverse applicant pool. The vast majority of its fellows have been those historically underrepresented in science: minorities, women, or both. Recipients are awarded $20,000 per year for up to six years.

http://www.npsc.org/

Norman F. Gant/American Board of Obstetrics and Gynecology (ABOG) Fellowship

The Gant/ABOG Fellowship helps talented and early-career health science scholars in obstetrics and gynecology. Nominations of underrepresented and minority candidates are especially welcomed.

https://nam.edu/programs/health-policy-educational-programs-and-fellowships/nam-fellowship-program/norman-f-gantamerican-board-of-obstetrics-and-gynecology-fellowship/

Ronald D. Lunceford Scholarship

This $4,000 scholarship is available to students from historically underrepresented groups in psychology, social services, therapy, or rehabilitation. Applicants must be pursuing admission to a graduate or doctoral program that will qualify them for licensure as a marriage and family therapist.

https://www.petersons.com/scholarship/ronald-d-lunceford-scholarship-111_151557.aspx

Tradition Bearers Bio Cultural Diversity Fellowship

The Seventh Generation Fund for Indigenous Peoples began in 1977. It aims to promote the self-determination of indigenous people and the sovereignty of native nations. It supports the development of grassroots efforts in indigenous communities. This fellowship is available to Native American and First Nations individuals focused on cultural identity and biological diversity. Recipients are awarded up to $10,000 toward their education.

http://www.7genfund.org/tradition-bearers-bio-cultural-diversity-fellowship

** Xerox Technical Minority Scholarship

The Xerox Technical Minority Scholarship supports full-time undergraduate and graduate minority students in chemistry, information management, computing and software systems, material science, printing management science, laser optics, physics, and engineering.

https://www.xerox.com/en-us/jobs

"Washington, D.C., has everything that Rome, Paris, and London have in the way of great architecture. Washington has obelisks and pyramids and underground tunnels and great art and a whole shadow world that we really don't see."

— Dan Brown, American author

SECTION 5:
Living in the Nation's Capital

The chapters in this section provide information and resources to help you live well — and thrive! — in Washington, D.C. We devote the most attention to housing, due to the challenges it poses. In 2018, Kiplinger (https://www.kiplinger.com/slideshow/real-estate/T006-S001-most-expensive-u-s-cities-to-live-in-2018/index.html) named Washington, D.C., the fifth-most-expensive city in America, noting that its housing costs were 2.5 times the national average. The median monthly rent for a one-bedroom apartment was $2,200 in 2016, as tracked by the Zumper (https://www.zumper.com/blog/2016/04/zumper-national-rent-report-april-2016/) rental-listing service. Knowing such facts and planning accordingly are vital to your success.

Some popular cost-reducing housing options include the following:

- living in university campus housing (for summer interns)
- sharing a group house, which costs roughly one-third to one-half the cost of a studio or one-bedroom apartment and offers additional social and networking (and occasionally romantic!) benefits
- subletting an apartment or a room in a group house
- living in the surrounding area (Maryland or Virginia)

Getting Around

Once you have found your pad, you can leave your car behind. Washington, D.C., offers all kinds of sustainable ways to get around, from old standbys like the Metro bus and Metrorail (https://www.wmata.com/) to innovative options such as BikeShare (https://www.capitalbikeshare.com/) and Carpool Now (http://www.commuterconnections.org/commuters/ridesharing/mobile-apps/). The latter enables you to request a carpool right when you need it via your smartphone, the same way you would request an Uber or Lyft. The GoDCGo (https://godcgo.com/commutator/) website has all the details. There is even a D.C. Streetcar (https://www.dcstreetcar.com/) line serving the H Street Corridor in Northeast.

The wide-ranging Metrorail and Metro bus system makes getting around Washington, D.C., quite affordable. Metro also has a special D.C. Circulator (http://www.dccirculator.com/) bus that costs just $1 and services popular spots including Georgetown, Union Station, Capitol Hill, and the National Mall. (It recently added some all-electric buses to its fleet, which offer free onboard Wi-Fi, as part of the greening initiatives of D.C.'s mayor, Muriel Bowser.)

Metrorail fares vary by time of day and distance between stations. You can use Metro's Trip Planner (https://www.wmata.com/) to calculate the fare for your trip (and how best to get there). Metro buses still take cash (fare is $2; exact change only), but you need a SmarTrip card to use Metrorail. They are sold online (https://smartrip.wmata.com/Storefront/ShoppingCart/AddAndPurchase?id=6745467) and at Metrorail stations, Metro sales offices, commuter stores, and retail outlets.

The Smithsonian's many museums, as well as numerous historical sites, are free to visit. Winters are relatively mild, though summer interns should be aware that the city's summers are extremely hot and humid.

Insider's Tip: Here is what another insider wished she knew (https://www.youtube.com/watch?v=bkqIJMZIFBc) before moving to Washington, D.C.

"A house is not a home unless it contains food and fire for the mind as well as the body."

— Benjamin Franklin, author, politician, inventor, and one of America's founding fathers

Chapter 25:
University Summer Housing

The following universities in Washington, D.C., offer relatively low-cost, short-term housing for visitors (including non-students) during the summer. Space is limited, so apply at your earliest convenience!

American University

American University offers summer housing to students who intend to stay for at least three consecutive weeks. It aims to reflect environmental sustainability in its housing policies and design. Summer costs range from $1,012 to $5,152, depending on length of stay, room size, and housing session.

https://www.american.edu/ocl/housing/

Catholic University of America

Summer housing at the Catholic University of America is available to students currently enrolled at the university, those who have graduated that year, and visiting students enrolled in summer courses. Rooms are offered at a nightly rate ($42 or $46) and for the entire summer session ($3,528 or $3,864).

http://housing.cua.edu/

George Washington University

At George Washington University, summer housing is available to students, interns, and conference attendees, regardless of enrollment. Housing is available at both the Mount Vernon and Foggy Bottom campuses. Rates vary by room type and length of stay.

https://living.gwu.edu/

Georgetown University

Georgetown University offers summer housing to students, interns, individuals, and conference and camp attendees. Their facilities have recently been renovated. Residents are charged on a weekly basis. Prices vary by room size and length of stay.

https://residentialliving.georgetown.edu/

Howard University

Howard University offers summer housing to interns and conference attendees. Students should be enrolled at Howard University. Rates vary by session and room type. Howard University also offers accommodations off-campus at College Hall.

https://residencelife.howard.edu/

"If you laugh with somebody, then you know you share something."

— Trevor Noah, comedian and author

Chapter 26:
District of Columbia, Maryland, and Virginia Neighborhoods

Living in the Washington, D.C., area can be a rich, multicultural experience. Here is a taste of what some safe, accessible neighborhoods have to offer.

One popular, affordable housing option for many young D.C.-area professionals is a group house, in which four to six people share a large house and split the rent and utilities. Note: If the total number of housemates exceeds six, be sure to check with local government to be sure it is legal.

Insider's Tip: We recommend the easy-to-navigate Hotpads (https://hotpads. com/washington-dc/apartments-for-rent), Trulia (https://www.trulia.com/for_rent/ Washington,DC/), and Zumper (https://www.zumper.com/apartments-for-rent/ washington-dc) websites to help with your housing search. It is generally best not to rent a place until you see it in person, but performing some research on these sites before you move can help you hit the ground running when you arrive. Craigslist (https://washingtondc.craigslist.org/search/hhh) can be a resource too, although it is often less user-friendly.

Washington, D.C.

Adams Morgan

This diverse neighborhood, located uphill from Dupont Circle, centers around 18th Street and Columbia Road. Adams Morgan is an urban area whose residents include students, diplomatic officials, and families. The area is moderately priced and is home to a vibrant nightlife with many bars. Although it does not feature a Metrorail station, it is served by Metro buses.

Cleveland Park

Cleveland Park is a historic neighborhood of single-family houses and large apartment buildings. The Metrorail station is conveniently located in an attractive area filled with small stores, restaurants, and a classic movie theater. Metrorail: Red Line.

Dupont Circle

Dupont Circle, located along Connecticut Avenue, is known for its lively urban lifestyle. The area offers various housing options, such as modern apartments, rooms in private homes, and older high-rises. The area is well connected, with cafes, shops, bars, restaurants, a Metrorail station, and Metro buses. Metrorail: Red Line.

Foggy Bottom

Foggy Bottom is located near the D.C./Virginia border. With its high-rent housing, it is not ideal for interns; however, it is home to George Washington University and may have some budget-friendly options for young professionals seeking a basement apartment or a group house. Metrorail: Blue/Orange Lines.

Friendship Heights

Friendship Heights, located around upper Wisconsin Avenue at the D.C./Maryland border, features numerous high-end department stores and shops. It contains high-rise buildings (including Microsoft's Washington, D.C., headquarters), boutiques, restaurants, grocery stores, and two large shopping malls. Regular Metro bus service; Metrorail: Red Line.

Georgetown

Georgetown, home to one of the city's most popular nightlife and shopping areas (as well as Georgetown University), has relatively high rents, and most apartment buildings do not rent to students. Limited opportunities are available, however, from homeowners renting out basement apartments and Georgetown students offering summer sublets. The area includes regularly running university shuttle buses that provide easy access to Metro bus stops and Metrorail stations, and even make stops on Capitol Hill.

Glover Park

This quiet neighborhood, sometimes referred to as Upper Georgetown, is located near the National Cathedral, around Wisconsin Avenue. In addition to many group houses, it also sports smaller apartments with reasonable rents. It is particularly popular with graduate students and young professionals. Although it has no Metrorail station, it is served by Metro buses.

Logan Circle

This area, north of downtown and east of Dupont Circle, consists mainly of Victorian mansions and townhouses, many of which are currently being renovated and revitalized. It features a mixture of accommodations. It is served by several Metro bus lines and within walking distance of the Dupont Circle Metrorail station: Red Line.

Northeast

Northeast is the area around Catholic and Gallaudet Universities as well as Union Station, a large shopping and dining complex housing Amtrak and regional bus terminals. Metro buses travel regularly through all major arteries within Northeast. Metrorail: Green and Red Lines.

Southeast/Capitol Hill

This historic area is well known for its many federal and governmental offices, as well as the Library of Congress and the Capitol. Many federal employees, as well as students, live in Southeast. Due to the diversity of its residents, affordable, safe housing is available, but rental rates vary widely. Metrorail: Blue/Orange Lines (Capitol South, Eastern Market).

Southwest

Southwest is the area near the Smithsonian museums on the Mall and the waterfront. It is served by Metro buses and Metrorail: Green Line (Waterfront), Blue/Orange Lines (Smithsonian), Blue/Orange/Yellow/Green Lines (L'Enfant Plaza).

Van Ness/Forest Hills

Van Ness/Forest Hills is a residential area just north of Cleveland Park. Housing ranges from high-rise apartment buildings to full-size houses. Close to the University of the District of Columbia, American University, and many embassies, the area caters to college students, families, and diplomats alike. Served by Metro buses and Metrorail: Red Line.

Woodley Park

Woodley Park, a comfortable neighborhood of town houses and large apartment buildings, has a suburban feel and is located between Dupont Circle and Cleveland Park, just west of Adams Morgan. It is home to the Smithsonian's National Zoological Park (a must-see zoo that offers free admission — ideal for cash-strapped interns and young professionals). The Metrorail station is in the middle of a small but attractive shopping area. Metrorail: Red Line.

Maryland

Bethesda

Downtown Bethesda, under rapid development, has a suburban feel. Many people who live and work in Washington, D.C., make their homes in this city, which is also home to the National Institutes of Health. It features numerous extensive, new apartment buildings and restaurants of all types and price ranges. Metrorail's station is centrally located on Wisconsin Avenue. Metrorail: Red Line.

Silver Spring

Located not far from Bethesda, Silver Spring features several large apartment buildings that are accessible to the shopping district on Colesville Road and Georgia Avenue. Metrorail's station is central to the neighborhood and above it all; here, the subway is actually elevated. Metrorail: Red Line.

Takoma Park

Takoma Park offers various group houses and is located in Maryland, just over the border. This area is well known and popular among young professionals. It is served by Metro and Ride On buses, which service Montgomery County in Maryland. Metrorail: Red Line.

Virginia

Alexandria

The historic, charming city of Alexandria lies just outside Washington, D.C. It is home to many students and families. Varieties of housing options are available, including affordable housing for those who qualify. Metrorail: Yellow Line (Braddock Street, King Street).

Arlington

Arlington sits adjacent to Washington, D.C., immediately across the Key Bridge overlooking the Potomac River in northern Virginia. It features a variety of housing types, including townhouses, garden apartments, expansive high-rises, luxury apartments, and single homes. In addition, a number of apartment buildings have been constructed at Pentagon City, adjacent to the Fashion Centre shopping mall. Metrorail: Blue/Orange/Yellow Lines (several stops).

"We must discover the power of love, the redemptive power of love. And when we discover that, we will be able to make of this old world a new world."

— Bishop Michael Bruce Curry, first African-American head of the Episcopal Church

Chapter 27:
Other Housing Resources

Co-Living Spaces

This interesting new housing type is a sort of formalized group house, where the monthly rent for a fully furnished private bedroom within a shared suite includes weekly cleaning and Wi-Fi. A developer called Common offers furnished rooms in the Chinatown and Shaw neighborhoods.

http://www.common.com/

Craigslist

You can use the Craigslist.org website to search online for housing: a solo apartment, a group house, or a roommate situation. Its for-sale section is an excellent source of affordable furniture; the Letgo app/website may be helpful as well.

http://www.craigslist.org/

D.C. Intern Housing

D.C. Intern Housing provides affordable, furnished housing for students, interns, and fellows.

http://www.cheapdcinternhousing.com/

Hostelling International (HI Washington)

HI Washington, a youth hostel in the heart of downtown, offers a temporary place to stay while you conduct your housing search. (The maximum stay is 14 days within a 12-month period, and accommodations are available only to travelers from outside a 55-mile radius of the hostel.) It offers lower-cost multi-occupancy rooms, along with free breakfast and Wi-Fi. HI Washington is near Mount Vernon Square on the Yellow/Green Line. Note that quoted daily rates generally do not include taxes;

instead, a hefty 14.5 percent local-government tax will be added to your bill.

http://www.hiwashingtondc.org/

Hostels.com

Hostels.com, an independent website, lists hostels in the Washington, D.C., area. See the important caveats in the above listing regarding the limitations on hostel stays and the 14.5 percent tax.

http://www.hostels.com/

Hotpads.com

Many young D.C. insiders recommend Hotpads.com for its clear, easy-to-navigate website. It lists sublets; rooms in group houses and in other shared living situations; and apartments. Use the "More" drop-down menu to view sublets or rooms for rent.

http://www.hotpads.com/

International Student House (ISH-DC)

ISH-DC, a nonprofit in Dupont Circle, is home to graduate students from 40 countries, which share rooms and engage with each other on a daily basis. Meals are provided. Alumni include journalists, professors, ambassadors, and directors of nonprofit organizations. ISH-DC provides residential scholarships to a small number of residents each year, based on need and academic promise. These scholarships support ISH-DC residents studying at Washington-area universities.

http://www.ishdc.org/

InternHousing.com

InternHousing.com matches interns with suitable property owners close to their internship's location, allowing interns to connect directly with people offering affordable intern housing. Users can also connect with other interns looking for roommates.

http://www.internhousing.com/

Roommates.com

Roommates.com is an online roommate matching service. Users can look for roommates in thousands of cities.

http://www.roommates.com/

Sublet.com

You can use Sublet.com to find furnished and unfurnished short-term apartments and rooms to sublet. You can rent directly from landlords as well.

http://www.sublet.com/

The Washington Intern Housing Network (The WIHN)

The WIHN, a company started by former interns, provides housing to interns in the Washington, D.C., area. Housing includes all furnishings and accoutrements, and tends to be more upscale than what is found on other sites. The WIHN also offers group pricing.

http://www.thewihn.com/

Trulia

Trulia.com is recommended by young D.C. insiders as a helpful website for finding an apartment or a room in a group house (in the "More" filter, choose "Room for Rent").

http://www.trulia.com/

Washington Intern Student Housing (WISH)

WISH has provided housing to interns from all over the world for over 25 years. Their buildings are conveniently located on Capitol Hill and are open to individuals from around the world.

http://www.internsdc.com/

Zumper

Zumper.com is another helpful website for finding an apartment or a room in a group house (under the "See all" filter, choose "Room" as the Type).

http://www.zumper.com/

Tuition-Based Programs

The Washington Center

The Washington Center arranges internship placement and housing for participants, who also attend an evening course and a colloquium. Participants should be undergraduates who have completed their freshman year.

https://www.twc.edu/programs/academic-internship-program

Washington Internship Institute

The Washington Internship Institute helps interns in nonprofits, the private sector, and the federal government find jobs in the Washington, D.C., area. It also offers housing to participants.

http://wiidc.org/living-in-dc-1/

Additional Tips

Alumni chapter: If your college/university has an alumni chapter in the Washington metropolitan area, it can be a good source of housing information. The alumni office on your campus can provide you with the chapter's contact information.

D.C.-area university off-campus housing offices/services: See resources below. In some cases, you may need to be a student at the university to use its resource.

Trinity University

Trinity University provides resources for students looking for off-campus housing near Trinity Washington University.

http://www.forrentuniversity.com/

D.C.-area university Facebook groups: See resources below. You need to be a student at the university to be a member of their group.

- Georgetown Housing: Spots to Fill (https://www.facebook.com/groups/414404978616662/)
- George Washington University Housing, Sublets & Roommates (https://www.facebook.com/groups/770438619740282/)

"My mission in life is not merely to survive, but to thrive; and to do so with some passion, some compassion, some humor, and some style."

— Maya Angelou, American author, poet, and civil rights activist

SECTION 6:
Thriving in the Nation's Capital (and Beyond)

Coming to a city like Washington, D.C, can be overwhelming at the best of times. When you're also trying to acquire an education, you may feel like it's an impossible task. However, underneath the hubbub of the city, precious gems await your discovery, ranging from listening to jazz at the tabard inn to dancing at an embassy ball!

"I think one of the things that we are facing right now is that we've stopped listening to each other in our politics."

— Michael Bennett, Seattle Seahawks football player and activist

Chapter 28:
Developing a Sustainable Lifestyle

Sustainable Lifestyle Tips for the Young Leader

Working in a demanding environment like Capitol Hill, you may feel tempted to purchase food from a street vendor or hit up the vending machine for a snack instead of making time for real meals. You may also find it challenging to make time for your normal exercise routine, working long hours as an intern with many responsibilities.

If you don't make healthy lifestyle choices, dealing with high-profile people all day and using your best professional skills, while highly important and beneficial for your career, can make you feel drained and unhappy.

These behaviors could not be worse for your mental and physical health! Try to achieve a balance between work and the rest of your life. It's not difficult to stop by a grocery store for fresh produce on your way home from work, take a walk during lunch, or prepare large meals over the weekend to enjoy as lunch and dinner all week.

The truth is, without excellent coping skills and the ability to balance and prioritize different aspects of your personal and professional life, you will not be able to achieve your full potential living in Washington, D.C. The pressure to succeed can sometimes be brutal, and it may seem like a good idea to give up literally everything except work, but if you choose that route, you will eventually burn out and actually become more inefficient than if you take the time to care for yourself properly.

While it takes some effort, being your best self is entirely possible during demanding situations such as working in a Capitol Hill internship. The key to success is finding a balance that works for you!

Eat Healthy Food

Washington, D.C., is a health nut heaven. Everywhere you go, you can see Whole Foods, Trader Joe's, and small health-conscious food places. Still, it's easy to get stuck in a bad junk food habit that it would be better to avoid.

Preparation is key here. You may want to stop by the grocery store on your way home from work every week or so to pick up some fruits, vegetables, and other wholesome foods to enjoy. You can spend some time preparing meals over the weekend to have lunches and dinners ready for a few days.

You can also cook your own meals cheaply and easily. If you are not a great chef, consider buying a slow cooker — many online recipes involve simply dumping some cans of broth or sauce, frozen vegetables, and chicken breast (or tofu) into your slow cooker to create a quick and easy meal. Slow cookers are versatile and the typical cook time is 4-8 hours, so you can leave a slow cooker on overnight and have a meal ready in the morning.

Drink Enough Water

The average person needs at least six to eight eight-ounce glasses of water a day. Add in the awful, swampy D.C. summers, and that number should be closer to eight or nine glasses a day. You can drink a glass of water first thing in the morning to get one or two cups of that daily requirement out of the way.

Water has many incredible benefits for your body. It reduces sugar cravings, gives you more energy, helps your digestive system run better, makes your skin look clearer, keeps you from getting dehydrated, and helps you feel fuller at mealtimes. Your body is 74 percent water, so don't forget to drink up! Make sure to avoid excessive caffeine (such as coffee or tea) and alcohol, which are both diuretics, meaning they rid your body of water and cause dehydration.

Get Enough Sleep

Sleep is an incredibly important part of your life, as it is a restorative process. When you sleep, your memories become consolidated. Failing to get enough sleep can put you at risk for a host of health problems, such as heart attacks and even Alzheimer's disease.

Without sleep, your immune system weakens, making you more prone to illness and mood swings. Of course, being tired is the most obvious consequence of not sleeping, which can lead to burnout and poor productivity. Therefore, aim for at least seven to eight hours of sleep each night. While you may feel like a loser turning down a late night out with friends, you will feel amazing in the morning after a full night of restorative sleep!

Exercise

The federal government recommends we exercise for 150 minutes each week. One easy way to get exercise in D.C. is by walking. Most people in D.C. do not have cars, so they walk everywhere or take the Metro.

However, for those looking for an endorphin rush, D.C. has a variety of exercise classes at gyms across the city (SoulCycle, CrossFit, Barre, etc.), a happening yoga scene, and excellent hiking opportunities at nearby national parks, such as Shenandoah National Park in Virginia. D.C. also features several running trails, as well as scenic locations such as the National Mall.

Exercise can help you stay in shape so that you can look good in your suit while also reducing your risk of heart disease, arthritis, diabetes, and cancer. It's also an amazing stress-buster!

As an intern, you may not be able to make time for long exercise sessions, but you can work hard during the week and catch up on life during the weekend. If you are a runner, you can always dedicate the weekend to a longer run and use the week to perform more routine activities, such as walks or a gym class before or after work.

Another great form of exercising is dancing. The DMV (D.C., Maryland, Virginia) area is known for having some of the best Latin dancers in the country. All of us need to take some time off from work every once in a while. It is important to disconnect from your regular job routine and go have some fun. It will refresh your mind, and surprisingly, help you become even more productive when you return to work.

You will be healthier, happier, and more at peace with the world around you. In addition, it is an excellent way to make new friends, and may even offer the perfect opportunity to meet that special person that your heart desires.

To start with, here are some of the best Latin dance places to check out:

- Salsa With Silvia (https://salsawithsilvia.com/)
- The Salsa Room (https://www.facebook.com/thesalsaroom/?rf=303398683006780)
- D.C. DanceSport Academy (https://www.dcdancesportacademy.com/)
- Chevy Chase Ballroom (http://www.chevychaseballroom.com/)
- DanceSport Dupont Circle (http://www.dancesportdupont.com/)
- Capitol Ballroom Dance Studio (https://www.capitalballroomds.com/)
- Crown Dance Studio (https://www.crowndancestudio.com/)
- Cuba Libre (http://www.cubalibrerestaurant.com/en/washington/)
- Cafe Citron (http://www.cafecitrondc.com/)

Insider's Tip: To participate in another exciting form of exercise, be sure to look into Washington, D.C.'s BikeShare (https://www.capitalbikeshare.com/) program.

"Washington is a city of Southern efficiency and Northern charm."

— John F. Kennedy, former president of the United States

Chapter 29:
Insider's Delights in Washington, D.C.

Work is not everything; pursuing your interests and following your passions are important as well. As you build a successful career, remember to enjoy the process, take time to smell the roses, and have fun. Leisure refreshes your mind. It brings you "outside the box" and gives you new perspectives and ideas.

Our research team pooled our knowledge to compile this list of lesser-known ways (mostly free or inexpensive) to spend your leisure time in our nation's capital. (For transportation options to each site or event, visit the webpage in its listing.)

Insider's Tips:

- The Free in D.C. (http://freeindc.blogspot.com/) blog suggests multiple free or low-cost events to fill every day and night of your week. Twitter: @ FreeinDCBlog
- A night at the theater in Washington, D.C., doesn't have to cost a fortune: www.todaytix.com.

Year-Round

Belmont-Paul Women's Equality National Monument

Situated in a historic 200-year-old house on Capitol Hill, the Belmont-Paul Women's Equality National Monument is also home to the National Woman's Party, which today focuses on education about the women's suffrage movement. Admission is free; no tickets or passes are required. The museum is open only from Wednesday through Sunday.

https://www.nps.gov/bepa/index.htm

Frederick Douglass National Historic Site

The Frederick Douglass National Historic Site offers guests a tour of Cedar Hill, the home occupied by Douglass from 1877 to 1895. The home has been restored to its 1895 appearance. Don't miss the Growlery out back, Douglass' version of the man-cave. Admission is free; however, obtaining a reservation online in advance (inexpensive) is recommended.

Home: https://www.nps.gov/frdo/index.htm

Growlery: https://www.nps.gov/frdo/learn/historyculture/the-growlery.htm

Kennedy Center Millennium Series

The Kennedy Center, which opened in 1971, is a hub for performing arts in the D.C. area. It offers free performances, ranging from stand-up comedy to opera, at 6 p.m. every night. Arrive early, as seating is limited.

http://www.kennedy-center.org/

National Air and Space Museum

The National Air and Space Museum is part of the Smithsonian museum complex on the National Mall. Admission is free (although IMAX movies have an admission fee), and the museum is open every day except Christmas. Visitors can attend events and see exhibits on American aviation and space flight, including the *Mercury Friendship 7*, the historic capsule that NASA astronaut John Glenn used to establish the United States as a major player in the space race, which has been on display at the museum since 1963.

https://airandspace.si.edu/

National Museum of African-American History and Culture

Christened by President Barack Obama at its opening in 2016, this museum is a recent addition to the Smithsonian family of free, top-quality museums in the city. Obtaining a free timed entry pass online in advance is recommended.

https://nmaahc.si.edu/

National Portrait Gallery

Founded in 1962, the National Portrait Gallery displays a range of portraits, from first lady Eleanor Roosevelt to poet Allen Ginsberg to Bill and Melinda Gates. Portraits of the Obamas debuted in early 2018. Michelle Obama's is particularly popular. Admission is free. No tickets or reservations are required to view the portraits.

http://npg.si.edu/home/national-portrait-gallery

Politics & Prose

This bookstore presents readings nightly (some free), by authors ranging from Ronan Farrow to Tom Hanks, at its several locations and other venues throughout the city. The original store, on upper Connecticut Avenue, includes a coffeehouse and wine bar.

http://www.politics-prose.com/

Rock Creek Park

An urban oasis in the northwest quadrant of the city, the 1,754-acre Rock Creek Park offers foot and horse trails along the creek and through the woodlands. Features include an outdoor concert and theater, a tennis stadium, a planetarium, and an equestrian center offering horseback riding lessons and guided trail rides. A boat center rents bikes, kayaks, canoes, and sailboats. The park is also a haven for birds and other urban wildlife. Park admission is free.

http://www.npca.org/

Smithsonian's National Zoo

Admission is free, and the zoo is open 364 days a year. It is famous for its giant pandas, who are internet rock stars and can be seen 24/7 on the Smithsonian's Giant Panda Cam (https://nationalzoo.si.edu/webcams/panda-cam).

https://nationalzoo.si.edu/

Tabard Inn

Visitors are welcome to drop in to the Tabard Inn, the oldest continuously operated hotel in Washington, D.C. (since 1922), to enjoy jazz in the fireplace lounge Sunday through Tuesday nights.

http://www.tabardinn.com/

Annual Events

April: National Cherry Blossom Festival

Every April, magic happens in D.C. Near the Jefferson Memorial and reflecting pool is a prime viewing spot, but cherry trees are also scattered throughout the city, bursting into giddy pink and white blossoms. Free!

http://www.nationalcherryblossomfestival.org/

May: Embassy Open Houses/Tours

On one Saturday in May, you can visit more than 40 foreign embassies on the free Around the World Embassy Tour, part of the monthlong Passport D.C. celebration. Experience the food, art, dance, fashion, and music of different countries — along with karate performances, sari-wrapping lessons, and henna demonstrations. The following Saturday, the embassies of more than two dozen European Union countries host their own free open houses.

http://www.culturaltourismdc.org/
http://events.euintheus.org/landing_page/euopenhouse/

September: Library of Congress National Book Festival

This popular book festival featuring noted authors is held at the beginning of September at the Washington Convention Center. Admission is free.

https://www.loc.gov/bookfest/

September: WalkingTown D.C.

WalkingTown D.C. features more than 50 free walking tours led by historians, licensed tour guides, community leaders, business owners, enthusiasts, and docents. All tours require reservations in August.

https://www.culturaltourismdc.org/portal/about

Splurges

Embassy Ball

Embassy balls occur throughout the year in Washington, D.C. These events may feature food, films, art, and more at embassy locations throughout the city. Most balls require business casual dress, at minimum. Prices vary by event, and tickets are available in advance.

https://thingstododc.com/events/embassy-culture/

Studio Theatre

Studio Theatre produces exceptional contemporary theater in deliberately intimate spaces, seeking to foster a more thoughtful, empathetic, and connected community. It works to cultivate a diverse audience and hosts conversations following selected performances. It costs $20 tickets for college students; two tickets may be purchased per order.

http://www.studiotheatre.org/

"Think like a queen. A queen is not afraid to fail. Failure is another stepping stone to greatness."

— Oprah Winfrey, American actress, producer, and philanthropist

Chapter 30:
Coping with Rejection

Coping with rejection is undoubtedly one of the biggest roadblocks that most people face. On one side, many people who love us and care for us don't want us to fail. On the other side, you will never achieve anything if you don't try.

Some people want to protect you from making the same mistakes that they made. Some of them automatically put you in a box just because they failed at something in the past, and believe that because they failed, you shouldn't waste your time trying. That's quite noble of them.

Nevertheless, my view is, "Why should I not try something just because someone else failed at it?" Of course, I can learn from their mistakes, and try not to repeat the same things, but that does not mean I shouldn't try!

In other words, I always listen to people and consider their advice, but I always take it with a grain of salt. I am my own man. I think critically for myself, and I should be allowed to make my own decisions. In this spirit, I am always prepared to deal with the consequences of my actions. This context is truly applicable when you are applying for internships and scholarships.

What's the point of applying for a job that you know would not be difficult or nearly impossible to get? While I understand that you should not throw yourself in a hole and do something that is beyond your ability, that in itself does not mean you should not stretch yourself. Everything has a fine line.

If you are not a neurosurgeon, you have no business operating on someone's brain. If you are not a lawyer, you have no business representing someone in court. However, if you have a strong academic background, some professional experience, and the passion and determination to succeed, you should always stretch your capabilities and apply to jobs that would challenge you.

However, in the process of challenging yourself, embrace the possibility of failure or rejection. You should never take it personally. In fact, think of failing as an indication that you are trying. That is all that matters. At the same time, be strategic: Learn something each time you fail, and try to be more innovative when submitting your next application.

Albert Einstein once said that the definition of insanity is doing the same thing over and over again, and expecting different results. Therefore, make every failure a lesson rather than a roadblock in your path to your success.

"The future belongs to those who believe in the beauty of their dreams."

— Eleanor Roosevelt, humanitarian and former first lady

Chapter 31:
A Parting Thought

My primary passion is helping people achieve their dreams and realize their full potential. It brings me great joy to know that a person's life has been improved after working with me. I have always focused on bringing value to those around me, to help them improve their lives. At the same time, I realize the importance of taking care of myself first so that I can be in a position to help others.

My other passion is dancing. Being a dancer is tough. In order to progress, you must be very disciplined, continuing to practice even when your entire body hurts and, at times, when you cannot even feel your feet. You must push yourself every day.

Ballroom dancing is the most difficult thing I have ever done in my life. Yet, because it is my passion, I continue to hone my skills in an effort to be the best I can be on the dance floor. I have learned more about myself from dancing than from anything I was taught in a classroom. I admire all kinds of dancers for their passion, creativity, and dedication.

No one will understand why you spend so much time on your passion. Probably, most people will think you are just wasting your time. This makes no difference; always be true to yourself. Whenever you make a decision, own it. You have to be willing to deal with the consequences. Therefore, whatever you decide to do, keep on fighting, and focus on the prize. Who is the most important person in your life? You!

"Optimism is the faith that leads to achievement."

— Helen Keller

Epilogue:
Call to Action

I compiled this guide with one goal: to provide you, the young leader, with all the information you need regarding internships, scholarships, and fellowships as you advance and flourish in your career.

If you are an aspiring leader who plans to make an impact on the world, I hope the valuable resources in this guide will help you achieve your career and academic goals.

For information on how I can provide individualized advice and even mentor you during your internship or next career move, please contact me at http://www.steevesimbert.com/.

"It's hard work that creates change."

— Shonda Rhimes, American television producer

Section 7:
Appendices

On the following pages, you will find various excellent sources that we utilized during the compilation of this guide, stunning cover letter samples, and examples of résumés that will inspire you to write the best résumé your future boss will ever read, as well as a wide selection of useful email and letter samples. These samples feature a variety of differences from one to the next, demonstrating various ways to showcase your knowledge and expertise.

Appendix A:
Sources and Resources

Here are the sources we used and others we recommend, including job boards and other websites that are well worth your time to check out.

How to Use This Guide
Websites: www.TheHill.com's online job board, Public affairs jobs blog

Section 1: Preparing for Success

A Positive Mindset
Kathy Campbell, "Career Guide for Bachelor's and Master's Students," Stanford University, 2015. https://beam.stanford.edu/sites/default/files/stanford_cg15-161.pdf

Kendra Cherry, "Why Your Mindset Really Matters," VeryWellMind, March 21, 2018. https://www.verywellmind.com/what-is-a-mindset-2795025

Jocelyn K. Glei, "Talent Isn't Fixed and Other Mindsets That Lead to Greatness," 99u, 2013. https://99u.adobe.com/articles/14379/talent-isnt-fixed-and-other-mindsets-that-lead-to-greatness

Anthony Moore, "How to Unlearn Limiting Mindsets and Become the Best Version of Yourself," Medium, February 4, 2018.https://medium.com/@anthony_moore/how-to-unlearn-limiting-mindsets-and-become-the-best-version-of-yourself-42cb4ca18794

Deep Patel, "8 Mindsets That Will Set You on the Path to Success," Entrepreneur, November 3, 2016. https://www.entrepreneur.com/article/283988

The Art of the Interview
Career Services at Princeton University, "Preparing for Interviews." https://careerservices.princeton.edu/undergraduate-students/interviews-offers/preparing-interviews

"Clinton vs. Bush in 1992 Debate," YouTube, March 19, 2007. https://www.youtube.com/watch?v=7ffbFvKlWqE

Richard Harroch, "10 Essential Steps to Prepare Yourself for a Job Interview," Forbes, March 31, 2017. https://www.forbes.com/sites/allbusiness/2017/03/31/10-essential-steps-to-prepare-yourself-for-a-job-interview/#708369457c72

"How to Prepare for a Job Interview," WSJ.com Guides. http://guides.wsj.com/careers/how-to-succeed-in-a-job-interview/how-to-prepare-for-a-job-interview/

Jacquelyn Smith, "How to Ace the 50 Most Common Interview Questions," Forbes, January 11, 2013. https://www.forbes.com/sites/jacquelynsmith/2013/01/11/how-to-ace-the-50-most-common-interview-questions/#7579766c4624

"The Ultimate Interview Guide: 30 Prep Tips for Job Interview Success," The Muse. https://www.themuse.com/advice/the-ultimate-interview-guide-30-prep-tips-for-job-interview-success

Section 3: Interning in the Nation's Capital and Beyond

Websites: D.C. Public Affairs + Communications blog, www.Internships.com, www.Monster.com, www.SimplyHired.com

Charles Davis, "The Exploited Laborers of the Liberal Media," Vice, December 2, 2013. https://www.vice.com/en_us/article/mv5ekb/the-exploited-laborers-of-the-liberal-media

Alex Debelov, "How to Meet Anyone from Steve Wozniak to the President," Lifehacker.com, November 5, 2012. https://lifehacker.com/5956035/how-to-meet-anyone-from-steve-wozniak-to-the-president

National Association of Colleges and Employers, "Intern to Full-Time Hire Conversion: 'Returning' vs. 'Nonreturning' Interns," July 21, 2015. http://www.naceweb.org/talent-acquisition/internships/intern-to-full-time-hire-conversion-returning-vs-nonreturning-interns/

Chriss W. Street, "Despite Silicon Valley, Most Interns Who Earn, Earn Little," Breitbart News, July 11, 2014. http://www.breitbart.com/california/2014/07/11/most-interns-now-paid-but-not-much/

U.S. Government Internships and Fellowships

Christina Miracle Bailey and Jennifer E. Manning, "Internships, Fellowships, and Other Work Experience Opportunities in the Federal Government," Congressional Research Service, September 30, 2016. https://www.senate.gov/CRSpubs/1f2aeca3-772c-4de2-a991-cb47a02967b5.pdf

Congressional Management Foundation, Congressional Intern Handbook: A Guide for Interns and Newcomers to Capitol Hill. Washington, D.C.: 2006. http://www.congressfoundation.org/publications/intern-handbook

Rebecca Gale, "Best Intern Ever: Roll Call's Guide to Acing Your Internship," Roll Call, 2014. http://cdn.videos.rollcall.com/files/HN-Best-Intern-Ever-FINAL.pdf

Georgetown University Career Center, "Sample of Popular Federal Government Internships," 2018. https://careercenter.georgetown.edu/industry-resources/government/federal-internships

GovCentral, "Top Ten Federal Internships," Monster.com, 2018. http://govcentral.monster.com/education/articles/1214-top-ten-federal-internships

Internships.com, "Government Internships," 2018. http://www.internships.com/government

Robertson Foundation for Government, "Guide to Getting into Government for High Achievers," August 2015. https://rffg.org/wp-content/uploads/2015/08/Guide-to-Getting-into-Government-for-High-Achievers.pdf

Robertson Foundation for Government, "Guide to International Jobs in Government," August 2015. https://rffg.org/wp-content/uploads/2015/08/Guide-to-International-Jobs-in-Government.pdf

Robertson Foundation for Government, "Guide to Internships and Fellowships in Government," August 2015. https://rffg.org/wp-content/uploads/2015/08/Guide-to-Internships-and-Fellowships-in-Government.pdf

Robertson Foundation for Government, "Guide to Managing the PMF Application Process," August 2015. https://rffg.org/wp-content/uploads/2015/08/Guide-to-Managing-the-PMF-Application-Process.pdf

U.S. Office of Personnel Management, "Working in Government," USAjobs.gov, 2018. https://www.usajobs.gov/Help/working-in-government/unique-hiring-paths/students/

The Washington Post, "Intern City: Your Guide to Interning in D.C.," 2018. https://www.washingtonpost.com/interncity/

Virtual Student Federal Service https://vsfs.state.gov

Advocacy Organizations and Foundations
"Encyclopedia of Associations." Farmington Hills, MI: Gale Cengage, annual.

Michelle Leach, "10 Most Powerful Special Interest Groups in America," Listosaur.com, July 2, 2014. https://listosaur.com/politics/10-powerful-special-interest-groups-america/

Thought.Co, "Top 10 Conservative Advocacy Groups," March 3, 2018. https://www.thoughtco.com/top-conservative-advocacy-groups-330361

Public Policy Research Organizations
Gordon Barnes, "Think Tank Jobs 14," DC Public Affairs + Communications Jobs, January 10, 2017. https://publicaffairsjobs.blogspot.com/2017/01/think-tank-jobs-14.html

Alejandro Chafuen, "The Most Influential Think Tanks in the United States: A New Social Media Ranking," Forbes, December 16, 2015. https://www.forbes.com/sites/alejandrochafuen/2015/12/16/the-most-influential-think-tanks-in-the-united-states-a-new-social-media-ranking/

Dr. Amarendra Bhushan Dhiraj, "The 100 Most Influential Think Tanks in the World for 2017," CEOWorld Magazine, January 31, 2017. http://ceoworld.biz/2017/01/31/100-influential-think-tanks-world-2017/

TheBestSchools.org, "The 50 Most Influential Think Tanks in the United States," 2018. https://thebestschools.org/features/most-influential-think-tanks/

International Organizations
Websites: www.Devex.com, https://ngojobboard.org/

Financial Supervision Authority, "List of International Organizations." http://www.finanssivalvonta.fi/en/Regulation/Regulations/New/Obsolete/Documents/10507L5.pdf

United States Institute of Peace, "International Organizations." https://www.usip.org/publications/international-organizations

Leading Companies
Jeff Kauflin, "The 20 Most Prestigious Internships for 2018," Forbes, 2018. http://www3.forbes.com/leadership/the-20-most-prestigious-internships-for-2018

Sam Levin, "How Much?! Snapchat Interns Earn $10,000 a Month, Twice the Average U.S. Worker," The Guardian, April 29, 2016. https://www.theguardian.com/technology/2016/apr/29/tech-intern-wages-snapchat-twitter-apple

Political and Business Consulting Firms
Vault, "Most Prestigious Consulting Firms," 2018. http://www.vault.com/company-rankings/consulting/best-consulting-firms-prestige/

Top Law Firms

"Vault Law 100," Vault, 2018. http://www.vault.com/company-rankings/law/vault-law-100/?pg=3

Section 4: Financing Your College and Graduate Education

Websites:

http://www.collegescholarships.org/

http://profellow.com/

http://scholars4dev.com/

http://scholarships.com/,

http://scholarships.org/

http://scholarshipsforwomen.net/

U.S. Scholarships and Fellowships

Elizabeth Hoyt, "Prestigious Scholarships and Fellowships," Fastweb.com, 2017. https://www.fastweb.com/college-scholarships/articles/prestigious-scholarships-and-fellowships

Lynn O'Shaughnessy, "10 Most Prestigious Scholarships in America," CBS News, 2011. https://www.cbsnews.com/news/10-most-prestigious-scholarships-in-america/

University of Illinois Springfield, "A Selected List of National Scholarships and Fellowships," 2018. https://www.uis.edu/diversitycenter/resources/scholarships/national/

Scholarships and Fellowships for Study Abroad

www.Scholars4dev.com, "Top 10 Prestigious Scholarships for the Best International Students," 2017. http://www.scholars4dev.com/6268/top-10-scholarships-for-international-students/

Scholars4dev.com, "25 Fully Funded Scholarships for International Students," 2017. http://www.scholars4dev.com/8319/fully-funded-scholarships-international-students/

Pre-Law Programs and Law School Scholarships

American Association for Justice, "Scholarships," 2018. https://www.justice.org/

search/site/scholarships

UCI Law, "Outside Scholarships," 2018. http://www.law.uci.edu/admission/tuition-aid/outside-scholarships.html

University of California, Berkeley Law School, "Scholarships for Minority Students," 2018. https://www.law.berkeley.edu/admissions/jd/financial-aid/types-of-aid/scholarships/outside-agency-scholarships/scholarships-for-minority-students/

Yale Law School, "Outside Scholarship Resources," 2018. https://law.yale.edu/admissions/cost-financial-aid/financial-aid-forms-resources/outside-scholarships

Women's and Diversity STEM Scholarships and Fellowships
Scholarships.org, "STEM Subjects [for Women]," 2018. http://www.collegescholarships.org/women.htm

ScholarshipsForWomen.net, "Scholarships for Women in Science," 2018. https://www.scholarshipsforwomen.net/science/

Society of Women Engineers, "SWE Scholarships," 2018. http://societyofwomenengineers.swe.org/scholarships

Section 5: Living in the Nation's Capital
Websites: www.Craiglist.org, www.Hotpads.com, www.Trulia.com, www.Zumper.com

Jessica Blut, "What I Wish I Knew Before Moving to D.C.," YouTube.com, April 20, 2017. https://www.youtube.com/watch?v=bkqIJMZIFBc

Dan Burrows, "10 Most Expensive U.S. Cities to Live In," Kiplinger.com, March 19, 2018. https://www.kiplinger.com/slideshow/real-estate/T006-S001-most-expensive-u-s-cities-to-live-in-2018/index.html

Office of U.S. Senator Patty Murray, "Intern Guide to Finding Housing in Washington, D.C.," 2018. https://www.murray.senate.gov/internship/dchousing.cfm

Devin O'Brien, "Zumper National Rent Report: April 2016," Zumper.com, April 7, 2016. https://www.zumper.com/blog/2016/04/zumper-national-rent-report-april-2016/

Smithsonian Institution, Office for Fellowships and Internships, "D.C. Metro Area Housing Guide," 2017. https://www.smithsonianofi.com/wp-content/uploads/2017/01/2017-Housing-Guide-1.pdf

Appendix B:
Cover Letter Examples

Kate Bullett

1234 A Street | Washington, DC 12345 | (000) 000-0000 | email@
gmail.com

January 1, 2019

The Office of Senator XYZ

0000 Longworth House Building

Washington, DC 12345

Dear Mr. [Chief of Staff's Last Name],

I am writing to express my strong interest in the internship position in your senate office. My ability to translate complex concepts into simple language will allow me to effectively communicate the senator's message to his constituents.

With a solid grasp of French and Haitian Creole, as well as conversational Spanish, I am particularly attuned to different people and cultures, which will assist in meeting the concerns of diverse constituents.

My expertise lies in successfully managing a broad portfolio of policy matters, including energy, natural resources, appropriations, Social Security, veterans' issues, technology, cybersecurity, transportation, and infrastructure.

When assisting the senator, I will leverage my expertise to advance his legislative goals. Through my extensive experience in the U.S. Congress, I have become adept at working with the Congressional Research Service, committee procedures, and leadership offices to advance legislation.

The following achievements demonstrate my unique qualifications for this position:

- Spearheading the appropriations process, including drafting, reviewing, recommending, and submitting requests;
- Staffing the Small Business Committee;
- Developing and analyzing policy recommendations, drafting remarks, speeches, and correspondence;

- Completing extensive CRS legislative process trainings on raising and considering measures, amending measures, monitoring committee procedures, and resolving differences between the chambers;
- Co-writing Harvard Journal on Legislation article "Prohibiting Federal Funding for Confederate Symbols";
- Excelling in demanding, high-pressure, and ever-changing environments with unpredictable work hours.

My proven ability to optimize operations and team success, along with my solid skills in communication and problem-solving, will contribute immensely to the success of your team. Thank you for your consideration. I look forward to hearing from you soon.

Yours sincerely,

[Signature]

Kate Bullett

Jane Doe

1234 A Street

Winthrop, Massachusetts

(123) 456-7890

brilliantstudent1@futuredcintern.net

November 10, 2020

Human Resources Department — Internship Program

National Public Radio

123 Government Street

Washington, DC 20301

Dear Mr. Jones,

After reading about the internship position within the communications, public, and media relations department available within your organization during the winter quarter, I feel that my qualifications strongly align with the necessary credentials.

As a junior at Harvard University, I am currently pursuing a bachelor's degree in American studies with a minor in communication. My research experience has sparked my interest in how media is delivered through marketing and advertising. I believe in the mission of National Public Radio and welcome the opportunity to intern with your organization.

This summer, while studying abroad, I examined American culture from a different perspective than I ever had before. My findings during this process increased my interest in news delivery and the various ways in which it helps inform citizens.

As the only freshman elected to the position of senator for the Associated Students of Massachusetts, I rose to the challenge of representing first-year students while collaborating on larger university issues. Through these experiences, I learned the value of effective communication through all forms of media.

I feel confident that my experiences, skills, and strong interest in the goals of NPR have adequately prepared me to be a strong intern within your program. I have attached my résumé to this letter and look forward to discussing my qualifications with you. Thank you for your time and consideration.

Sincerely,

[Signature]

Jane Doe

Matt Castle

brilliantstudent1@futuredcintern.net

+1480) 639-8909

June 7, 2018

Re: Regional Manager, Francophone Africa, Design & Implementation Team

I am writing this letter to express my interest in working as the regional manager for Francophone Africa in your Dakar office. I am a recent graduate of the Master in Public Policy program at Harvard Kennedy School (HKS) with experience in advising and report writing in the government and NGO sectors in Rwanda.

I learned about Viamo through the Mobile Engagement Project Manager in your Dakar office, Alison Thurston, who informed me of the vacancies at Viamo. Upon further research, I became intrigued by the way your company leverages technology to enable its clients to make a meaningful impact. As someone passionate about tech for development, I see joining Viamo as a logical and exciting next step in my path to becoming a leader in global development.

My professional experience has equipped me with the skills in project management and strategic thinking, as well as the understanding of emerging markets that you seek in a regional manager. For example, as a summer associate at Rwanda Development Board (RDB) in Kigali, I enabled the RDB management to address the needs of business leaders by evaluating the energy demands of 13 firms in Kigali's Special Economic Zone.

Moreover, as a reports officer at the UN World Food Program, I excelled in a variety of relevant tasks, such as engaging UN and NGO partners to coordinate various projects, including mobile money transfers in three refugee camps in Rwanda. These experiences revealed that I not only enjoy but also thrive in a collaborative and international work environment, similar to that which I would encounter at Viamo.

A self-starter, I also excel at team motivation. I demonstrated these qualities most recently in my role as co-chair of the 2018 Black Policy Conference at HKS. In this role, I enthusiastically managed a team of 13 panel organizers; coordinated logistics such as flight and hotel reservations for 40 guest speakers; devised and implemented a marketing strategy; and co-managed a $30,000 budget.

As co-chair, I also raised the international profile of the conference by spearheading a partnership with the Gender, Diversity and Public Policy Initiative at the University of Toronto, and my team proudly increased ticket sales from the 2017 Conference by 71 percent (from 175 to 300).

From my extensive international exposure, I would additionally bring to Viamo a nuanced and comparative perspective on the intricate developmental challenges affecting these markets: I have lived in and traveled to over 10 countries in the developing world and possess a working proficiency in French and Spanish.

Ultimately, what attracts me to Viamo is its unwavering mission to improve human welfare. As someone passionate about social and economic empowerment, I would be thrilled to work as part of a like-minded team. If you seek a regional manager who is eager to learn and enjoys the challenges of problem-solving in a fast-paced work environment, I hope you consider what I have to offer. Thank you for your time and consideration.

Most sincerely,

[Signature]

Matt Castle

Lizzy Lipscomb

Something@gmail.com

000-777-7777

July 6, 2018

Stanford Law School

559 Nathan Abbott Way

Stanford, CA 94305

Dear Human Resources Administrator,

I was thrilled to learn about your empirical research fellowship position on The Princeton University Career website. A senior at Princeton University majoring in sociology and minoring in law and society, I am strongly interested in taking some years off to conduct empirical research after graduating with my bachelor's degree. I plan to attend law school in the future.

Working as an empirical research fellow at Stanford Law School would allow me to continue my commitment to both research and law, and I feel confident that I could contribute substantively to the work of your department while strengthening the skills I'll need for a career in legal research.

Although I do not have extensive empirical research experience, what I do have has only furthered my commitment. I believe my enthusiasm to become an effective and committed legal professional and my ability to learn fast are my greatest assets.

Through my studies for an associate degree in Pre-Law at Alamo Community College, I gained strong skills in conducting legal research and a broad knowledge of the legal system. I am eager to employ my research and writing skills in the area of empirical research, and I believe that my experience drafting legal documents and meeting deadlines will serve your team well.

I have had the opportunity to develop strong legal writing and analysis skills in my pre-law studies. Highlights of my background include conducting legal research for judges, mastering Westlaw Next and Lexis Nexis, and being admitted to law school during my junior year. I am now looking forward to applying my skills and knowledge in a new setting, where I can continue to meet new and different challenges.

Outside of the classroom, my position as a court-appointed special advocate has allowed me to acquire extensive experience with many aspects of the law. I have a solid understanding of court proceedings in both civil and criminal cases, and I look forward to applying these skills as a research assistant at Stanford Law School.

In addition, my experience working as an editor-in-chief for GW Hatchet and my internship at the United States Senate Foreign Relations Committee have allowed me to improve my communication and problem-solving skills. My work ethic includes a near-perfect attendance record, a willingness to go above and beyond what's expected, and the ability to work long hours when necessary. I have excellent references, and I show up even when no one else does.

The position of Empirical Research Fellow is more than a job to me. It is my passion. Assisting your team, working closely with others, creating improvements, and providing ideas that support the research is what I can offer Stanford Law School.

I have enclosed a résumé highlighting my education and work experience. I hope to have the opportunity to interview with you about the empirical research fellowship position, and I will call your office in a few weeks to see if I may schedule a time to speak with you. Thank you in advance for your time and consideration. I look forward to hearing from you.

Sincerely,

[Signature]

Lizzy Lipscomb

Enclosure (1)

Appendix C:
Résumé Examples

PATRICIA SMITH

patricia@gmail.com – Jacksonville, FL - 000-000-0000

Overview

A diverse leader with experience leading technical teams, as well as performing technical roles that include Information Security Engineer, Project Engineer, System Engineer, and Technical Lead.

Critical Skills/Knowledge

- Service Level Management
- Technical Lead
- Technical Planning
- TIL v3 Foundation
- Service Management
- Process Integration
- Knowledge Management
- Project Management
- Metrics Development
- Workforce Management
- System Engineer
- Technical Troubleshooting
- Data/Process Analysis
- Testing Plan Development
- Information Security Engineer
- Cloud Computing
- Vulnerability Management

Experience

Lockheed Martin Corporation 2005 – Present

Information Assurance Engineer Sr. 2015 – Present

- Ensure that operating systems, web applications, and databases are in compliance by leading a team effort on a monthly basis.
- Provide security engineering support for new and existing systems that are integrated into the Lockheed Martin network infrastructure.
- Evaluate VPN remote access requests for contractors in accordance with Lockheed Martin access matrix guidelines. Processed over 900 requests in 2016 and 700 as of August 2017.
- Proposed process improvements for VPN remote access requests to expedite approval workflow. Proposal increased time resolution by 60 percent, compared to previous process.
- Lead effort to evaluate and approve requests to add restricted websites and SSL decryptions to the whitelist that allows control access through proxy servers.
- Provide enterprise tool support, including but not limited to, company document exchange system (Sharing Document technology).
- Represent Information Security organization within the Defense Contract Management Agency (DCMA) access review board to evaluate and approve DCMA user access.
- Completed an assessment to improve existing support model for both technical and information security engineer support.
- Led security categorization process to rank security risks on new or existing systems within the company's infrastructure.
- Responsibilities include, but are not limited to, coordinating the review board to evaluate and approve requests, identifying risks and making recommendations for implementation. As team lead, I discovered opportunity for process improvement, which increased process resolution. My recommendation was considered for integration on existing tools within the corporation.

Advanced Technical Leadership Program (ATLP) 2013 – 2015

Data Center Infrastructure – IT Hosting Services – Project Engineer Senior

- Provided leadership, oversight & integration of Data Center Infrastructure Services (DCI).
- Reviewed project proposal and design execution plan, including decommission of legacy DCI environment.
- Scheduled weekly meetings with solution engineers to track project execution.

- Provided primary partner interface and accountability for DCI projects.
- Provided cost & schedule oversight to senior and executive-level leadership as required.

IT Service Delivery Lead - Lockheed Martin EBS – Site Point of Contact (SPOC) 2012 - 2013

- Designed effective strategies and procedures to maximize communications between the LMSD analyst and LMSD SPOC.
- Developed and implemented effective short- and long-range operational support, service plans, and business cases to support operation of SPOC and LMSD performances.

IT Service Delivery Lead – Lockheed Martin EBS – Remote Deskside Support (RDS) 2008-2012

- Developed tactical strategies and procedures to maximize resources in support of Lockheed Martin business areas.
- Analyzed and evaluated technical resources and developed creative techniques to attain efficient performance in cost, client loyalty/satisfaction, and user growth.

Education

Master of Science in Computer Science (Colorado Technical University).

Bachelor of Science – Information Technology (University of Central Florida)

Additional Certifications

System Engineering Principal (SEPP) | ITIL v3-Foundation Certified | Threat-Driven Methodologies (Cyber Security)

Common Body of Knowledge (CBK) | HDI- Knowledge Management Foundation (KCS) | Support Center Team Lead Certified (HDI)

Awards

STEM Volunteer Lead of the Year 2017 | RMS-Orlando STEM Council

President's Volunteer Service Award 2016 & 2017 | Corporation for National & Community Service

Spot Team Award 2014 & 2015 | Spot Individual Award – 2014 | ATLP System Engineer Sr.

HENNAC Nominee – 2012 | Great Minds in STEM

Alberto S. Barcane

123 Martin Luther King St., Washington, D.C. 21000 | (200) 000-000 | 000@harvard.edu

EDUCATION

SCHWARZMAN SCHOLAR, TSINGHUA UNIVERSITY **Beijing, China**

Master of Global Affairs with Focus in Economics & Business **2018 – 2019**
- Winner of the highly selective Schwarzman Scholarship to study U.S.-China relations (less than 5% acceptance rate)
- Coursework in finance, strategic risk management, international business development, accounting, and Mandarin
- Dissertation focused on regulatory and governance approaches to cryptocurrency, digital assets, and blockchain startups

UNIVERSITY OF OXFORD, BLAVATNIK SCHOOL OF GOVERNMENT/ST. ANTHONY'S COLLEGE Oxford, U.K.

Master of Public Policy **2017 – 2018**
- Startup Nation Scholar with full funding for course emphasizing economics, policy evaluation, and international trade
- Elected Class External Affairs and Alumni Director | Oxford Union Debate Team | Editor-in-Chief, BSG Policy Journal

HARVARD COLLEGE **Cambridge, MA**

A.B. Degree in Government Cum. GPA 3.8 **2008 – 2013**
- Center for American Political Studies Research Fellowship | Undergraduate Council Rep. and Winthrop House Rep.

PROFESSIONAL EXPERIENCE

KARAKUL – *Blockchain advisory and digital asset fund* **Beijing, China**

Co-Founder & Partner **Oct. 2016 – Sep. 2017**
- New firm based between Paris, Silicon Valley, and Beijing, focusing on arbitrage opportunities between the West and China
- Initial limited partner funding from California and European family offices, including from Lord Jacob Rothschild

ENERGY ACCESS VENTURES Nairobi, Kenya

Venture Capital Summer Associate **June 2015 – Sept. 2016**

- Prepared and conducted due diligence, market reviews, revenue forecasting, and political risk analysis for ~$75 million VC fund, focused on energy access projects in sub-Saharan Africa
- Outlined comprehensive overhaul of fund's website, messaging, collateral, and overall messaging strategy
- Initiated and executed effort to build relations for fund with Silicon Valley VC firms with aim on impacting investing

THE WESTLY GROUP – *California-based Cleantech venture capital firm* **Menlo Park, CA**

Political Director with additional research and fundraising responsibilities **Jan. 2012 – Jan. 2015**

- Chief political and policy advisor for former CA State Controller, venture capitalist, and major political donor Steve Westly
- Managed political and fundraising efforts, including events for President Obama and Senator Tim Kaine, raising hundreds of thousands of dollars for candidates
- Conducted political intelligence on behalf of Mr. Westly's venture fund to provide accurate assessments of regulatory trends that could impact investments into his portfolio of seed stage and series A companies

CITY OF MADERA Madera, CA

Senior Advisor and Legislative Director **July 2015 – Sept. 2016**

- Managed staff of three on issues ranging from rent control to emergency disaster preparations and budgeting
- Assisted in pension reform negotiations that, when finalized, locked in over $2 billion in long-term structural savings
- Led effort to revamp city's small and local business incentive and retention policy that loosened burdensome regulation

LEADERSHIP EXPERIENCE

THE HISPANIC HERITAGE FOUNDATION Washington, D.C.

Board Member and Program Director, Latinos on the Fast Track (LOFT) **Aug. 2012 – Jan. 2016**

- Created and directed LOFT Actionable Leadership Summit now held annually in Washington, D.C., where over 50 student leaders from across the nation participate in two-day leadership training. Raised over $25,000 each year. Sponsors have included The White House, The Congressional Hispanic Caucus, Southwest Airlines, and TFA. Summit has been featured in *The Washington Post*

BANK OF AMERICA – *Regional bank with over $250 million in assets* **San Jose, CA**

Bank Board Director & Strategic Planning Committee **Dec. 2014 – Jan. 2017**

- Negotiated merger with California Bank of Commerce, resulting in a combined institution with $650 million in assets

ADDITIONAL INFORMATION

Languages: English (native), Spanish (professional), French (professional), Mandarin (beginner)

Published in: *The New York Times*, CoinDesk, *The San Jose Mercury News*, *San Jose Metro*, and the *Huffington Post*

MATT CASTLE

7434 S. 25th Way Phoenix, AZ USA 85040 brilliantstudent1@
futuredcintern.net +1 (480) 000-0000

EXPERIENCE

Summer 2017

RWANDA DEVELOPMENT BOARD (RDB) — Kigali, Rwanda

- **Summer Associate**

  - Spoke with business leaders and assessed energy demand.

  - Enabled RDB management to address energy needs of eight firms in Kigali's Special Economic Zone.

  - Analyzed and created tool to better track and visualize business conversion rates.

2015 – 2016

UNITED NATIONS WORLD FOOD PROGRAMME (WFP) — Kigali, Rwanda

- **Reports Officer (Princeton in Africa Fellow)**

  - Provided timely and high-quality reporting:

  - Wrote quarterly project evaluation reports.

  - Developed narratives for 12 projects for brochures and donor briefs.

  - Wrote and edited monthly monitoring and evaluation bulletins and commodity price watch bulletins.

  - Monitored French and English news sources to disseminate updates on industry trends to staff.

  - Strengthened project coordination by liaising with NGO partners and sub-office staff.

  - Enhanced government partnership by creating a compendium on key national policies.

2014 – 2015

TEACHING ASSISTANT PROGRAM — Beauvais, France

- **English Teaching Assistant**

  - Increased students' oral language skills and broadened their understanding of U.S. history and culture.

  - Planned and facilitated daily lessons for four high school classes.

  - Prepared classroom materials, administered exams, and evaluated assignments.

2013 – 2013 **COMMITTEE ON U.S./LATIN AMERICAN RELATIONS** — Ithaca, New York

- **Communications Intern**

  - Coordinated and created press releases for committee events.

  - Composed content for website.

  - Served as assistant editor for Fall 2013 newsletter.

  - Authored two articles in newsletter.

EDUCATION

2016 – 2018 **HARVARD KENNEDY SCHOOL** — Cambridge, Massachusetts

- **Master in Public Policy**

  - Courses include: Operations Management; Budgeting; Public Service Innovation; and Business Strategy.

2010 – 2014 **ITHACA COLLEGE** — Ithaca, New York

- **Bachelor of Arts in Culture and Communication**

  - Completed minor in Latin American studies.

  - Became a Martin Luther King Scholar.

  - Became a member of Model UN team.

OTHER

Activities BLACK POLICY CONFERENCE 2018 — Cambridge, Massachusetts

- **Co-Chair**

- Managed a team of 13 panel organizers, including two remote panel organizers.

- Led weekly meetings to develop conference panel topics, vision, and content.

- Increased ticket sales from the 2017 conference by 71 percent (from 175 to 300).

AFRICA POLICY JOURNAL — Cambridge, Massachusetts
- **Senior Editor**

- Developed content ideas and revised materials for publication.

Technical
- Advanced knowledge of Microsoft Office software (Excel, PowerPoint, Word, Publisher, and Visio).
- Basic knowledge of STATA.

Languages
- Native fluency in English.
- Working proficiency in French and Spanish.

Benjamin Bennet

brilliantstudent1@futuredcintern.net | +00 (0)0 00 00 00 00 | 0, rue Victorian 75016 Paris, France

Sciences Po Paris (Paris School of International Affairs) September 2017 – Present, Paris, France
- Dual Degree with Columbia University (SIPA)
- Master's in International Public Management

Georgetown University (Walsh School of Foreign Service) September 2014 – June 2015, Washington, D.C., U.S.A.
- Exchange year - Security Studies Thesis: "Transatlantic Defense Cooperation in the 21st century"

Sciences Po Paris September 2012 –September 2015, Paris, France
- B.A. - Double major: Political Science – International Security Summa Cum Laude

French Navy — Foreign Affairs Officer (LHD Mistral) September 2016 – September 2017, Toulon, France (full time)

- Jeanne d'Arc 2017 deployment to Asia-Pacific (India, Vietnam, China, Japan, Guam, Australia, Singapore, Sri Lanka)Acted as the liaison officer for allied nations (U.S. Marines, Japan Maritime Self-Defense Force, British Royal Navy) during the the ARC 17 exercise held in Guam and Tinian
- Acted as the deputy chief of staff to the naval task force commander in charge of diplomatic relations

European Union Delegation to the United States — Summer Intern (Political Section) May 2016 – August 2017, Washington, D.C., U.S.A. (full time)

- Presented daily press briefings to European diplomats regarding U.S. defense policies (PACOM and EUCOM)
- Researched and reported on legislative, foreign affairs, and defense issues
- Represented the EU delegation at the P3+ ECOWAS Partners Meeting hosted at the state department

French Embassy in the United States — Fellow (Defense Cooperation Office) May 2015 - June 2016, Washington, D.C., U.S.A. (full time)

- Areas of expertise: U.S. Navy and U.S. Pacific Command
- Attended and reported on congressional hearings and think tanks events (CSIS, Brookings, Atlantic Council, CFR)
- Drafted policy memos, fact sheets and strategic analysis reports to senior military officers and diplomats

UNESCO — Assistant to the Chief of Staff (Permanent Delegation of Morocco) November 2012 – December 2013, Paris, France (part time)

- Prepared talking points for the ambassador and drafted summaries of relevant meetings
- Drafted analytical reports and fact sheets regarding the African Group
- Assisted in the preparation of the delegation's strategy for committees elections

J-PAL Europe Massachusetts Institute of Technology — Summer Consultant June 2012 – August 2012, Paris, France (full time)

- Conducted post-electoral field surveys in working class areas of Paris suburbs
- Reported results on online databases

Girls Rise Up! — Co-Founder and Vice-President July 2015 – Present, Washington, D.C, U.S.A./Kaduna, Nigeria

- Co-founded a yearly summer program in Kaduna, Nigeria to encourage

and support young female athletes, especially in basketball, with an emphasis on education
- Received the "Georgetown University Social Innovation and Public Service Fund" 2016 grant ($5,000)

Youth Diplomacy — Global Security Department Director September 2014 – June 2015, Paris, France

- Organized and coordinated workshops and conferences with French defense officials, diplomats, and researchers
- Attended the Elysée Summit for Peace and Security in sub-Saharan Africa (December 2013)

Sciences Po United Nations — Vice-President September 2013 – May 2014, Paris, France

- Managed a team of 28 members for the organization of the second edition of the Paris International MUN

Languages

- Native in French | Fluent in English and Arabic | Conversational in Spanish

Model United Nations

- Participated in various MUN (London, D.C., Moscow)
- Best Delegate Award (NSC, Washington, D.C., 2015)

Computer

- Microsoft Office (Word, Excel, PowerPoint)
- Python Programming
- Adobe Premiere Pro

Basketball

- Sciences Po's women's varsity basketball team captain (2013)
- Regional Champion (2012)

Hiking

- Challenged myself to complete solo hikes during each port visit

Appendix D:
Miscellaneous Email and Letter Samples

Reaching-Out Email Sample

From: pauline@georgetown.edu

To: brown@mail.house.gov

Subject: Georgetown SFS Student Seeking Advice

Dear Mrs. Brown:

I hope this letter finds you well. My name is Pauline Blitzberg, and I am a rising senior at Georgetown University's School of Foreign Service. As I was navigating the Hoya Gateway online platform, I discovered your information. Given my passion for public service and the inner workings of Congress, I would be honored to meet with you and ask for your advice, as I am considering interning on the Hill in the near future.

My previous internship experience includes the City of Madera Council in the office of Councilman Roberto Gate. I also worked on the presidential campaign canvassing. I would love to further my internship experience in this field.

I am fascinated by your position as chief of staff for Senator John McCain, and I would enjoy learning more about you, such as how you made your way from the School of Foreign Service to Capitol Hill. I understand how busy you are, but I would greatly appreciate the opportunity to meet briefly with you to ask for your advice about Congress and learn from your experiences.

My schedule is flexible. You can contact me by phone at (000)000-0000 or by email at pauline@georgetown.edu. Thank you kindly in advance.

Sincerely,

Pauline Blitzberg

Thank-You Handwritten Letter Sample

July 13, 2020

Dear Mrs. Brown:

Thank you so much for taking the time to meet with me.

Your advice was truly priceless. I feel very excited about the possibility of interning on the Hill next semester. I have already submitted my internship application for the office of Congressman Mark O'Neill.

Thank you again for everything you have done for me. I look forward to keeping you posted on my progress, and to staying in touch with you in the months and years ahead.

Sincerely,

Pauline Blitzberg

"Every great dream begins with a dreamer."

— Harriet Tubman, American abolitionist and political activist

About the Author

Born into poverty and raised in Haiti, Steeve Simbert moved to the United States in 2010 to continue his studies after a catastrophic earthquake devastated his home.

As he recovered from this setback, Steeve earned his bachelor's degree in government from Georgetown University. He also studied abroad, attending both the Institut d'Études Politiques de Paris (Sciences Po) in France and the University of Cape Town in South Africa.

In 2013, Steeve became a Public Policy & International Affairs (PPIA) fellow at Princeton University's Woodrow Wilson School. After that, he became the first Haitian American in history to receive a Master of Public Policy from the University of Oxford, Blavatnik School of Government.

Currently Steeve works as a contractor with the Department of the Navy, which falls under the jurisdiction of the U.S. Department of Defense. Prior to that, he worked in the U.S. Congress and the Department of State as a contractor. Additionally, he interned in the U.S. Senate, the U.S. House of Representatives, the French Ministry of Foreign Affairs, and the Organization of American States.

As an alumni board member and the social chair for the Oxford University Society of Washington, D.C., Steeve hosts a monthly happy hour in the capital city and has fostered partnerships with alumni groups from Ivy League and other top-tier universities worldwide. He is also the Alumni Point of Contact in North America and Washington, D.C., for the University of Oxford, Blavatnik School of Government.

Steeve is passionate about ballroom dancing and competes with the Georgetown University Ballroom Dance team. He has won numerous competitions, including first place in Bronze International Latin at the Mid-Atlantic Championships, first place at the UPenn Classic, and second place at the USA Dance National DanceSport Championships.

Steeve is the founder and chief mentor of the Young Leaders Mentoring Group, a highly selective mentorship program that focuses on career, internship, leadership coaching, and university admissions. He recently published his memoir, *Finding Hope in Chaos: Rising from Crisis into the American Dream.*

www.steevesimbert.com

Made in the USA
Middletown, DE
09 March 2020